Selling Hope and College

SELLING HOPE AND COLLEGE

*Merit, Markets, and Recruitment
in an Unranked School*

ALEX POSECZNICK

ILR PRESS

AN IMPRINT OF
CORNELL UNIVERSITY PRESS
ITHACA AND LONDON

First published 2017 by Cornell University Press
First printing, Cornell Paperbacks, 2017

Printed in the United States of America

Library of Congress Cataloging-in-Publication Data

Names: Posecznick, Alexander, author.
Title: Selling hope and college : merit, markets, and recruitment in an
    unranked school / Alex Posecznick.
Description: Ithaca ; London : Cornell University Press, 2017. | Includes
    bibliographical references and index.
Identifiers: LCCN 2016037422 (print) | LCCN 2016037909 (ebook) |
    ISBN 9781501707582 (cloth : alk. paper) | ISBN 9781501709821 (pbk. : alk.
    paper) | ISBN 9781501708398 (epub/mobi) | ISBN 9781501708404 (pdf)
Subjects: LCSH: Universities and colleges—United States—Admission. |
    Universities and colleges—United States—Administration.
Classification: LCC LB2351.2 .P675 2017 (print) | LCC LB2351.2 (ebook) |
    DDC 378.1/610973—dc23
LC record available at https://lccn.loc.gov/2016037422

Cornell University Press strives to use environmentally responsible suppliers and materials to the fullest extent possible in the publishing of its books. Such materials include vegetable-based, low-VOC inks and acid-free papers that are recycled, totally chlorine-free, or partly composed of nonwood fibers. For further information, visit our website at www.cornellpress.cornell.edu.

This book is dedicated to everyone who has hoped to overcome the invisibility that comes with mediocrity—that is, most of us

CONTENTS

PREFACE

"Hey Bernard," Dean Levitz said leaning into the office, "I want you to meet Alex—he's going to be doing a research project with us." My heart soared. For months I had been meeting with admissions officers from across the region in an attempt to gain access to a research site for this ethnography of college admissions. I had been refining my approach and arguments, but responses from admissions officers ranged from exasperation to offense. Over six months, most of my attempts had been bottom-up approaches, but at Ravenwood, it was the top-down approach that finally yielded a site willing to work with me. A Ravenwood dean in my personal network introduced me to Ravenwood's new president, who then introduced me to the dean of admissions, Karl Levitz. When Levitz offered to introduce me to his staff after our first meeting, I thought it was just a polite gesture—until the above exchange. "Access achieved," I thought to myself.

Of course, in retrospect, this notion of access seems almost quaint, and in putting together this book, I have thought long and carefully about just what I had access to and how my point of entry has shaped whatever that was.

Here I briefly outline how I both came to and went about this study to shed a bit more light on what access may mean with this kind of research and in this case. After some reflection, a constellation of factors seemed to have facilitated my access to Ravenwood when many other institutions had turned me down. First, the president was new and was himself trying to better understand the organization and the challenges it faced; my study would not reflect on his performance. Likewise, Dean Levitz was new in the role, and enrollments had stabilized under his recent tenure; he may have seen this as an opportunity to document his successes to internal factions. In addition, some of the concerns with granting access—even with assurances of confidentiality—expressed by institutions had been about the possibility of tarnishing the institution's brand. Ravenwood, however, did not have a strong and cohesive brand, and so there was not a strong public image to blemish. And, of course, there was the privilege I carried with me—my class, my race, my gender, my credentials, and the personal networks that introduced me into power networks at Ravenwood. These were all particularly relevant, given my object of inquiry.

It is almost taken for granted that college admissions should be a simple matter of sorting students into meritorious bins, with the best heading off to Harvard, Princeton, and Yale, and the rest taking up their appropriate slots. Many assume that there is nothing really wrong with this system. Aside from some hiccups, proponents of the current admission system might say sorting people in this way works out quite well. Standardized exams, high school transcripts, essays, recommendation letters, and interviews supposedly capture the objective merit in each individual, and prestige is well deserved at the most elite levels. Admissions at selective institutions is based on extremely fine distinctions, and students line up to take every open seat.

And then there is college for everyone else.

The roots of this project can be traced back to a simple observation: although every college and university has an Office of Admissions, some of these offices are tasked primarily with bringing people in, while others are tasked primarily with keeping people out. And despite this contradiction, institutions of both types contribute to our so-called meritocracy. *Meritocracy,* the notion that social structures are built to recognize and reward persons solely on individual merits (and that they largely succeed in this effort), has long been at the heart of debates about the place of education in American society. Our resultant notions of *merit* are most often understood as inhering in consistent and individual personality traits, such as competency, intelligence, and diligence. And yet, as individuals, we are embedded in complex social worlds that are culturally specific and historically contingent, and these notions of merit arise from them. It is this culturally specific and historically contingent aspect of merit that I am most interested in throughout this work, and thus the reader should take note that I reference merit throughout more as a cultural and ideological outlook than I do as the particular "something" that individuals or institutions have or should have.

On the whole, we seem more concerned with the institutions that keep people out than we are with the ones that focus on bringing people in. I suppose it is natural to be interested, to wonder who the "best" are, how they are identified, and how we (or our children) might get classified in the same way. Yet it seems odd to spend so much time on the institutions that least reflect the norm. And so in preparation for this study, I was determined to explore these processes in a place that was not in a position to sit back and wait for the lines of applicants to beg for admission. Of course, sometimes this took some explanation. When I tracked down a well-regarded sociologist to ask his advice on the project, he asked me, "What's interesting about mediocre students attending a mediocre college?"

In many ways, this book is my response to that admittedly rhetorical question.

One clear reason for the need to study less selective colleges and universities is that, by many accounts, it is precisely such institutions that are in crisis. The project to extend higher education to everyone has been somewhat successful in the United States: record numbers have been attending—and, to a lesser extent, graduating from—college. Yet, despite data suggesting that college graduates have been cushioned from the brunt of the economic crisis, confidence in the value of college degrees has been shaken.[1] Selective institutions live in privileged bubbles (ones built out of large endowments, pervasive brands, and momentum) that cushion them from the vicissitudes of the market.

Ravenwood College, where I spent one year doing ethnographic research, was a small, private, nonprofit institution dedicated to social justice and serving traditionally underprepared students. Ravenwood was not shielded from the market. To survive in the higher education marketplace, the college had to operate like a business and negotiate complex categories of prestige. In fact, a few years before my study, student enrollment had fallen, and the institution had been forced to lay off about a hundred staff and five faculty members. Rather than having the luxury of long wait-lists to take open seats, admissions staff were burdened by low enrollments and worked tirelessly to fill empty seats with students. Despite being a small local college without a broadly recognized brand,[2] Ravenwood remained an expensive investment—one that about 80 percent of its students took out student loans to pay for. Such students demonstrated a hope that Ravenwood and the credential they conferred would be valuable in the labor market; Ravenwood needed to cultivate that hope in their students.

I take as a starting point the notion not only that questions of recruitment and admissions are as relevant for less selective institutions as they are for selective ones but that due to the precarious financial position of many less selective institutions, the consequences of these activities are more visible; there are pressing tensions for these institutions. I untangle these tensions with ethnographic encounters, such as when admissions counselors at Ravenwood poach applicants from one another, when prospective students cheat on entrance exams, when the college recruits homeless students, or when an admissions officer invites an applicant to "take a red pen to" her essay as a condition of admission.

"Ravenwood College" is a pseudonym, as are the names of all of my interlocutors described in the book. I respect the rights and privacy of both research participants and the institution more broadly, and I have taken a great deal of time and care to protect the identity of the institution and those within it, both in terms of its precise location in the region and its characteristics. Specific numbers (costs, enrollments, and so forth) have been systematically altered to make it more difficult to identify the institution in which this study took place while preserving the character of the real Ravenwood College. I do not intend for this book to be an exposé of Ravenwood, however—I do not think that there are terrible secrets being revealed or extraordinary practices. In fact, it has become clear to me, at least anecdotally, that many of the quotidian affairs I encountered at Ravenwood are playing out across all sorts of institutions of higher education.

In terms of traditional measures of academic performance, Ravenwood College and the people in it were (are) often labeled as mediocre, and it would be dishonest of me to say otherwise; however, it is also true that I found both the institution and the people in it to be extraordinary. Rankings, scores, affiliations, policies, and mission statements delimit the socially permissible position of individuals and shape their opportunities, but these social markers do not constrain the range of human possibility.

Given my mode of entry from the top down, I tried to alleviate any impression that my presence was one of a spy or interloper, and I attempted to build rapport over time just as any ethnographer would with homeless heroin users (Bourgois and Schonberg 2009), with mothers struggling with violence and death in Brazil (Schepper-Hughs 1993), with privileged, high-achieving high school students (Demerath 2009), or with Wall Street investment bankers (Ho 2009). Conversely, I was acting as a *participant* observer; members of the Admissions community knew that I had experience in higher education administration and would sometimes ask my opinion or feedback, which I always provided with honesty. I shared my thoughts on marketing images, event management, letters to prospective students, and interpretation of admissions data. At times I could explicitly feel myself being constructed as "expert"—clearly fueled by my Whiteness, maleness, and growing credentials, and I attempted to mitigate this positioning with humor, honesty, and a little time. Despite recent shifts, colleges and universities remain strongholds of White, male, affluent authority—and a look at faculty membership and university leadership shows that in many ways, it remains so. I was at all times a "political actor in the everydayness of [my] practice" (Jackson, 2010, p. S284); and that everydayness was as complex and layered for me as it was for members of the Ravenwood community.

Throughout the course of this study, I discovered that college admissions infiltrated every aspect of the institution. As the study continued, I moved beyond the Office of Admissions to interview, observe, and interact with a variety of constituents: the Testing Center, faculty, Student Services, students, numerous deans, executives, and board members. I tried to carefully navigate the various internal factions and allegiances. There were those who likely supposed I had an agenda connected with some internal faction or were anxious that I might unwittingly align with one, both of which I did my best to avoid. I took the participants and my research very seriously but tried not to take myself too seriously. Despite the president's support and introduction, the relative prestige of my own doctoral institution, and the sensitive nature of the research, in the end, I felt like I was a marginal figure at Ravenwood.

For example, I was eventually able to procure an office space—during quiet moments, I would hide away and write up some field notes or consult one of a few books. One day while I was not on campus, I received an e-mail that I would have to move my things because they would need that space, though they might be able to find another one for me. The next day, I went to the campus and found that all of my personal possessions had been stuffed into a box and that someone else had moved in already. Not only had someone gone through my personal items (I was thankful I stored my field notes on my laptop, which traveled with me), but the professor who took the space had actually taken some of my books and put them on her bookshelf and tossed out some "unimportant" papers (which, again, I was thankful were unrelated to the study). I had known that others would have access to the space and so did not leave any data lying about, but it clearly demonstrated to me how peripheral my position was in this setting. Despite Ravenwood's relative lack of prestige and resources compared to institutions with which I was affiliated, it is important to recognize that I was "studying up"—that is, heeding Nader's (1972) call to examine the privileged rather than the oppressed. My position in the college hierarchy was unclear and, in most ways, powerless. In contrast, many of the men and women I met were educated and powerful in the institution—making this study more akin to Ho's (2009) ethnography of Wall Street investment bankers than to Bourgois and Schonberg's (2009) ethnography of homeless heroin users.

As with any such study, I attempted to navigate various forms of asymmetry by building some kind of meaningful, professional, long-term relationships. Despite a few tense moments, the majority of staff members with whom I met seemed friendly, and we developed almost coworker-like camaraderie, with good humor, talk about weekends, and kids' birthdays. Because the work in Admissions was very cyclical, there were long periods when there was nothing to do and other periods when the staff were too busy to be bothered with me. Although I used these busy times to examine documents, reports, and application processes or to help out, there were times when I found myself checking Facebook, looking at the clock and thinking about when the next commuter bus could take me to my family. In many ways, I began to feel like a coworker and often found myself using first-person inclusive when discussing the college (e.g., "tell me about *our* students," or "what do you think *we* need to do to reach other prospects"). I found myself addressing Ravenwood as "our" college and wanting to help these (mostly) good-hearted people to move the college forward. Nonetheless, I was clearly not an employee. I did not report to the dean of admissions, I made my own schedule, and I constantly reiterated that any information shared with me would not be (directly) reported back to management. Again, I tried to avoid any political factions, and I was also not beholden to the recruitment numbers that drove much of the everyday activity; I was not being evaluated by anyone in the institution. Some staff members readily consented to participate, even finding my presence therapeutic and telling me things to "get it off their chest" as there were few others with whom they could share such information without there being possible consequences. A few admissions staff also taught courses in the college as adjunct instructors and came to me to discuss teaching, as I had extensive experience teaching as an adjunct. As expected, a couple of staff members simply ignored me as irrelevant or gave me the cold shoulder despite my efforts to reach out.

I collected data on campus between November 2008 and November 2009, observing a full cycle of enrollment activities. For much of that time, I spent between thirty and forty hours a week on campus, including the days between Christmas and New Year's Day when a few lonely staff would hold down the fort while others celebrated with family. Like many employees of Ravenwood, I commuted daily, ate my lunch out of Tupperware containers, and spent my free time with family. Personally, I very much liked not only most of the employees of Ravenwood but also its students. Ravenwood's curriculum was unique, many of its faculty members seemed dedicated to their students, and the students were inspirational—many having overcome personal adversity. There was also a friendly camaraderie on campus. A security guard would call me aside to seek advice about some relationship trouble he was having, a technophile administrator would send me a link about the upcoming release of GoogleWave, the dean of admissions made sure that everyone saw Susan Boyle's stunning performance on *Britain's Got Talent*, and everyone was deeply moved by the election of Barack Obama. At times, and based on my own previous experiences having worked in higher education administration, I grew to feel very much a part of the everyday activity in Ravenwood. At other times, my lack of belonging was felt more keenly. My journals and field notes highlight such experiences.

I limited my participant observation largely to a support role, helping with organizing events, guiding applicants to locations, putting packages together, or giving feedback on various activities. I also attended various staff meetings, in-house recruitment events, student orientations, graduation, off-campus recruitment events, and some informal gatherings, such as the staff Christmas party. Although real students populated that landscape, their active role as individuals began to fade: they were no longer quite as important as individuals as they were as aggregates on paper. Nearly all of the admissions counselors with whom I met described how important it was to them that they were actually "counseling" students and felt that they were providing personal career guidance as much as they were "selling" the college. Nearly all of them mentioned working directly with students as their "favorite" part of the job. But the numbers, or the lack of them, were always there waiting.

Although to preserve student privacy I did not review applications directly, admissions counselors would discuss applications, policies, and procedures in public spaces where I could readily join in (and was frequently invited in). Because admissions counselor turnover was somewhat high, it seemed that there was always someone who was relatively new and needed to learn these things themselves. These incidental hallway conversations seemed to be a primary method through which admissions counselors would learn the purpose of some form or the proper procedure for some activity. I also attended a number of staff meetings in which I would, like everyone attending, quietly take notes—although I always asked Dean Levitz about joining the meeting and was occasionally asked not to.

On the basis of this research, I aim to fulfill two broad goals with this book. My first goal is to provide a detailed account of how higher education is run for a certain class of institution in America by looking at real people making hard decisions. I describe the interpenetrating layers of bureaucracy (both local and distant), the big-picture financial aid processes, educational policies, recruitment strategies, and politics involved in operating a small college struggling to keep its doors open. Rather than offering a caricature of the faceless bureaucrat, however, I share stories of good-intentioned people doing the best they can both to pursue the college's educational mission and to ensure that it remains fiscally sustainable. This book offers a glimpse into the life of a particular type of institution as it went about the business of producing itself on a daily basis. Thus, readers can expect to see how institutions balance the desire to empower students with the need to exploit markets— or what the counselors themselves described with the contrasting idioms *counseling* and *selling*.

My second broad goal is to examine the ways that Ravenwood College operates as a node in a massive educational infrastructure that is continuously measuring, evaluating, diagnosing, converting, processing, explaining, and positioning individuals; it is node in a *culturally configured meritocracy*. This sort of activity is not a cold, machine-like set of procedures but rather one that is deeply layered with meaning: anticipation, expectation, possibility, desire, and hope. But the very real and valuable services and credentials that Ravenwood provided to nontraditional students was overshadowed by the pressure on it to maintain its position in the meritocracy and marketplace. I show how these systems are shaped by contradictory dynamics: cultural understandings of merit on one side and a tightly stratified market on the other. It is in this context that good-intentioned people attempt to navigate and manage these contradictions with an air of hope. Thus, I describe how, despite the sometimes extraordinary stories I encountered, Ravenwood came to inhabit a mediocre position in the meritocracy—which can tell us a little something about all of our positions in that meritocracy.

Some may find my decision not to interview Ravenwood students and applicants or not to observe classrooms puzzling. There are many powerful and insightful ethnographic depictions of education, and the majority of these are centered in the experiences of students and teachers in and out of classrooms.[3] Yet it strikes me that a majority of what those students and teachers deal with emerges not from classrooms but from offices and on paper. In the end, the central questions of my study were not about the experiences of students but about the bureaucratic machine that they moved through—and I hope that limiting my work with them helped me to better understand that particular social world.

The bureaucratic, social world at Ravenwood was inhabited by lots of documentation on paper. Again, although I was unable to actually review applications, numerous parts of applications were shown to me as examples or discussed openly in meetings or corridor conversations. Even within my field notes, I carefully recorded the content of these discussions but not the identifying information of the applicants. Despite not collecting actual student records, I still collected vast numbers of documents that were relevant to the daily activities of a college Office of Admissions, particularly as most applications were still done on paper at the time. I collected copies of e-mails, applicant reports, self-studies, reports about recruitment trips to China, more than ten years of catalogues, accreditation reviews, advertisements, websites, brochures, guidebooks, flyers, strategic plans, viewbooks, sign-in sheets, memos, endless forms, and even some video clips of ads run on local television.

I therefore focused on the administrative spaces peripheral to the classroom and to the growing layer of educational administrators that operate and are tasked with the (re)production of colleges and universities. I am more interested in schooling as infrastructure, or as "networks that facilitate the flow of goods, people or ideas and allow for their exchange over space" (Larkin 2013, 328), than in what takes place in classrooms. And this in turn tells us something about the ways the inequality gets reproduced in the United States.

Since I completed my fieldwork in November 2009, I have been back to the Ravenwood campus only a few times. I have kept my eye on Ravenwood's website and news and stayed in touch with a few key people. On the few occasions when I have stopped by campus since the completion of my fieldwork, staff members have treated me not unlike how they treated me during the course of the study: those who were friendly remained friendly, and those who were aloof remained so. Ravenwood, like any setting, is a universe unto itself—and my presence seemed little more than a blip.

I am an academic, but this professional identity does not automatically mitigate my deep internalization of and participation in American race relations. Research of this sort is deeply personal, and I embrace the notion that my access, perceptions, and interpretations are deeply colored by my own identities and life path. This is equally true for my sexual orientation, gender, breadth of professional experience, and so on. More so, this is a social world that I also participate and am complicit in, and my depiction of it should be weighed against my own lived experiences. My credentials have served me well, and it would be hypocritical of me to carelessly indict the entire system to which I have dedicated my professional life. I am an insider and outsider, and I am faced with some of the same challenges and compromises that my interlocutors were faced with in higher education.

And yet, as an educator and as an American, I also embrace the liminal (and maybe naive) space between desire, hope, and expectation (Crapanzano 2003); I am "caught" in it. I am tantalized by the possibility of social mobility for those seeking to better their circumstances through education and those willing to provide it. Although American meritocracy may be a myth, we remain "caught in the structure of these truth-bearing myths, and though challenged by empirical reality, [we] are ill equipped to find truth in that new reality" (Crapanzano 2003, 24). The arc of my own story has shifted through the collision with the stories at Ravenwood, and I hold on to the greater hope that the stories yet to be written can be empowering ones for all of us.

Acknowledgments

It is overwhelming to think about all of those who should be acknowledged in a work that has so profoundly affected my life. When I began this study, I was a graduate student encountering a fascinating yet familiar social world, and there was so much yet to learn—what I encountered at Ravenwood shaped my view of that world. Moving from a study about admissions and higher education into an administrative/academic position at a selective institution has blurred the lines between theory, practice, and life path. Although they are differently configured, I face the sorts of dilemmas and fissures that I observed at Ravenwood daily, and I find myself at a loss for how to resolve the broader structural forces that I see at play. There were many key people who figured into how I have grown to handle these tensions personally. But how can I acknowledge everyone who has shaped the outlook that has informed this book? Where can I begin?

Clearly, I must offer gratitude to the students, staff, faculty, and leadership at Ravenwood College who welcomed me into their institution for about a year. College admissions and recruitment is a contested and sensitive area, and it takes a degree of bravery to allow an outsider to poke his nose around. Particular thanks to Dean of Admissions Karl Levitz, whose bravery and spirit survived his passing away a couple of years after this study. As a role model and an organ donor, he continues to live on in the lives of others.

Special thanks must be offered to the Wenner Gren Foundation for their bravery in funding a young, unproven scholar, bringing anthropology to a space where anthropologists do not usually go. Although our mutual support is now some time in the past, Torica Webb, Serah Shani, and Carly Hutchinson have earned a permanent place in my heart through their encouragement and feedback in our writing group, as have many other peers from those years.

I was humbled to learn from world-class scholars who deeply informed this work. Ida Susser continuously challenged me to keep the ethical dimensions of this work front and center. Chuck Harrington provided a rich and systematic framework for collecting and handling my data. Lesley Bartlett taught me a lot about how to inhabit a scholarly life—how to balance open inquiry, intellectual rigor, supportive critique, and positive reinforcement. Wes Shumar's expertise on higher education has been a pillar of rich intellectual, engaged, and thoughtful debate; I have been fortunate enough to have continuous and sustained dialogue with him as I have grown as a scholar. His professional and personal support has been invaluable to me. Finally, I remain forever grateful to Hervé Varenne for the broad intellectual legacy he has given to the anthropology of education and for his mentorship; I am very proud to be counted among his students. During the study, I would come to see him with a nugget of data: a shiny, red apple of data to share and discuss proudly. His insights were such that when I walked out, he had shown that I did not have an apple at all but a banana—something less symmetric and that needed to be peeled. I frequently return to his works, which with each rereading reveal new, more layered insights into the human experience.

Since my appointment at the University of Pennsylvania's Graduate School of Education (GSE), I have been particularly fortunate to have amazing colleagues and mentors who have each provided guidance and support in different guises. Thanks to the mentorship and support of Stanton Wortham, Kathy Hall, John Puckett, Sigal Ben-Porath, and Nancy Hornberger. Jen Moore, GSE's indefatigable editor and faculty writing coach, has been a treasure. Additional thanks to Robert Moore, Ameena Ghaffar-Kucher,

Gerald Campano, Veronica Aplenc, Elizabeth Mackenzie, Rand Quinn, Dan Wagner, Jessie Harper, Krystal Strong, and many others for their collegiality and wisdom. Francisco Ramos has been an amazing thought-partner in considering the implications of education as infrastructure, and continues to push the line of inquiry in new and thoughtful ways. Lauren Scicluna-Simon's support as a program assistant at GSE has helped make my professional life a pleasure and allowed me to make meaningful progress on this book. I am also so grateful to the graduate students who have taken a journey with me through my courses *Anthropology and Education* and *Merit and America* and who have shaped me as much as I have shaped them—particularly Troy (Yifeng) Cai and Anna Smith, who further provided some support in putting together this book.

The American Anthropological Association's Council on Anthropology and Education has been a wonderful space to find mentorship and colleagues, including David Long, Greg Tanaka, Bonnie Urciuoli, Matt Carlson, Joe Henderson, Shabana Mir, Marki LeCompte, Fida Adeley, Katie Anderson-Levitt, Jane Jensen, and Eli Thorkelson.

I am thankful to Fran Benson, Emily Powers, and the whole editing team at Cornell University Press for their interest in and support of my vision for this project—and for their patience. Thanks also to the editors of *Ethnography and Education* (Routledge, Taylor and Francis) and *Policy Futures in Education* (Sage), for publishing articles based on this study, some of which overlaps in spirit and content with this work as a whole.

Finally, I offer thanks to my family. Thank you to my daughters, Maya and Roxanna, who are the soul of everything I do. And thank you to my partner in life, AeSook, the most generous, brilliant, hard-working, and amazing person I have ever met. She is the fire behind everything I do, and has been more impactful on my success than anyone I know; I am privileged to have her in my corner.

Selling Hope and College

INTRODUCTION

An Uncertain Beginning

Ravenwood is only for the serious students and I would recommend that only
the serious apply. The pace of the instruction commands attention to detail
and mimics real life workplace experience.

I think the educational experience at Ravenwood was exceptional and
rewarding. I think the institution needs to get a doctoral program in there.

The education model for adult learning at Ravenwood is extremely helpful.
The admission standards should be raised, as should the expectations—both
of students and professors. It must be added that several of the Ravenwood
professors are extremely good and dedicated.

ANONYMOUS COMMENTS, RAVENWOOD GRADUATION SURVEY 2007–2008

Beginning at the End . . . Which Is the Beginning

I headed to the commencement ceremonies of Ravenwood College at a large
hall in the city center on a warm afternoon in June 2009.[1] I knew I was in
the right place when I spotted all of the caps and gowns worn by passengers
on the bus and in the street leading to the hall. Although I was committed
to going, I was not looking forward to the day. As someone who has been
around colleges and universities for some time, I had grown to expect a
somewhat dull event in which lines of people would file in and stand for too
long while listening to droning speeches that were all inspiring in the same
uninspiring way. The new chair of Ravenwood's Business Programs and I
had both reacted with astonishment upon learning that the last ceremony
had been over three hours, particularly considering that there were only a

few hundred graduates. As we entered the hall, I awaited the long, dull speeches and reading of names with a sort of numbness. I did not expect what I encountered next.

The students at Ravenwood College were overwhelmingly Black and Hispanic adult women, and many were also first-generation college students. According to the popular *U.S. News & World Report*, Ravenwood was an unranked institution—indexed in the rankings and yet without a calculated score. Ravenwood was a private, four-year, nonprofit college in the urban Northeast Corridor of the United States. For those who had heard of the college, and even according to many who were part of its community, Ravenwood was mediocre. But the crowds of students and families at the commencement ceremony did not seem to care about rankings, and they were vocal in their joy: cheering, shouting, and making catcalls throughout the ceremony, often encouraged by the speakers. The student speakers that afternoon described finding hope in the face of obstacles, always obstacles. These women of color spoke about being strong in the face of difficulties: exams that terrified, studying till the morning light, working forty hours a week, taking care of children, relying on friends and families, coming to know their faculty as mentors, and always refusing the negativity of others. These speeches were punctuated by shouts from the audience, "tell it girl!" and "that's right!" At times it felt almost as if we were listening to a sermon in a stereotypical Black American church, and the best speakers that day stoked such sentiment rather than discouraged it.

The crowds fell silent when listening to the story of one young woman. She was graduating with her bachelor degree, and her mother was to graduate with her master's degree from Ravenwood that very day. But only a couple of weeks before the ceremony, the mother died suddenly, and the young woman accepted that degree on her mother's behalf. The audience rose from their seats to honor this woman and her mother who had not made it to the ceremony.

Nearly every one of the seven student speakers referred to or directly quoted from newly elected President Obama, and at one point the crowds spontaneously took on his "Yes we can" campaign slogan, chanting in unison that shook the walls: "Yes we did! Yes we did! Yes we did!" A guest receiving an honorary degree from the college was not scheduled to speak but took the microphone from the college president nonetheless and spoke directly to the graduating students, stating "I am in awe of you." The keynote speaker said that he had given speeches at commencement ceremonies across the United States, including Harvard, and that the other ceremonies could not hold a candle to what he was seeing at Ravenwood College. When specific faculty members were called upon to speak, there were cheers; when the popular dean of the School for Business and Technology rose, he was greeted by a deafening roar of applause. As students' names were called and they crossed the stage, different parts of the hall would likewise erupt with cheering. When the recessional began to play, it was not the traditional *Pomp and Circumstance* but the R&B disco favorite by McFadden & Whitehead, "Ain't No Stoppin' Us Now." By the time the recessional moved past the students, not only were they dancing, but so were the families and the faculty. The students had not let anything stand in their way; hope for the future was palpable. During my time at Ravenwood College, I had encountered cynicism from students, faculty, and staff alike, but on this day, everyone was hugging everyone else amid laughter and tears, and the three hours passed very quickly.

The ebb and flow of college has become so etched into the American imagination that it marks the seasons like a force of nature: while old leaves fall, college application narratives are blooming each autumn; the spring brings exhilarating possibilities and crushing disappointments; offices of admission watch decisions unfold throughout the summer; new crops of hopeful students arrive with the next autumn and return to their home as young adults over the holidays; and summers also bring caps and gowns. But despite these rhythms that resonate with the natural world, colleges and universities are not natural features of our landscape; they are the product of particular histories, agendas, and cultural understandings. Neither are they all the same.

Ravenwood College was the product of the counterculture and alternative educational movement of the 1960s and 1970s, and many members of the campus considered it progressive. Like many other colleges of this type, it was founded by charismatic individuals and was dedicated to providing education to nontraditional students who emerged in the era of L. B. Johnson's Great Society. Although the founders passed away some years ago, the mission of the college retained their vision through terms such as "empowerment," "positive change," and "community." It was a commuter college for working adults, most of whom were women (about 75 percent of the student body) of color (about 91 percent of the student body). It is also suggestive that according to one internal survey,[2] 80 percent of respondents had studied at a four-year institution at some point in their life; the traditional path had not worked for these students. And so the graduation ceremony drove home to me something that had been on my mind: despite what many thought of Ravenwood, in my eyes it was far from mediocre. But why, then, did the college always find itself positioned as mediocre? And what were the consequences of that label? This book attempts to answer these questions.

When I arrived at the Office of Admissions a couple of days after the graduation ceremony, a small assemblage of staff were chatting about it; Dean of Admissions Karl Levitz, who was at the center of the buzz, immediately greeted me. Despite the generally positive tenor of the event, he was concerned about one particular speech.

One student speaker had departed from the theme of overcoming obstacles and pride in achievements. She had issued a call to her graduating classmates, not to simply achieve beyond the college, but to dedicate themselves to improving and being a part of the Ravenwood community. Specifically, she asked graduates to donate money to the college, to pursue their graduate degree at the college, to send their family members to the college, to tell their coworkers about the college, and to tell friends about the college. She urged the audience to donate once. She did it twice. She did it again and again. Although Dean Levitz was pleased with the sentiment, he disapproved of her repeating it as often as she did. Whether these repeated calls for money were made out of nervousness or love for alma mater, Levitz was concerned that her speech lacked subtlety and would be perceived as "pandering," a "sales pitch," or "over the top." As the person who oversaw admissions to Ravenwood, Levitz thought that this was an opportunity gone awry. It was his job to think about such things.

Messaging and image were particularly important given Ravenwood's recent enrollment history. A few years before this study, student enrollment had fallen dramatically, and the institution had laid off about a hundred staff and five faculty members; at about the same time, Ravenwood had closed four satellite campuses. Without the luxury of long wait-lists to take open seats, admission staff members had been schooled on the consequences of low enrollments and worked tirelessly to fill empty seats with students. Whether they were mediocre or extraordinary, Ravenwood College had to have students. Every opportunity counted. Every message counted.

I quickly found that admissions work was not bound to that one office, space, or even institution. Instead, the work of recruiting and admitting students was drawn into many overlapping and competing aspects of life at this small, less selective, less prestigious college. Ravenwood College operated in a metropolitan region along with at least 166 other accredited colleges and universities within a hundred miles. Ravenwood offered associate's, bachelor's, and master's degrees. With some important exceptions, the college had been hovering at a student population of around 1,500 for the past few years but lacked a recognizable brand even by residents in the region.[3]

The students of Ravenwood were interesting and worthy of attention in every way; many seemed to have extraordinary life stories about overcoming obstacles and setting aspirations in the face of them. This book, however, does not tell their stories. This is the story of the "mediocre" college in which they enrolled, which was not really mediocre at all. This is the story of the individuals tasked with the perpetuation of the institution and how they tangled with categories and processes not of their own making. I offer here a snapshot of an institution occupying a precarious position in the higher education marketplace—neither particularly selective nor particularly affordable, rooted in local communities but lacking strong brand awareness even locally. It is an institution that ekes by each year, semester by semester, in its tiny corner of the marketplace. Hope, in all its manifestations, is central to what takes place at Ravenwood: dreams and waking dreams; patience and waiting; doubt, fear, and joy; illusion, fantasy, and the future; revolution, utopia, and apocalypse; salvation, redemption, and expiation; anticipation, expectation, and possibility; realism and resignation (as adapted from Crapanzano 2003, 6). It is a place not only with a special spirit and some unique challenges but with a story that may be relevant to others outside its walls. I argue that through Ravenwood's story, we can learn something about hope, credentials, and the massive educational infrastructure that builds and maintains them.

Ravenwood's Struggles with Mediocrity

As per my agreement with the institution, Ravenwood College and the names of all persons related to this study are pseudonyms. I have taken numerous steps here to protect the identity of the institution less because I think it needs to be protected and more because I want the reader to focus on how other institutions struggle with these questions, not on the particular decisions made at Ravenwood. Although I do not argue that what I observed is generalizable to all higher education institutions, neither do I want the readers to dismiss everything here as an aberration; although these particular people tangled with tensions in particular ways, the tensions themselves are deep and wide. But where exactly is Ravenwood College?

It is true that the college was located within a physical plant, included a particular set of people, circulated around a set of ideas, created a particular pathway for participation, drew on a group of students, and can be considered, as a whole, a thing called Ravenwood College. Ravenwood College was not bound to or by any one of these individual components, however. Historically there were different staff members tasked with different (although similar) activities to perpetuate the institution, different faculty teaching, different students to participate, and even different ideas encountered. Ravenwood College was once located in another building and moved to its current home in the 1990s. So where is Ravenwood College, if not in a particular building or set of individuals? Exactly what is it that is being perpetuated? Ravenwood College is no more than the locus identified as Ravenwood where multiple networks meet and around which a great deal of activity takes place. Staff, faculty, and students are pulled together in and around the imaginary of the college, but government policies on financial aid, private lenders, marketing agencies, communities, neighborhoods, student and alumni employers, individual families, and so on all acknowledge and are implicated in this space. Further, this circulation is knotted together in unique ways around differing institutions, like Ravenwood, that then regulate or facilitate that flow. But this is not a cold and alien infrastructure; it is layered with culturally and historically contingent affect, hopes, desires, and fantasies. In this book, I describe Ravenwood College as I found it in 2008–2009, a material, semiotic, and social node for moving around people and ideas. I readily acknowledge that this may not be the Ravenwood College of today; the strands in the infrastructure are always shifting, and given its precarity, there may no longer be a Ravenwood College at all by the time you read this. And although I share my sincere reflections and observations, this story is filtered through—and cannot be separated from—my own particular experiences.

Ravenwood of 2008–2009 was located in an eighteen-floor building in an urban neighborhood that was once industrial but was quickly becoming trendy and hip; the college leased four floors plus a large suite on the first floor for the Office of Admissions. Although the building entrance was on the neighborhood's main thoroughfare, a secondary entrance was designated for college use only and was staffed by Ravenwood security. Near this secondary entrance, large "Ravenwood" banners gave the impression that the institution took up the whole eighteen-floor building. Not far away were small art galleries, thrift shops, and trendy young people. To the east was a growing community of Russians and Eastern Europeans, with fresh produce, hidden bakeries, and very strong coffee. A number of businesses in this neighborhood were pushing to re-label the area in an attempt to give it its own character and designation, but those in the college remained uninterested, as this new name had no cachet; administrators in the college seemed happy to be part of the trendy nearby neighborhoods. Staff indicated that even ten years earlier it was difficult to find more than one or two places to eat lunch, but at the time of this study, there were strings of eateries within walking distance: trendy coffee shops, gourmet sandwich joints, soup shops, Starbucks, and Dunkin' Donuts. Over the course of the year of this study, a nearby empty lot was transformed into a park with fountains, benches, and gardens, and an art gallery had been slated to open on the first floor of the same building as Ravenwood. At one time, the only people on the street would be locals going to and from work, but by 2008–2009, many others passed through the area daily; the neighborhood was clearly gentrifying.

There were other postsecondary institutions and their satellites in this neighborhood: a culinary arts school had moved into the eighth floor of the same building, and a university from the greater metropolitan region had opened a small site across the street from Ravenwood. Furthermore, Ravenwood "sublet" space to two institutions: an English-as-a-second-language school and a German liberal arts college that maintained an exchange site in the United States.

Ravenwood's halls were wide but poorly lit; the layout was a bit confusing and contained some passageways that were not intuitive. The facility was generally clean and well maintained, and during the day, the campus was somewhat quiet. As the evening hours approached, students would begin to arrive for the many night classes and could be found meandering around the massive concrete pillars, which were painted Ravenwood blue. As the building was by far the tallest structure in the neighborhood, it afforded amazing views of the city skyline, which appeared with almost astonishing suddenness upon coming around a corner or entering a classroom.

Divided into two academic schools with mostly professional majors, the college offered both undergraduate (59 percent of Ravenwood students) and graduate degrees (41 percent of Ravenwood students).[4] Among undergraduates, 73 percent were female and 27 percent were male. In terms of reported race and ethnicity, 70 percent were Black, 21 percent were Hispanic, 3.4 percent were White, and 3.2 percent were international students.[5] The average undergraduate student was 32.8 years old (more heavily distributed with those in their twenties and others in their forties). Graduate students had similar traits: 75 percent female (average age 35.7) and 25 percent male (average age 34.4); 61 percent Black, 18 percent Hispanic, 11 percent White, and 7 percent international. Among full-time, first-time undergraduates, 94 percent received some form of financial aid, 72 percent of students received federal grants, 58 percent received state or local grants, 75 percent received some institutional grants, and about 84 percent were taking out student loans. Roughly 30 percent were married, 43 percent had children under their care, and 27 percent were first-generation college students. Students came primarily from four different, local townships or communities in the region. According to internal data, Ravenwood College's acceptance rate had varied dramatically over the years, from 74 percent in 2000, to 97 percent in 2006, to about 40 percent in 2008. The freshmen retention rate was only about 40 percent, meaning that nearly 60 percent of freshmen dropped out at some point in their first two semesters.[6] In many ways, Ravenwood fits Astin and Lee's (1972) description of relatively small, private, less selective institutions with limited resources.

The Ravenwood tuition rate was between $450 and $850 per credit, which translated into between roughly $15,000 and $26,000 per year depending on the program in which a student enrolled. Ravenwood College was about twice as expensive as local public institutions and priced similarly to other four-year, private institutions operating in the region.

The college was founded as an alternative educational institution designed to empower women of color and had originally operated under another name. As part of its attempt to rebrand itself, the college's name was eventually changed to Ravenwood College, but the founders' activist heritage was still enthusiastically celebrated on campus. Several important terms were peppered throughout its literature on the school's vision, mission statement, and values, including *social justice, experiential learning, applied scholarship, positive change, communities,* and *empowerment.* The college was regionally accredited and successfully renewed its membership after each review.

Ravenwood College had a curriculum design that some praised and others lamented. Ravenwood offered a limited number of degree programs in its two academic schools; the majors offered tended to be those often referred to as careerist, professional, or vocational in orientation. The college operated one "traditional" liberal arts program, which had one of the lowest enrollments of any program. For all degree programs, students at Ravenwood would enroll not for a single course but for a cluster of courses that integrated material from a variety of disciplines into a single theme based on that major. Therefore, students would enroll in "Learning Community Clusters" (or LC Clusters) topically relevant to their major with a cohort of other students doing the same (thus, students had courses only with other students of the same major, moving through all the same courses for that semester). A capstone project for each semester would explicitly link the coursework for that cluster and some sort of internship or professional experience. Many faculty and administrators at Ravenwood felt that this alternative curriculum design not only was at the heart of their activist heritage but also appealed to adult students. Students took these LC Clusters as a cohort and were then encouraged to continue taking LC Clusters with the same cohort. When many students graduated, they were doing so with students with whom they had taken dozens of courses over the entire course of study, creating the sense of a very close-knit community (although one, like all others, with internal conflicts). At the graduation ceremony, many students talked about their cohorts as a powerful and important support group that they drew upon semester after semester, although there were also cohorts of students rife with conflict and disagreement.

Another aspect of this curriculum design, however, was that it limited choices. Unlike some other colleges with similar curricula, the LC Cluster was the only option at Ravenwood. There were no electives, no traditional departments, and although students had some choice in terms of which LC Cluster to take, they could not opt out of any courses within that cluster. The advantage of this accelerated, integrated approach was also that it allowed students to complete a bachelor's degree in fewer than four years. Adult students were thus able to take LC Clusters of courses every semester (including the summers) in the evenings and weekends, while working a full-time job. The intense series of demands that were placed on students left little time for extracurricular activities or student activities and left students with less need for academic advisement.

Although there were both full-time and part-time faculty at Ravenwood, there were no traditional departments, and there was no tenure or faculty ranks. There were approximately forty-eight full-time faculty, fifteen of whom were women. Among the full-time faculty, twenty-nine self-identified as white and nineteen as people of color. With some important exceptions, teaching and service were generally the focus of time spent by faculty. Under the presidency of Saul Hartwick, Ravenwood had attempted to move toward a more traditional university model, with an emphasis on ranking, research, and prestige. As will be seen, faculty expressed a great deal of dislike for former President Hartwick during this study, and many of his changes were rejected after his departure. Faculty who came in under this presidency found themselves with different responsibilities—including rules for sabbatical and an expectation of publication—that differed from those who came in before or after. In addition, a veritable army of part-time, adjunct faculty worked on a course-by-course contract.

The degree of student satisfaction was difficult to measure, and of course, there were many ways that one could point to this or other related measures. One such attempt to uncover student satisfaction was in a detailed survey of recent graduates implemented and analyzed by a research company hired by Ravenwood College to measure likes, dislikes, and perceptions that the program "helped students develop marketable strengths and achieve goals." The survey was sent to 750 alumni (of both undergraduate and graduate programs), of whom 174 (or 23 percent) responded. Graduates whose first year at Ravenwood was anywhere from 2004 to 2007 made up about 90 percent of respondents.

Broadly, the questions asked alumni to reflect on their opinions either of the college or of the students themselves; although the response rate was only 23 percent, the results show a great deal of support for what Ravenwood was doing. Eighty-six percent of respondents were either "Very" or "Somewhat" satisfied with their experiences, and 85 percent said they would recommend Ravenwood to a friend. The survey allowed students to write in comments as well, and many of these rich, anonymous comments provide an interesting window into alumni perceptions. I draw on these at the head of this and the other chapters of this book to bring forward the voice of students. This light peppering of student voices is intentional, not because student voices are not valuable, but rather because comment sections such as these were the primary media through which administrators heard those voices.

In these comments, there is little consensus about whether Ravenwood was a good or bad place to pursue one's education. This book follows in that tradition of Varenne and McDermott (1998), in which they set out not to answer why certain schools are successful or failing but rather to engage in a dialogue about how these categories are actively constructed in context. Or as applied to this case, my goal is not so much to ask how much merit this institution warranted, but rather to understand why hierarchies of excellence are the starting point of most discourses about colleges and universities, and how persons deal with this fact. I am not trying to answer the question of whether Ravenwood was a "good" place to pursue postsecondary education, which is why these students are not at the center of this book. The quotes from students here also demonstrate how student voices are deployed and made sense of within institutional bureaucracies.

The fates of institutions such as Ravenwood are the result of continuous, joint activity by all sorts of actors, from administrators and professors to magazine editors and accrediting agencies. Ravenwood is both a locus, or node, for these activities, and also the end result of those activities identified as "Ravenwood." In the end, therefore, this book is not about Ravenwood *being* mediocre but about how Ravenwood comes to be *classified* as mediocre by many constituents, and the consequence of that mediocrity for those affiliated with it. And the consequences of inhabiting a mediocre label shaped not only how activities were enacted but also how individuals layered meaning into their pasts, presents, and futures. Likewise, the Office of Admissions was a locus for certain sets of activities within Ravenwood, but particular actors (admission counselors, college presidents, professors, prospective students, current students, and so forth) participated to varying degrees in those activities.

Welcome to the Office of Admissions

Although rife with tension, work in college admission has a somewhat predictable rhythm. Ravenwood operated with three full semesters every year: fall (September to December), spring (January to May), and summer (May to

August). Offering a full set of courses in the summer was one way that Ravenwood allowed for students to complete requirements more quickly than many of its peers. Unlike at many other colleges, new students (both undergraduate and graduate) were admitted each semester, including summers. This created a near constant stream of activity, culminating in the weeks leading up to a semester start and the few weeks after that start date, which were at a breakneck speed. At other times, admission counselors were able to operate at a slower and independent pace—coming to the office at 10:00 or 11:00 AM, attending meetings, traveling to events, making presentations, and planning where or how to find prospective students. At high points, however, admission counselors spent every moment of their day managing communication with prospective students in "conversion," the process of moving one from *prospective* status to enrolled *student*. Despite the dean's pride in teamwork and team goals, the counselors did much of this work independently—in parallel, and they often saw themselves in competition with one another. Sitting in the Office of Admissions during these frenzied "conversion" periods, I would note a steady stream of students being let in to sit and wait in the reception area, while counselors rushed throughout. They ran from their office, to the administrative center, to their office, to the waiting students, to the files, to Dean Levitz's office for special approval, to their office, to the tuition planner's office; sometimes there was a student in tow and usually a clutch of papers under the admission counselor's arms (as most of the process at Ravenwood was not digitized). At their frequent stops in their offices, counselors would make a phone call, listen to eighteen voice mails, and send off an e-mail or two. All of the activity by these six or seven men and women ensured that the college would continue to exist from semester to semester.

Prospective students and guests entering the Office of Admissions would generally be greeted at the front desk by student workers, usually young women responsible for providing forms and contacting admission counselors. Behind the desk were the three "ladies in the back," the administrative support staff who processed the vast amounts of documentation that streamed into the office every semester.

The rest of the Admissions suite was a large, open hall with offices around the perimeter. The main hall could be arranged for either small group conversations at individual tables or with rows of seats for large presentations. Admission counselors, who were the main face of the institution to prospective students, had window offices along the outer wall. In contrast, the administrative support staff were in a shared, interior space without windows, individual offices, or general access.

At any given time, there were six admission counselors whose primary duty was to recruit students and "convert" them into students. Admission counselors tended to be young, and turnover rates were typically high. Upon my arrival, the admission counselors were Bernard, Maggie, Nadira, and Louisa. There were two open positions at that time, which were almost immediately filled by Aaron and Jaleel in November. In March 2009, Nadira resigned and was soon replaced by Kenya. In September 2009, Louisa resigned and was replaced by Julian, who started in October. According to the College and University Professional Association for Human Resources (2010), the national average salary for an admissions counselor in a "Master's University" was $33,361 per annum, and the salaries at Ravenwood College were close to this figure.

Other staff members were also peppered throughout the office. Andrei and Sam worked with graphic design and website, respectively. Cole was a part-time tuition planner working out of the office to help applicants think through the financial decisions.

At the time of this study, Dean Levitz was a long-standing member of the community and remained so until his passing in 2012. At one point, he had moved from admissions work to development and marketing but had returned to the Office of Admissions shortly before my research began. He laid out goals, established policies, and provided leadership for the office. Dean Levitz was supported by Madelyn, the assistant director of admissions, who was tasked both with recruitment responsibilities and with the daily operations of the department.

These were the men and women I came to know most closely at Ravenwood. They shaped my understanding of how the institution struggled with recruitment, legitimacy, and precarity.

Capturing and Complicating the Special Spirit of Ravenwood

Ostensibly, this book is about one particular place; it is about the individuals I encountered from 2008 to 2009 engaged in the ongoing activity required to produce Ravenwood College on a daily basis. It is about their struggles, competing agendas, tensions, triumphs, and deliberations as they went about these activities. Layered through this work, however, is the broader cultural context in which these activities made sense. Although this work was necessary for the continued existence of Ravenwood College, much of it also reproduced the institution's position in a hierarchy of excellence or merit—in particular, on the lower end of that scale. Only about 30 percent of Americans have a bachelor's degree (Ryan and Bauman 2012), and as such, we must reject the notion that Ravenwood and its students represented the most marginalized or dominated groups in the United States. And yet, in the ongoing, postsecondary hierarchy premised on elitehood, selectivity, resources, and prestige, Ravenwood was peripheral at best.

Much of the educational infrastructure is intended to make diverse institutions and students commensurate with one another—so that they may be better compared. But this also serves to mask the incommensurate nature of race, gender, and class. Explicit talk about race, gender, and class were difficult in the administration—either because of formal organizational culture and conventions or perhaps because it was just difficult to perform in front of an outside observer such as myself. Regardless, these three hovered beneath the surface of nearly every interaction, unspoken and unexplored. Despite the extraordinary commencement ceremony, and what some term Ravenwood's "special spirit," the American context positioned the institution as mediocre; in many ways, its service to nontraditional students (in terms of race, gender, and class) was starkly overshadowed by the pressure to maintain its position in the meritocracy. The chapters that follow highlight particular aspects of these activities and work in relation to this central concern.

In chapter 1, I provide a historical analysis of the American culture of meritocracy as I understand it and as it is made manifest in education broadly and in higher education in particular. This chapter thus lays out the broader understandings that inform this work as a whole and provides the context in which Ravenwood can best be understood.

In chapter 2, I describe Ravenwood's position in the higher education market and the kinds of persuasive arguments that members of the community deploy to recruit new students every year. As I attempt to do throughout the book, I attend to the views and realities of administrators making decisions.

Chapter 3 brings to the fore the day-to-day activity of the admissions team with a particular emphasis on the bureaucratic process through which *in-*

quiries become *applicants* and then *students*. Of particular importance in this section is the semiotic place of numbers and how they are understood and deployed at Ravenwood. In fact, "numbers" are an important aspect of the cultural life of organizations and are layered through the chapters that follow as well. In chapter 4, which focuses on how Ravenwood's community thinks about and tangles with merit, numbers have a privileged place in conversations about entrance examinations, accreditation metrics, and so on. I also, however, unpack how "merit" gets folded into ways of talking and walking or even in the physical plant of Ravenwood—and the contradictions that these ways of being then entail.

Chapter 5 focuses entirely on the most pressing and consequential of numbers: fiscal ones. In this chapter, I show how the financial conditions that disciplined the Ravenwood community shape the way the college operates and drive the ways that they resolve problems. As in chapter 4, I also examine how notions of merit become entangled with this sort of number through access to resources, financial decisions, and financial knowledge.

Finally, in the conclusion, I attempt to bring these various strands together to provide a fuller picture of life in institutions such as Ravenwood—disciplined by market and merit. In this book as a whole, therefore, I share the very real dilemmas and deliberations that the members of the Ravenwood community encountered every day. Despite faculty stereotypes, administrators were not universally malicious, incompetent, apathetic, or obsessed only with dollars. Administrators can be a convenient symbol of the corporatization of higher education in the last forty years, and certainly, university administration has been radically transformed over the course of the twentieth century (Bok 2003; Shumar 1997, 2014; Shumar and Canaan 2008; Sunderman 2010; Trencher et al. 2013; Tuchman 2011). Based on both this study and on those whom I encounter in my own professional experiences, however, there are many well-intentioned and deeply moral administrators; it seems unfair to impugn an entire class of person for the ills of the era.

Thus, one of my central goals here is to draw a face on the faceless bureaucrat. As is the case with any good ethnography, I hope to depict cultured agents moving through structures; Ravenwood was inhabited by real people making hard decisions about a risky social world that they did not build themselves but with which they were faced daily. Although it was not always clear how well it was working out, it was crystal clear to me that there were individuals at Ravenwood who had spent their lives devoted to improving the condition of others. There were persons at Ravenwood who deeply believed in the empowerment of the marginalized and did not hesitate to act when it was easier to simply shake one's head at the futility of it all. Ravenwood faced challenges, and the persons involved were deeply human—with shortcomings, failings, and idiosyncrasies like any other. But any such shortcomings only highlight to me how important their work was; their words, their actions, and their lives helped transform constraints into possibilities. Although I present a complicated and critical picture here, I do so while paying homage to the hopeful and special spirit that I also felt at Ravenwood College.

Chapter 1

Extraordinary Mediocrity

I have already recommended some of my clients. This program is very
challenging but for working individuals with a family, the outline
and schedule is one of the best in the nation.

They need to have more experienced teachers who understand
that the older you get the harder it is to learn.

I would have recommended this program to both friends and family
members, because the program is great for working adults and it did help
change my life. I entered Ravenwood raw. When I say raw, I mean the last
time I set foot in a school it was over 20 years to the date. I was working
and doing things that I could not put a name to, and Ravenwood
College helped me to not only place a name on what I was doing,
but helped me to perfect what I was doing.

Try to have a smaller class roster so that the teachers can give the students a
one on one tutoring session when needed. Also try to compensate the tuition
when you are a re-entrant back to school. In other words, work with the
student so that going to school will not be a heavy burden to them.

<small>ANONYMOUS COMMENTS, RAVENWOOD GRADUATION SURVEY 2007–2008</small>

The student opinions quoted above reveal the hidden struggles that
nontraditional students might have with the category of *merit* and the
hope that they can find their place within it. Merit is most often understood as being a personal matter, as inhering in enduring and individual
personality traits such as competency, intelligence, and diligence—which
are themselves rooted in cognition, biology, and morality. Although those
things are certainly at play, it does not take into account a twenty-year
hiatus from education. By others, merit is imagined in aggregate as a massive bell curve with the mediocre bulk in the middle and tails of exceptionality and incompetence on either side. And yet, as I describe in this
chapter, every individual is embedded in complex social worlds that are

culturally specific and historically contingent and through which notions of merit arise.

This work is rooted in many core assumptions and arguments about the world, which I explore in this chapter. Individuals make choices and take action, but they do so within the confines of their cultural understandings and as these conform to the existing social order; education as a formal institution is organized in a particular way and around particular logics. Although there is an infrastructure to education, educational institutions also operate *as* infrastructure, in that they act to facilitate the movement of individuals and ideas, literally and figuratively, across different social institutions over the lifetime. Much of the work of educational institutions is therefore less concerned with teaching or learning (although those things certainly take place) and more concerned with sorting or positioning everyone in relation to the others around them, and then in communicating that position to other institutions through a process that can broadly be called credentialing. Additionally, the ways that educational institutions are built are more likely to maintain or reproduce the status quo than to challenge it. Particular students have been served well by these institutions, and others have been systematically marginalized from it. I will also argue that although schooling is certainly more meritocratic than it once was, the credentialing process involves much more than just individual traits in individual students. This is largely because the structures of schools emerge from a particular history, and so do the ways that we think about individual traits and their various merits. There are deeply entrenched paradoxes and contradictions built into the way we see merit, which is cultural and deeply informed by our particular ways of thinking about race, class, and gender and which education attempts to resolve in a rather patchwork way.

Individuals with resources and privilege, quite rationally, do an awful lot to keep those things and to give others the impression that they deserve them (or that they are legitimately theirs, or merited). They also do the same for their children. These people are more central to the centers of power and so can hold on to resources very efficiently. Those without resources and privilege attempt to obtain both tangible resources and pride in themselves but have a much more difficult time doing so because they lack privilege but also because they lack a finer-tuned understanding of how the whole system works. They are more peripheral to the centers of power, and so this process is marked by struggle.

In financially insecure times (such as 2008–2009, when this study took place), education is seen as a way to better manage the risk of an uncertain future in supposedly meritocratic societies and is tightly wrapped up with our understanding of the market. Those with privilege seek to protect it, and their position in the market, through education, and those without it want to use it as a mechanism for social mobility (or at least to shield them from economic decline). Like individuals, institutions act to secure their own futures by taking on the markers of privilege and bestowing them on their students as best they can. Like individuals, institutions are either central or peripheral to centers of power. Institutions do a tremendous amount of sorting and positioning work, and how well they do this will either cement or undermine their position in the meritocracy. The way they approach this work, however, both reflects where they currently stand in the meritocracy and reinforces that position. In the remainder of the chapter, I therefore explore the extraordinary, and contradictory, nature of merit as it emerges from American history and political economy.

Merit and American Higher Education

I have been asked, "What is interesting about mediocre kids going to a mediocre college?" Mediocrity, in essence, is about having a certain amount of merit—not too much and not too little. Thus, to answer this question, it is to merit that we must first turn. Merit is a social construct against which we evaluate people and institutions as legitimately aligning with culturally constituted and historically relevant values. In classical China, in order to be appointed as a civil engineer, one demonstrated merit through an ability to recall from memory various works of classical literature, such as Confucius's *Analects*. In medieval Europe, a man's right to rule was merited in part by his ability to ride a horse and knock another man off of his—even if he never went to war. Today, one's position in the market economy is largely merited by the ability to perform well on standardized tests and to become affiliated with others who perform as well, regardless of whether one will ever encounter an algebraic expression after the schooling days have passed.

The intellectual genius stands as a contemporary icon of merit and meritocracy. The genius is understood as an extraordinary class of person who possesses natural inclinations and competencies that will allow him or her to individually overcome most circumstances and obtain public recognition of those achievements.[1] As McDermott (2004) has demonstrated, however, this is only one version of genius that has emerged and grown to dominate Western notions of merit, while others have slowly faded from memory. McDermott describes at least four other understandings of genius, all of which point to not a class of person but rather a moment of clarity or inspirational experience (thought by Pascal, for example, to be bestowed by God) that anyone might encounter. This shift in how we think about genius is instructive in how we have come to think about intelligence and schooling more broadly. There are extraordinary people born with extraordinary talents, and then there is everyone else.

To be extraordinary is to stand out from others around you; the genius is the icon of this side of the binary. In contrast, to be mediocre is to be similar to the others around you, to be invisible. But this simple binary is specious. A great deal of diversity of experience is hidden in that "mediocre" label— nuance is erased or dismissed as irrelevant. Further, mediocrity is not a fixed position but one that we may all experience at different points in our lives. The valedictorian is a local hero who finds herself suddenly mediocre at the elite university, only to be extraordinary again when she returns home for Thanksgiving dinner. Merit is a fundamentally relational and comparative quality, and thus it depends on those with whom one is compared.

De Botton (2004) has argued that tensions about meritocracy are real; they are internalized as status anxiety, which has emerged under the conditions of modernity and from the democratic egalitarianism engendered by the radical reconceptualization of rights in the Enlightenment era. In the medieval era, in contrast, there was no expectation that the masses could or should do anything other than toil for the benefit of their "betters," whose position in the hierarchy was ordained by God. But, he argues:

> The rigid hierarchy that had been in place in almost every Western society until the late eighteenth century, denying all hope of social movement except in the rarest of cases . . . was unjust in a thousand all too obvious ways, but it offered those on the lowest rungs one notable freedom: the freedom not to have to take the achievements of quite so many people in society as reference points—and so find themselves severely wanting in status and importance as a result. (De Botton 2004, 35)

As the formal channels of privilege were replaced with more subtle ones, and as our ability to observe the conditions of others was expanded via the media, the cultural interpretation of the hierarchy made a significant shift. Rather than the invisible persons at the bottom being "unfortunate" in God's plan, they came instead to be seen as the producers of their own misfortune: failures. Meritocracy, the notion that social structures are built to recognize and reward persons solely on individual merits (and largely succeed in this effort), when paired with our late capitalist political economy creates an endless tide of unfulfillable expectations for ourselves.[2] In other words, as merit is relational and comparative, it requires that that which cannot be seen is made visible. To be clear, like Young (1958), who coined the term, I do not believe that our society (or any other) is structured as a real meritocracy, and I instead reference merit throughout this work more as a cultural and ideological outlook than as an objective reality. Despite the near impossible odds of any particular individual achieving the material wealth of Bill Gates (and the impossibility of many individuals achieving such wealth, as its concentration produces inequality that makes that impossible), his story reinforces the notion that with some hard work and innate ability, anyone can.[3] Within a meritocracy, inability to achieve material success points to personal incompetence or moral failing (such as laziness), even when such success is statistically implausible.

In the context of colleges and universities, people and institutions mutually constitute one another's position in the structure and mobilize one another as symbolic capital. An alumnus of a prestigious institution proudly wears his or her affiliation to demonstrate merit—particularly through the initial job search after college. If an extraordinary individual graduates from a particular institution, that institution shouts it from the rooftops to reinforce the notion that through the institution one will be affiliated or branded with that extraordinary individual. And achievement as measured by standard metrics like SAT and ACT scores are deployed in aggregate to likewise suggest a certain profile of attendee. Of course, if scores are not toward the top of the curve or alumni have not moved mountains, then there is a resounding silence on these matters. Institutions deploy those traits that are most favorable for cultivating enrollments. Some institutions, like some individuals, are the object of attention, high regard, and privilege—and others are invisible. Just as it is difficult for individuals to significantly change their position in the meritocracy, so too is it challenging for institutions. And these challenges have an enduring history in the United States.

The Jeffersonian Paradigm and Higher Education

Perhaps one of the most enduring and deeply rooted tensions about merit and higher education is the fundamental cultural and ideological contradiction of the American project as both deeply egalitarian and capitalist. The Enlightenment-era notions of human equality were radical in their time, and the Declaration of Independence built upon these notions to apply them to a more democratic alternative than what was widely available in that era. Declarations about "all men being created equal" and being "endowed with certain inalienable rights from their Creator" obviously conflicted with the ways that Native Americans, African slaves, and women were systematically oppressed and even non-land-owning European males were marginalized from the initial democratic experiment. If all men were created equal, why were all men not living as equals? And according to the capitalist ideology requiring competition to act as the agent of stratification, all people should not be equal. This contradiction needed some sort of resolution, which the capitalist ideology was able to partially reconcile by suggesting that the focus shift from *equality* to *equal opportunity*. Thus, the critique of the old, European models of social hierarchy was not that inequality existed but rather that those differences were handed down through arbitrary bloodlines and not on the basis of individual merits.

Thomas Jefferson, a key figure in crafting the educational dialogue of the era, in founding the University of Virginia focused on the project of schooling not only as a site for learning but primarily as a systematic means to sort people. He described his vision in a letter to John Adams, arguing that one of the state's goals should be

> to establish in each ward a free school for reading, writing and common arithmetic; to provide for the annual selection of the best subjects from these schools who might receive at the public expense a higher degree of education at a district school; and from these district schools to select a certain number of the most promising subjects to be completed at a university, where all the useful sciences should be taught. Worth and genius would thus have been

sought out from every condition of life, and completely prepared by education for defeating the competition of wealth and birth for public trusts. (Jefferson 1959)

Although learning would clearly be integral at each stage of this sorting process, Jefferson was one of the earliest thinkers in the United States to imagine the role of school in society as an infrastructure to identify, evaluate, measure, and reveal the natural talent and intelligence in individuals that would warrant their promotion through the education system.[4] Thus, the old aristocracy would be replaced with a new one based upon ability rather than bloodlines; in other words, Jefferson did not reject the notion of aristocracy or inequality—just the premises on which it had been based. Jefferson's "natural aristocracy" was grounded in "virtue and talents," in stark contrast to the "artificial aristocracy founded on wealth and birth, without either virtue or talents" (Jefferson 1959). By implication, an intellectual elite existed invisible to the naked eye, which schooling would make visible through the process of sorting. Those who completed university studies were marked as the most elite, and thus the most deserving of authority and positions of leadership. Education thus acts as a revelatory infrastructure: revealing what is hidden. I refer to this way of thinking of education as the *Jeffersonian paradigm*.[5]

Although Jefferson's own efforts at school reform were not particularly successful in his lifetime (or even the generation after), the Jeffersonian paradigm of schooling as centered as much in sorting as learning would become a powerful strand of ideological thought in twentieth-century American educational thinking. James Bryant Conant, the Harvard University president directly responsible for many of the features of present-day college admissions systems,[6] believed in a perhaps radical meritocracy. A powerful public figure and a bundle of contradictions,[7] Conant tirelessly promoted "Jefferson's Ideal" as critical to the national project of the United States,[8] largely centered in educational testing as a means to identify and classify all members of the population in order to align their talents with their role in society. For Conant, perhaps naively, these roles were intended to have no stigma or privilege associated with them and rather to be a neutral and objective space for this sorting process. At one point, he even suggested that wealth should not be passed on from one generation to the next in order to disrupt the ways that affluence corrupts meritocratic sorting (Lemann 1999, chapter 4). Ironically, while Conant was busy professing a new period of radical meritocracy in his written works, in admission policy he was inventing systems designed to sharply reproduce existing elite structures, including access for students from elite families, strict quotas for Jews, and tactful strategies for turning away virtually all Black applicants (Karabel 2005, chapter 6) regardless of their merits.[9]

After some false starts with explicitly sexist, racist, and elitist logics, Karabel (2005) demonstrates how the Ivy League universities devised both a system and a logic that included understanding merit not only as academic tests (upon which Jewish applicants were scoring well) but also as a more holistic review of individuals that included athletic ability, legacy, personal character, extracurricular activities, letters of recommendation, and all of the other accouterments that American college applicants are familiar with. The logic averred, in the vein of the Jeffersonian paradigm, was that the universities were looking not just for intellectuals but for true leaders and well-rounded people who would be the future leadership of this country. This system also allowed for the possibility that a Jewish kid from Brooklyn with excellent academics could be denied admission, while a White prep-school athlete with mediocre grades could be admitted. Conant, of course, was not alone in this project but rather was working alongside admission officers in Harvard, Princeton, and Yale to identify undesirable applicants who might otherwise meet the academic criteria (with a particular emphasis on Jewish students), and a strictly enforced quota system was enacted to keep such "undesirables" to a minimum. Karabel's work thus demonstrates how merit has historically been racialized in the United States. Today, as I discuss below, the reality is now largely inverted, as privileged parents who have engaged in a lifetime of systematic and concerted cultivation (à la Lareau 2003) may see testing (which their children have been trained in their whole lives) as reliable and consistent markers of their children's merit. Given the prevalence of this paradigm, the very existence of nonelite, less selective colleges is itself extraordinary.

On a visceral level, the policies Karabel (2005) describes are clearly anathema to the American notions of equal opportunity, and yet it is important to recognize that they are logically implicated in capitalist understandings of schooling and merit—where competition for few resources will incentivize those with access to resources to fight ferociously to keep them and pass them on to their children. The contradiction has been wrapped up in the language of education for the "public good" versus the "private good" and is partly at the root of Labaree's (2010) "School Syndrome"—the compulsiveness Americans demonstrate when "we keep turning to school for the answer to every social and individual problem" (222) despite evidence that it is not an institution suited to that task. These contradictions were further captured by John Adams, who argued against Jefferson in his written response, suggesting that a democracy should not have any aristocracy—old, natural, or otherwise. Or, as McDermott and Raley (2010) point out, "the problem is not that some children are on the bottom. The problem is that there is a bottom, a carefully crafted bottom, that defines a top eventually available to only a few" (37). The capitalist enterprise of education as resolved by "equal opportunity" could put only a bandage on the contradiction of embracing both equality and unfettered competition. Embracing education as relational and competitive must by definition produce inequality and mediocrity. But in order to take any sort of action about these assumptions, instruments, tools, and processes must be put in place.

Instruments for Sorting in the Credential Arms Race

Pyschometricians today design tests that presuppose that intelligence and performance conform to the bell curve mentioned earlier, with a tail on either end and a bulge in the middle. But this so-called normal curve does not merely capture some reality—it produces a particular reality. For example, Herrnstein and Murray's (1996) influential work *The Bell Curve* took up the Jeffersonian paradigm, arguing with statistical data that educational tests accurately measure IQ, which fits a normal distribution (i.e., a bell curve), which in turn demonstrates the existence of a cognitive elite. They argued, however, that given the "objective" nature of this process, this advantage represents an *inherited* intelligence, because smart, educated individuals tended to procreate with one another. As such, we were seeing a genetically predetermined hierarchy of intelligence unfold in America— again in the Jeffersonian vein, as revealed by the "objective" sorting infrastructure in place at schools. They also argued that particular racial, ethnic, or cultural groups occupied particular places in that hierarchy because of these inherited differences.[10] Again, the underlying assumption in this position is that *education is more revelation than production.* That is, although education may produce something in students, its core function is rather to reveal something about them that has always been there. Just as the notion of God was used in medieval Europe to justify and explain rampant inequality as natural, Herrnstein and Murray (1996) do the same with a resuscitated, socially Darwinist cognitive elite.

In certain circles, critiques were swift and manifold.[11] Varenne and McDermott (1998) pointed out that schools in this model were tasked to make fine distinctions, sort students into appropriate piles, and then legitimate their position in those piles through whatever means necessary.[12] One key critique lies around the misunderstanding of the term *normal intelligence* in reference to a normal curve.[13] It certainly implies that most people should be or score as normal; this is not the case. If one were to position everyone into the normal curve, one would see that by definition, half of the population will be below normal and half will be above normal. "At worst, the identification of a child by a score on a test locks the child in position. . . . Whether a test is normed on a scale of 1600 (the SAT) or on a scale of 2 (Pass/Fail), the structural properties are the same. The possibility that one will 'fail' is there, inescapable" (Varenne and McDermott 1998, 216). One's position in relation to others takes precedence over learning, as there are a finite number of seats in the above-normal category. And about half will always be below normal.

Test designers partly define a valid test by its ability to produce a normal curve, which is considered natural.[14] Thus, if too many individuals score high in the design phase, more difficult questions are introduced, or if too many score low, easier questions are introduced; the test will be revised until it produces a normal curve again. Such number crunching makes sense only if you presume a priori that intelligence is one-dimensional (or frequently two-dimensional—mathematical and verbal), captured objectively by such instruments, and normally distributed. Educators, who understandably focus on their individual students' successes and failures, can lose sight of this big picture. Moving an individual up the curve, in the long run, is simply moving someone else down, because there are a finite number of individuals in the below-normal and above-normal categories. If massive pedagogical revolutions took place in which academic scores were suddenly raised by hundreds of points for every category of student, we would still have half of the students falling below the norm; the testing industry is premised on the fact that there will always be those who perform above and those who perform below.[15] This contradiction is examined in works like Koyama's (2010), where for-profit industries crop up to help students improve test scores under No Child Left Behind reform and thus move up into a higher category—which actually pushes others down to the below-normal category, in an endless, profit-making machine of test preparation.[16]

The ethnic and racial component of inequality and attributions of merit is also a fundamental aspect of meritocracy in the United States. The measure of extraordinariness is not the same for everyone. Aside from historical, explicit exclusion from paths to mobility, people of color remain peripheral to the processes that facilitate meaningful social movement, as captured in President Obama's (2013) commencement address at Morehouse College:

> You are the mantle of Frederick Douglass and Booker T. Washington and Ralph Bunche and Langston Hughes and George Washington Carver and Ralph Abernathy and Thurgood Marshall and, yes, Dr. Martin Luther King Jr. These men were many things to many people and they knew full well the role that racism played in their life. But when it came to their own accomplishments and sense of purpose, they had no time for excuses. Every one of you has a grandma or an uncle or a parent who's told you at some point in life as an African American you have to work twice as hard as anyone else if you want to get by.

The notion that people of color have to work "twice as hard to get half as much" has circulated as anecdote for many years, but systematic research has been increasingly finding elements of truth in such adages, including the works of Desante (2013), Reardon, Fox, and Townsend (2015), and Cavounidis and Lang (2015). Racial and ethnic difference thus adds a new layer of anxiety and complexity to conversations on merit. The controversial work of Fordham and Ogbu (1986) captured this anxiety in their work highlighting the "burden of acting White" in educational and professional settings. As schools are fundamentally White spaces and institutions built and maintained around White cultural understandings, Black kids are burdened with the contradictions of needing to succeed in a space that is seemingly in opposition to their own racial identities. Although some have misinterpreted this to suggest that Black kids underperformed in school because of peer pressure from other Black kids, it is more about the added layer of anxiety that some kids have to deal with that others do not.[17] And although students of color may feel the tensions of structural inequality, they are also deeply informed by notions of meritocracy so prevalent and culturally reinforced in the United States.[18] Structural inequalities related to race, gender, and class are thus not adequately accounted for in the Jeffersonian paradigm.

The Jeffersonian paradigm for higher education leads to a contemporary contradiction: that an institution specifically designed for identifying and serving a small, elite group has become one that is practically a prerequisite for employment in the mainstream economy—and which therefore systematically acts to further marginalize people who struggle in that context. In other words, the notion of higher education as a site for open access (and as a product that is to be sold to as many people as possible) is in direct contradiction to the Jeffersonian paradigm of the university as identifying the most elite.[19] Furthermore, although I fully endorse an attainment agenda and access for traditionally marginalized populations, the democratization of access to higher education also serves to devalue the credential in a capitalist marketplace. In such a marketplace, as Labaree (2010) further explores, students are consumers and education a "badge" to be purchased and worn:

> What is most salient about schooling for them [consumers] is not its use value (what usable knowledge is provided) but its exchange value (what doors it will open). Front and center in the consumer agenda for gaining greatest benefit from schooling is to acquire its marketable tokens of accomplishment. (Labaree 2010, 237)

As more and more people have such tokens or credentials, one must continue to seek other ways to distinguish oneself, and thus just any academic degree is not enough; a distinctive credential sets one apart. Or one must consider going to graduate school. As Labaree (2010) repeatedly invokes, "the race continues" (240); what I would call an unsustainable, *credential arms race*.[20] And this tension is exacerbated by the concomitant, ever-rising costs of higher education as a proportion of annual income (Jones 2011; Snyder and Dillow 2012). At this point, one contradiction falls like a domino to another.[21]

The next domino is that some academic programs become more and more focused on specific, instrumentalist, vocational training to prepare a graduate for a particular job with particular skill sets—such was the case at Ravenwood. The mark of elite training and symbolic capital as reinforced by centuries of traditional, elite, higher education, however, is abstract, theoretical, general knowledge. Ho's (2009) work shows how investment banking firms obsessively recruited from Ivy League universities because they believed that these were the best of the best and continuously reinforced the notion that involvement in their bank was the next natural step in these graduates' extraordinary lives. They did not particularly care what the student knew or majored in, whether business, art history, chemistry, or philosophy. Rather, if students had attended Princeton, they were desirable because they were marked for their distinctiveness. And these elite universities are well known for being the most theoretical, most abstract, and least vocational in orientation. Thus, in many ways, academic programs that emphasize vocational, instrumentalist skill training mark themselves as particularly not elite in the cultural logic. One could argue that cultivating very specific job skills in higher education is a cultural marker of mediocrity and is not distinctive in the marketplace. Elites have the luxury of ignoring such base concerns as vocational, marketable skill sets, while everyone else obsesses over them. This is not to say that there is not a tremendous amount of work involved in producing that eliteness, or that specific skills are not learned, or that there is not anxiety about obtaining skills, just that it is not marked by the skills discourse in the same way.[22] Although some might suggest that these are entirely different institutions serving entirely different kinds of students, I would argue that they represent different points in a continuum. Thus, there exists a large and comprehensive infrastructure—schools and the peripheral bureaucracies around them—that acts to position every individual into a massive, supposedly meritocratic curve and a marketplace. These credentials have real value, but the nature of these processes and understandings of merit through schools have a long and entrenched history in the United States that shape how those credentials are understood.

Educational Infrastructures

The entire logic of higher education can be understood as a technology through which cultural notions of merit and intelligence are made meaningful to and across various institutions. Higher education mediates high school administrations, college recruiters, College Board test designers, marketing teams, testing centers, university administrations, federal regulatory agencies, voluntary accrediting agencies, academic presses, authors of textbooks, professional organizations, student loan lenders, employers, college ranking publishers, faculty, students, and their families. Even student lending institutions are deeply complicit in constructing and reinforcing a meaningful notion of merit—taking a gamble on who "deserves" funding and will likely be able to repay that loan. These individuals, organizations, policies, and artifacts of contemporary life operate massive, complex, technical systems designed to put Jefferson's paradigm of merit into practice: the process of measuring, sorting, and selecting for leadership. From this point of view, education can be thought of as fundamentally *infrastructural*.

The growing anthropological literature on infrastructure highlights the "built networks that facilitate the flow of goods, people or ideas and allow for their exchange over space" (Larkin 2013, 328). By and large emerging from actor network theory, this approach has deepened the ongoing conversations about materiality and networks and the ways that various "things" (including people and ideas) circulate through them.[23] This focus on practices in an organization allows for a synthetic understanding of both the technical and nontechnical aspects of its management. In the case of schooling, much of these efforts are centered in sorting.

Thinking about schooling as infrastructure certainly aligns with the Jeffersonian focus on sorting, which requires technical evaluation and translation, and facilitates the circulation of people/ideas into different positions in society.[24] Stevens, Armstrong, and Arum (2008) take note of the power implicit in how "higher education connects and reciprocally blesses various forms of privilege" (137) through that evaluative activity. Conversely, they argue that such institutions are also fragile in that they become a site for political contestation and conflict when it comes to nearly all aspects of their administration—from admission to academic labor. Further, they are deeply implicated with other institutions for patronage in the form of revenue such as government-based financial aid, private donors, and so on—and this patronage makes them dependent on the good will of other institutions. Like roads, electricity, water supply, and other material infrastructures, education is fragile in the sense that it requires constant maintenance and any bottlenecks or slippages spill over to disrupt other aspects of life. We do not notice the road until it is filled with potholes and disrupts our commute to work. We do not notice schools unless our children are underserved or we are personally inconvenienced. Also like material infrastructures, education is an important symbol of the modern state that mobilizes "affect and the sense of desire, pride and frustration, feelings which can be deeply political" (Larkin

2013, 333). If the roads are always broken, that says something about who we are collectively. What if the schools are always broken?

Many material infrastructures are therefore implicitly connected to Enlightenment-era notions of progress and modernization, where the notion of the free circulation of people and ideas is intimately caught up with a sense of the modern world and orientations toward the future (Graham and Marvin 1996; Larkin 2013; Mattelart 1996, 2000). They implicate the semiotic sensibility of hope and desire in a "collective fantasy of society" (Larkin 2013, 329).[25] We have many fantasies about schools, as both the cause and solution to every social problem we face (Labaree 2004, 2010). They are the beacons of hope through which one's hidden talents may become visible—the institution that can facilitate our broader recognition in society.[26]

What began as technologies for the production of certain sorts of persons in local schoolhouses have been elaborated into a massive and complex infrastructure that reaches out endlessly into other realms in the modern world. The work involved in producing these spaces is not the product of consensus but is rather filled with voices that, according to Latour, are constantly "justifying the group's existence, involving rules and precedents and . . . measuring up one definition against all the others. Groups are not silent things but rather the provisional product of a constant uproar made by the millions of contradictory voices about what is a group and who pertains to what" (Latour 2005, 31). A cacophony of voices come together at a college, which is a node in a massive network, engaging in constant acts of evaluation, measurement, and translation. This infrastructure is important to understanding how opportunity (or the lack of it) unfolds; how one moves through that infrastructure can enable or disable future possibilities. My aim is to provide an account of some of the activity at such a node, which I argue has implications for the semiotic occupation of mediocrity in the public imagination.

Nespor's work (1994, 1997) set out to challenge our notion of schools as "containers" filled with students and teachers; instead, he explores "the contrary notion that the key to understanding education isn't to be found in what happens in classrooms or schools, but in the relation that bind them to networks of practice extending beyond" (Nespor 1997, xiii). In his ethnographies, he examined the movement and flow of persons and ideas as they connected to larger systems, communities, and networks. He describes how growing participation in the academic disciplines of physics and business management involved not only acquiring discrete skills or knowledge but also an ability to understand and navigate the complex web of relations that organize both the physical spaces involved and the assemblage of practices enacted within them. He goes on to describe how networks are infiltrated by asymmetrical power relations and hierarchies. Like Nespor, I aim in this work to demonstrate the fundamentally interconnected nature of education—to show that analysis of these settings cannot be limited within boundaries of brick and mortar.

The fact is that while all institutions of higher education can be thought of as nodes in complex networks, those various strands are knotted together in unique ways. An elite institution has a different position in and relation to those various strands of the network than does an invisible or mediocre institution like Ravenwood. These infrastructures are human ones, and so they are not simply cold, analytic classifications but are rather powerful, affect-laden ones layered with culturally reinforced meanings.

Sorting, Social Reproduction, and Concerted Cultivation

For many young people, the question of college attendance becomes the ultimate mark of the opportunity for entry into greater affluence and to strategically manage a potentially precarious future. The process of sorting so central to the Jeffersonian paradigm is premised on our recognizing merit in others. And a tremendous amount of work has examined the kinds of symbolic meanings that are layered into schooling experiences, activities, and settings and which in turn come to define merit. The work of Bourdieu[27] has contributed to our understanding that "the school contributes significantly to the reproduction of inequality because the cultural knowledge and skills acquired in middle- and upper-income families and neighborhoods are accorded greater value in schools than are the knowledge and skills of other social classes. . . . The families of each social class develop distinctive cultural knowledge ('cultural capital') and transmit this to their children" (Mehan 2012). This provides a way for us to think about merit as a symbolic and cultural construct and is broadly part of what is called social reproduction theory. Key to Bourdieu's interpretation of social reproduction, habitus is deployed as an all-encompassing, deeply internalized set of dispositions that shapes practices under particular structural conditions.[28] Like Foucault's notion of power as "psychologically deeply intrusive" (Ortner 2005, 6), Bourdieu's habitus is subconscious, internalized, and, by implication, best explicated by an outsider.[29] Habitus is also both structured and structuring, in that it is the product of social structures but also acts to reproduce those structures and provides a different vehicle to think about the status anxiety that De Botton (2004) describes in his work.

In elaborating Marxist notions of capital to include not only economic but also social and cultural forms, Bourdieu was able to open up new discussions about how social institutions could confer and invest different kinds of status in individuals. In *Homo Academicus*, Bourdieu (1988) described how academia shifted and responded to broader cultural, economic, and demographic trends, particularly those that were provoking conflicts on French campuses in the 1960s. In part, he found that these tensions were related to correlations between disciplinary prestige and faculty members' socioeconomic origins, which reiterated Bourdieu and Passeron's (2000) contention that school and social structures, rather than offering a vehicle for mobility, reproduced the class differences of faculty and students alike. Or one might say that different cultural positions enable and disable possibilities (Varenne 2001).

Although not the first to critique the school as a mechanism for social reproduction, Bourdieu opened up entirely new areas of inquiry, including how cultural and social capital operate within educational settings. Bourdieu examined how cultural knowledge (or capital) becomes embodied in lived practices through notions of "taste" as an acquired disposition that allows for the classification of acts, persons, and so on. Cultural capital may be acquired through the spending of money (financial capital) but also serves to legitimize economic capital when made visible. For example, an affluent family pays for (using financial capital) various educational opportunities for a child, leading to him or her acquiring the "right" accent, mannerisms, and a knowledge of violin and Homer (cultural capital). This cultural capital then facilitates access to an elite, selective university (social capital), where all three forms of capital continue to reinforce one another. Personal networks lead to more deeply internalized ways of being, which lead to more opportunities for getting well-paid jobs, and so on. The mutuality built into these forms of capital point to the specific ways that elite institutions and persons become intertwined and their privileges are (in part) reproduced.[30]

Classification is deeply embedded in the internalized habitus and thus in the seemingly innocuous things we do or say. Bourdieu (1984) explains how practices "embed what some would mistakenly call *values* in the most auto-matic gestures or the apparently most insignificant techniques of the body—ways of walking or blowing one's nose, ways of eating or talking—and engage the most fundamental principles of construction and evaluation of the social world" (466). Despite their subconscious acquisition, however, systems of classification are at the center of political struggles because they not only reflect political divisions and the social order but actually contribute to the maintenance of that order (480). Such systems, however, are not perfectly suited to the task of reproduction and allow for the creation of spaces in which individuals can exploit discrepancies (481). This allows individuals (or institutions) to appropriate the practices and symbols that signify a classifi-cation that they do not yet have legitimate claim to or to distance themselves from those things that classify them as vulgar, indicating that individuals actively don those insignia (especially those that mark distinction or stig-mata) that are most flattering to the position they seek. In other words, in everyday practice, people can strategically produce specific representations to better position themselves in the social order.[31] If we accept the notion that educational infrastructures are operating to evaluate and sort everyone, and that many people in turn are attempting to better position themselves in ser-vice to that sorting, than we can see how central ideas about social capital are in educational settings.

As Kusserow (2004) has argued, much of this process begins even in pre-school. Her comparative, ethnographic examination of three preschools op-erating in affluent, middle-class and poor and working-class neighborhoods shows the ways that young children come to be instructed in their relationship to the social institution of schools. At the poor and working class school, kids were expected to obey authority and conform to the rules and conven-tions of the institution. In contrast, at the affluent schools, "the teacher had to approach the child gently so as not to impede the delicate process of feel-ings and allow for enough space for the self to 'flower' " (Kusserow 2004, 113). Most adult figures of authority in this setting spoke to children as equals, literally bringing themselves down to eye level with them and engag-ing in soft-spoken conversation—even if the children were being disciplined. This finding aligns very well with Lareau's (2003) now seminal work on unequal childhoods, in which affluent parents spend a tremendous amount of time in what she terms "concerted cultivation." Lareau found that this ap-proach to parenting focused on resources, time, and energy dedicated to the cultivation of that self as delicate flower as it unfolded into the world (using Kusserow's language). The parents' careful management of time, activities, and relation with social institutions allow affluent children to cultivate a privileged position in relation to social hierarchies. Such children may benefit from tutoring, violin lessons, organized sports, and other extracurricular activities along a very strategic trajectory in which they are achieving competitive access to institutions through the display of intellectual merit from preschool to higher education. Access to elite universities is thus the result of nearly two decades of concerted cultivation—training kids on precisely how to get in—and although there is no guarantee that a particular child will gain access to a particular institution, there is evidence that by and large affluent kids go to elite institutions (see Bastedo and Jaquette 2011; Gerald and Haycock 2006; Hearn and Hearn 2015; Hoxby and Avery 2013). Parents endlessly trade tips on how one achieves access to the "right" preschool, elementary school, middle school, and so on. It also requires that parents spend their time and resources shuttling their children around from event to event, activity to activity, and group to group in ways that require surplus resources and time.

Similarly, Peter Demerath's (2009) work shows the labor (and anxiety) that high-achieving high school kids are themselves engaging in to secure access to these institutions, largely after many years of training. In conformance with Kusserow's (2004) and Lareau's (2003) accounts, these kids have been the recipients of concerted cultivation, which is both symbolically powerful and practical, in that it educates them on how to gain access to the most elite universities. It is not by accident that universities recognize some forms of music and art as legitimate for gaining access to education (as in violin practice or fine arts) while other forms that are associated with disadvantaged communities are interpreted as having no such value (as in graffiti or hip hop, see Johnson, Dowd, and Ridgeway 2006). The path toward access to and participation in privileged spaces is very carefully managed over the course of a lifetime. It is also no accident that arts programs that can mark one as a distinguished candidate for college admission are among the first programs cut in already marginalized schools. Much of childhood among affluent kids is spent in planning for the future acquisition of particular credentials.

Khan's (2012) work on privilege in boarding schools demonstrates both this concerted cultivation and the ways that privilege has evolved in such elite schooling spaces today. Khan himself was a graduate of the school he studied but found in this semi-autoethnographic account of life in the boarding school that the new generation of privileged kids had elaborated different ways of relating to privilege. Rather than as an inherited entitlement, the kids in this setting were taught to think of their privilege as a sort of blessing that needed to be appreciated and cultivated through constant hard work. Like Lareau's (2003) and Kusserow's (2004) parents and Demerath's (2009) kids, these privileged kids engaged in a great deal of labor to maintain and justify their position. They also thought about themselves as subject to the social institution but also as having certain kinds of authority over it, while learning to manage relations with social inferiors (such as custodial staff).

As one gains access to selective institution after selective institution over the course of one's life, one can acquire an intimacy with how these institutions operate, producing an increased momentum of cultural capital acquisition. Individuals who have not acquired the correct experiences, habits, and affiliations by the age of eighteen are unlikely to compete effectively against others who are products of such activities over the course of their lifetimes. Mitchell Stevens, in his ethnography on college admissions at an elite, liberal arts college, observes that

> The mechanisms of preference have changed. Measurable accomplishment is the baseline criterion selective colleges now use to sort applications. But in general, only the relatively wealthy are able to afford the infrastructure necessary to produce that accomplishment in their children. Upper-middle-class Americans have responded to the triumph of educational meritocracy by creating a whole new way of life organized around the production of measurably talented children and the delivery of news about kids to the right places at the right times. This system is expensive and time consuming. Consequently, the distribution of elite college acceptance letters is as skewed by class as it has always been. (Stevens 2007, 22)

Navigating educational infrastructure requires a great deal of hard work, a fact that can then be used to justify inequities in the distribution of opportunity and resources. And after a lifetime of training, competition, and award, one can come to see achievements as fully warranted results of all of that hard work vis-à-vis an ideology of merit. And of course, the experience of this infrastructure varies tremendously depending on where one stands in relation to it.

The privileged lives of education and work are further elaborated across other moments of the lifetime, as we can imagine the kids described by Kusserow (2004), Lareau (2003), Demerath (2009), Khan (2012), and Stephens (2007) becoming investment bankers. Ho's (2009) ethnography of Wall Street investment banking emphasizes the social construction of smartness and privilege as justified by intensive work experiences for new employees. Ho highlights how the "culture of smartness" of Wall Street is not only a way of seeing but a form of currency implicated in practice and ideology: an assemblage of individual traits (mental, biological, and material) that invest the individual banker with symbolic capital. It includes certain ways of performing smartness, as well as embodied ways of being, such as maleness, Whiteness, ways of talking and walking, and material markers including dress, fashion, and consumptive practices (Ho 2009, 40–41) even implicating how decisions are made.[32] Again, as suggested earlier, for investment banks, a philosophy major from Princeton was considered a viable candidate while a business major from a lesser-regarded institution was not, demonstrating the Jeffersonian paradigm of schooling at work once again: it is not about what you know but rather how you have been sorted by the infrastructure and what that sorting reveals about you symbolically.[33]

As these college students became investment bankers, they were subject to the risks of the economy, and they felt little empathy for workers being laid off when they dissolved a company for its assets. Such young professionals were asked to put in endless hours of work to secure and maintain their position in the investment bank but were not rewarded with job security in the institution—so why would they worry about the job security of faceless workers in some distant company? This focus on their individual talents, smartness, and hard work[34] hid the lifetime of concerted cultivation that they benefited from and instead reinforced the notion that their rewards were the product of their individual merits alone. Such a way of seeing does not make space for those who have not had a lifetime of concerted cultivation or have not acquired the various forms of cultural capital necessary to make such fluid labor transitions more manageable.

The ability to overcome obstacles not only is the result of individual choices and unique personality traits but rather references a whole constellation of both individual traits and positions in the social structure as cultivated over a lifetime. One could presume that Karen Ho's (2009) investment bankers would have children and begin again the process of concerted cultivation across the lifetime as described above, while highlighting the individual traits that constituted merit for their delicate children as flowers. For Madan (2007), the notion of merit is a powerful ideology resulting from a confluence of social tensions, including highly stratified social structures and a cultural faith in the possibility of social mobility; a cultural meaning system centered on individual effort; and assumptions about and acceptance of social inequality. The children of privilege described above are well served by the ideology of merit.

Despite aping more privileged populations, in times of economic crisis, middle-class parents have fewer resources arrayed for concerted cultivation and, as such, have less opportunity for gaining access to the most elite institutions. And the truly marginalized and disadvantaged have a sea of obstacles that make acquiring the right forms of cultural capital to mark them as meritorious and smart extremely unlikely (see classic accounts by Bourgois 1996; Macleod 2008; Willis 1977). The momentum of access to educational institutions is mediated by class-based positions. In addition, even if one has cultivated the right kinds of ways of being, had the right sorts of experiences, and has been schooled on displaying the right kinds of knowledge, one must still pay enormous amounts of money to attend the best universities. For this, and many other reasons, access to the most elite universities is difficult to obtain for less privileged, less affluent kids and families. And as class and race are so conflated in the United States, these challenges can become exacerbated for students of color.

Regardless, one must hedge one's bets by more carefully than ever cultivating the right pathways in one's own life or in the life of one's children. Every decision is seemingly a consequential moment measured against the project of one's life, and intense anxiety can become wrapped up in making the right decisions, which are all about managing a risky present and future. Aspiration and education are laden with hope. Ravenwood students were likewise hope-laden.

Ravenwood was a legitimate college, in that it had met the requirements of the state and thus conformed with the "socially constructed system of norms, values, beliefs and definitions" (Suchman 1995, 574) that its peers had set. Ravenwood was accredited, was eligible to participate in financial aid programs, and appeared in *U.S. News & World Report*. It was officially recognized by peer organizations and other social institutions as one legitimately participating in higher education. But Ravenwood was also peripheral. The most privileged and prestigious institutions of higher education in the United States tend to also be the oldest and are not only familiar with the infrastructure but have had a hand in building it. College rankings are by and large premised on the institutional trajectories of elite institutions and consider the number of volumes in a library, the size of endowments, the number of applicants rejected, reputation, and so on. These did not play to Ravenwood's strengths.

Ravenwood had evolved to serve nontraditional students, who had not benefited from concerted cultivation over the lifetime or had access to the same symbolic capital as those who attend selective colleges. Much of this chapter describes the elite infrastructure that Americans must be fluent in to navigate toward meritorious success—and most of the nontraditional students at Ravenwood seemed less fluent in them. Much of this chapter describes the social world that Ravenwood had to participate in and yet found itself peripheral to. Ravenwood faculty, staff, and students knew they were peripheral to this social world and dealt with that fact in different ways.

Like Labaree (2010), I find myself standing in awe of the "convoluted, dynamic, contradictory and expensive system" (7) that has evolved to this end. I encountered no consensus about where Ravenwood stood in that system, where it should go, or how it should get there but rather a cacophony of voices, each struggling with the tensions and fissures of higher education as enterprise. I do not set for myself the task that various college ranking systems apparently do: I do not wish to classify particular students or institutions into bins of exceptionality or mediocrity—to challenge one particular instance or another. Rather, in the chapters that come, I hope to highlight the ways that Ravenwood carved out a meaningful place for itself and its students given the culturally configured meritocracy described in this chapter.

Chapter 2

How to Sell Hope and Mobility

Ravenwood offers programs of study that are unique and contribute to the
overall development of its students. Its [capstone course] empowers students
to get up and make a difference in their lives, community and workplace.
I will definitely recommend my program to a friend.

I believe that Ravenwood should improve their communication skills,
as far as giving information to new enrollees and current students.

The [graduate program] at Ravenwood College is on par with
other well-known universities. The fact that it is only one year
puts this program above others.

I would like to see an increased focus on strong academics. Considering the
importance of accreditation as well as a strong academic foundation, it is
extremely important that the degree is competitive within the marketplace.
Furthermore, as an alumnus, I am committed to working with the school to
accomplish this goal in terms of material and financial support.

It was intense but worth it. I have already spread the word.

What kind of friend would I be if I were to refer
Ravenwood College to someone?

ANONYMOUS COMMENTS, RAVENWOOD GRADUATION SURVEY 2007–2008

In order for Ravenwood College to continue to exist, the institution
needed to locate and acquire new students. As higher education in the
United States is voluntary, market-driven, and diverse, all colleges and universities need to fully participate in the sorting infrastructure broadly but
also to persuade persons to become part of their particular community. In
doing so, they must negotiate both a practical value proposition and the
affect-laden landscapes that makes up the lives of prospective applicants. As
institutions identify processes of both kinds that work for them, and as they
become an established point in the meritocracy, they fall into an enrollment

rhythm. Corporatization in the university has brought the logic and language of markets to these processes, which align with the Jeffersonian paradigm of education and create a somewhat rigid interpretation of institutional mission and risk. In other words, for less prestigious, tuition-driven institutions, building on the markets one already serves is both easier and less risky than attempting radical departures that might not conform with the brand. And yet, it is also risky to be too narrowly focused on a small market, as if it suffers a particular economic setback, it may lead to institutional insecurity.[1] Diversification of student enrollment is a safety net from fiscal risk but also reflects the potential watering down of institutional brand. Administrators are thus constantly balancing competing and contradictory tensions in their attempts to secure fiscal security without sacrificing the mission or brand of the institution. Furthermore, individual counselors tackle similar propositions within the context of their own careers. This chapter highlights how this balancing act took place at Ravenwood College.

Brand, Image, Education

Colleges and universities cultivate brands, which involves a coherent relationship between, on the one hand, instances of brand (or tokens) and its qualities and, on the other, a brand identity (or type) and its qualities given the broader legal and cultural framework that makes such notions meaningful (ontology) (Nakassis 2012). For example, a particular token of the brand (a sneaker) cultivates a particular affective meaning (the desire and will to "just do" something), given our broader cultural understandings (the notion that professional athletes are role models to emulate and represent tough, American individualism). As such, it can be thought of as "the ongoing articulation between brand tokens, a brand type and a brand ontology. Minimally, the brand relationship holds when there is a sufficiently tight calibration of these various levels (token-type-ontology)" (Nakassis 2012, 628). More simply, it is an institutionally constructed set of symbols designed to index certain meanings and associations in the general public:

> Whatever brands are, they are classifications of a particular kind. To speak
> of brands is to reckon the sameness of and difference between commodities

and their associated accoutrement. . . . This Reebok T-shirt is different from that Puma T-shirt. This Disney cruise is the same as this Disney film. Brands group together certain commodities . . . while cross-cutting other classifications. (Nakassis 2012, 627)

Although both are institutions of higher education, Ravenwood College is different from Harvard University. In terms of brand recognition, Harvard University is closer to Reebok or Disney than it is to Ravenwood. What meanings and associations was Ravenwood able to foster through its literature (material/digital) and activity? In August 2009, a research group prepared a sobering report that measured Ravenwood's brand recognition. In a survey of undergraduate, adult students in the region,

> 55 percent were not at all familiar with Ravenwood College, while only 6 percent were either "familiar" or "very familiar."
> More than 50 percent associated programs of study with Ravenwood that were not actually offered by Ravenwood College.
> Only 41 percent knew enough about Ravenwood College to rate it.[2]

Ravenwood College was not extraordinary in the ways that made a difference to college rankings and that would make it relevant in the public imagination. In a meritocracy and in a crowded marketplace, it is absolutely critical both to stand out and to activate ensembles of affect. Ravenwood struggled with both.

For years, internal data and anecdotes had suggested that the vast majority of students had heard of the college through word of mouth, which meant a personal referral from an alumnus, current student, or member of the community. Despite having invested significant amounts in marketing campaigns over the years, the college was still having difficulty in differentiating the institution from the 166 institutions within a hundred miles and thus struggled with establishing and communicating its brand. Admissions counselors needed to persuade prospects that Ravenwood was the best option in a sea of institutions despite most of those students knowing very little about Ravenwood or what the institution was like. There were, of course, a number of unique qualities and resources that did differentiate Ravenwood from other institutions, but brand is about not the qualities that one has but rather how one stitches together identity and experience into a cohering narrative that circulates into and penetrates the public imagination. Ravenwood was not a traditional university and did not seriously seek out high school juniors and seniors as its primary market. Ravenwood sought out working, urban professionals of color. But how to communicate that?

Admissions counselor Aaron was among those who reported that he had ended up with a career in college admissions largely by chance. After completing an MBA, he had gone to Ukraine as a member of the Peace Corps, where he taught English and principles of business. Upon returning to the United States, he was looking for some way to combine his new interest in education with his background in marketing and business. College admissions seemed an interesting fit, and he was hired at nearly the same time that I began my research. In some institutions, there are entire marketing departments dedicated to ad work, but Ravenwood was small and everyone contributed to everything. Aaron had proven himself by writing a thirty-second radio spot and now found himself in charge of the redesign of the literature for a small liberal arts program.

One day in June, I happened into Aaron's office and found him working away intently on this literature. He had brought together material from the faculty of the program and liaised with the ad agency to produce a first mock-up for a cardstock, full-color brochure for the liberal arts program. He had then sent this mock-up to the dean, chair, and faculty; it had been returned and was laid out before him with scrawled comments from each. Aaron had found the experience educational as he realized that the literature was "expensive real estate": every scrap of space was valuable and had to be used wisely.

Many aspects of the brochure were reviewed by the various constituents, and comments were written in with different handwriting. The cover, for example, held a photograph of an attractive, studious young woman who appeared to be either white and/or Latina and was pointing out something in a book to a young, Black man in a sweater and glasses. In the background were what appeared to be two more Latina women, one of whom was middle-aged. A sole comment was scrawled in the margin: "sexier photo." This photo was not changed and appeared on the front of the brochure when it was printed in August.

Other changes, however, were made as requested. A message was written above an image of a woman walking through the center city corporate district: "photo is not our target audience, —Bryant." It was replaced with a close up of a young, Latino male staring straight into the camera. Professor Bryant had further written in a quote from himself: " 'Our goal is to help students become agents of change in their communities' —Stuart Bryant, associate professor and editor of the [neighborhood newspaper]" on the bottom of one page. When the final version came out, one of the inner stock photos of a young woman of color talking seriously with a colleague had been replaced by a photograph of the smiling, blond-haired Professor Bryant in front of a classroom, with his quote prominently displayed beneath it.

There were a number of factual errors that needed to be changed. "There are no liberal arts articulation agreements," read one comment; another circled a statement about transfer credits and noted "not true." Quotes from Professors Hansson and Stubbs were crossed out, with a note to replace it with "quotes from students," but were later replaced with a quote from a Ravenwood founder about making a "positive difference in the lives of others," which corresponded with a comment scrawled in another location asking for a "quote from [founder's name]." Every word, every image, and every color choice on the piece of literature needed to fit in with the representations of Ravenwood College in order to cultivate the right brand. Although there certainly were decision makers (Dean of Admissions Levitz being one of the most influential), the process through which this material was produced was one not of democratic consensus building or autocratic direction but rather of slow emergence from across a variety of players, stitched together to compromise in some areas while not sacrificing core messaging in others. This aligns with the ways that Moore (2003) has described the division of labor that goes into the production of a "branding personality" as it draws on the expertise sets of designers, social scientists, and management. Such materials needed to suggest the possibility of mobility and success as the result of affiliating with Ravenwood and could take the form of video as well as hard copy.

Ravenwood College ran a series of spots on the cable television networks that received some positive responses from prospects and seemed to be generating some inquiries. As with much advertising, the commercials blended fantasy and reality. The assistant director of admissions, Madelyn, reported seeing one such commercial while watching the National Geographic Channel. The commercial was sandwiched between a show about legalizing marijuana and another about the abuse of crystal methamphetamine. Though not aired in the best context, the crowd of admissions counselors hung on

Madelyn's words as she described seeing the ad come on. The one-minute spot included faces of grave, young-looking people of color, with voice-overs giving excuses not to pursue a degree, followed by a narrator in response. It began:

I don't have time to go back to school	[a still of a young woman's face]
Yes you do!	[from a cheerful narrator's voice]
I can't afford to get my degree	[a still of a young man's face]
Yes you can!	[from the same cheerful narrator]

The commercial went on to mention that Ravenwood had been the "school of choice for working professionals" for over forty years. The music then turned to an upbeat jazz track accompanying video scenes from around the campus: students in classrooms, students working in computer labs, talking professors, and so on.

The scenes were all filmed on campus, but when the commercial featured a crowded hallway with attractive, young, Black, White, and Asian "students" walking together and laughing, it was clearly scripted. Actual student scenes all took place in classrooms and tended to feature older, Black women. In my experience at Ravenwood, when "diversity" was spoken of, it was in the context of recruiting more White students. The ethnic diversity demonstrated in the commercial did not accurately represent the student body's diversity, unless one counted students from two other associated institutions, which I will call "Atlas" and "Geschaft."

Because Ravenwood College offered courses primarily in the evenings and weekends for adult students and had limited course offerings during the day, the administration decided to sublet space to two institutions in order to produce some income from its space during daylight hours. These were the "Atlas Language Center" and "Geschaft College." During specific seasons and times, international students would fill the halls of the college, giving the illusion that Ravenwood was more racially and ethnically diverse than it really was. Further, the classes were segregated de facto.

At night, the majority of classes were filled predominantly with Black and, to a lesser extent, Latino/a students. During the day, the tall, young, mostly blonde, German students of Geschaft College would be taught by their own instructors in their own classrooms. Atlas Language Center students were largely from East Asia, Europe, and Latin America and were likewise taught by their own instructors in their own rooms. If one walked the college hallways in the evening, one would encounter an entirely different population. One admissions counselor revealed that a student complained because she had been given the impression on a tour that the college was more diverse than it really was and was unhappy to be in classrooms with "all Black students." In conversation, the admissions counselor bemoaned this White student's implicit racism but did not carefully interrogate the institutional role in producing the situation. The television commercial seemingly indexed Ravenwood as diverse in a particular set of ways that largely erased a complex social landscape in deference to a racially diverse fantasy of Ravenwood College that was better suited to the brand.

A number of staff who worked with the Office of Admissions made an appearance in the television commercial: Dean of Admissions Karl Levitz was talking with a student in his office, Andrei (admissions graphic designer) was reading in the library, admissions counselor Nadira was laughing, and Professor Pedicini was talking seriously. During the remainder of the spot, the narrator mentioned the speed of degree completion, the granting of financial aid, the convenient location (there were a few shots of the main entrance and the trendy neighborhood), the evening and weekend coursework, and the school's contact information.

Ravenwood's catalogs and TV commercials portrayed not only fantasies of diversity but working class fantasies of affluence (see Shumar 1997) that evoked possibilities for prospective students. I found many of the images in Ravenwood's advertisements, flyers, catalogs, and related literature to be somewhat typical of institutions like Ravenwood and, at times, even difficult to distinguish from its competition. Like other colleges that had strong career and vocational orientations, less selectivity, and were generally less elite, the literature was filled with images of attractive, young, professional looking men and women (mostly of color) working studiously over a desk or engaged in deep conversation with an older person (likely imagined to be a professor or tutor). All of the various marketing literature was filled with smiling, happy, attractive faces. And like the TV commercials, models were blended into the brochures with actual students and faculty. Many Ravenwood advertisements that I noted on buses and bus stops in the region were essentially made up of a few such smiling faces with text describing programs, and apart from logo and school colors, the advertisements were not really distinguishable from the advertisements of Ravenwood's competitors at the same bus stop. Other photographs in the literature depicted the city in which Ravenwood was located in a way that was reminiscent of a travel brochure: aerial images of the historic city center, the sun rising over the cityscape, a trendy gallery, and other tourist attractions. What distinguished all of these representations, however, was that they depicted the student as a certain kind of person: a strong individual making choices and investments. The narrative found in the marketing reduced the individual's entire future to a choice about attending college.

Other similar TV commercials from Ravenwood included young actors and actresses of color sitting at bus stops or on benches and being approached by their future selves wearing professional business attire. These professional selves had returned to the past to persuade the past selves to attend Ravenwood. Another such commercial suggested that students would get "more money," "more respect," and a "better future" if they attended Ravenwood. The school was presented as the mechanism through which a specific kind of personal success and mobility could be achieved, a technology for managing prospective students' own risky futures.

The imagined or fantasy students in these commercials conformed to a particular way of thinking about individuals and achievement in a meritocracy. They seemingly lined up very neatly with the traits that Demerath, Lynch, and Davidson (2008) described in high-achieving students, including (a) an awareness of competition in the marketplace, (b) an emphasis on control of self-authorship, (c) individual confidence, (d) advocacy for self, (e) an attachment to success, and (f) a self-conscious cultivation of work ethic. The advertisements were inhabited by exactly these sorts of subjects while erasing sociopolitical history, race, gender, and acknowledgement of structural inequality; they fetishized competitive individualism and ignored structural conditions or constraints.[3]

Andrei, Ravenwood's in-house graphic designer, worked hard to portray Ravenwood a certain way and to insinuate certain ensembles of affect about Ravenwood into the public imagination. In the spring, he designed a simple Ravenwood logo that appeared to be entirely woven from grass with a single daisy. Another image had a flock of ravens hazily forming the Ravenwood College logo. Andrei was always busy doing graphic design work for nearly every department in the college, from commencement programs to workshop flyers. Many of his images adorned the TV flat screens announcing events around campus, but few made it to the public marketing campaigns. Unlike the advertisements and commercials, these drew on comforting or pleasant imagery (as in the creative iterations of the logo described above) without suggesting any particular aspiration. Much of this work focused on cultivating a cohesive brand about Ravenwood within the Ravenwood community, that is, primarily among the students, staff, and faculty. This sort of work was therefore not focused on recruitment but rather part of the ongoing performance of the Ravenwood brand at Ravenwood.

Andrei, who was also enrolled at Ravenwood as an MBA student, worked closely with the ad agency on more typical marketing campaigns, with which he was generally pleased. He felt that the current advertising campaign looked clean, had a clear and simple message, included a diverse set of people (in terms of age, ethnicity, and so forth), and overall made Ravenwood look like a university. He had seen some advertisements for Ravenwood's competition that did not look like a college at all—they had all the gravitas of an advertisement for a "foot doctor," he said. In contrast, he thought that the current marketing campaign drew upon the "Yes We Can" spirit, energy, and optimism that was still at a high after the Obama election. On the website and in literature, he had worked to eliminate what he called the "flashy" or "gimmicky" images, such as blinking "Apply NOW!" buttons. He was very aware of the need to conform with the conventions of higher education and attempted to divest Ravenwood from those messages that he felt indexed anything that might suggest that it was counterfeit, illegitimate, or not real in some way. Very often, he would be heavily involved with the ad agency, liaising between it and the dean of admissions on various images.

Andrei described the biggest challenge as finding ways to package the intangible concept of "education" with meaningful imagery. He wanted the college to have a certain brand; he wanted to look at an image and get a certain feeling of comfort and then associate that feeling with Ravenwood College. For example, to capture the accelerated nature of the programs, Andrei designed a series of images that drew upon traffic signs: taglines on a bright yellow traffic sign suggested both speed and an urban setting. Dean Levitz described the advertising as "aspirational"; he wanted prospects to look at the image and aspire to be part of it. He wanted the prospective students not only to colonize their own future but to see Ravenwood College as an essential component in bringing that future about.

Although print advertisements have faded in favor of digital as I write this, in 2008–2009 it was still necessary to produce such materials in hard copy. Shumar (1997, 131) describes the ways that institutions began in the 1990s to engage in "aggressive advertising campaigns and computer-designed, individualized, direct marketing campaigns" in order to expand applicant pools that had declined because of population changes. By the time of this study, when dozens of postsecondary institutions had billboards along highways, posters in every subway, and Twitter accounts, ignoring the role of advertising in higher education would have been naive and risky. Indeed, Shumar (1997) saw trends in advertising as producing

> a system of highly prestigious sought-after institutions in high demand, a second layer of less illustrious institutions doing their best to imagine themselves illustrious and a huge number of institutions using all the market techniques they can get their hands on to sell their product to a consuming public. The rapid growth of adult student populations, which is the result of the survival strategies of many universities, shows that the buying public can, and will, be wooed successfully with images of prestige and credentials promising to get you out of your humdrum life and into an exciting new career. (134)

Ravenwood broadly fit into the last category, one of a huge number of institutions drawing aggressively on as many techniques as possible to package themselves as a particular set of experiences.

In order to differentiate the Ravenwood experience from its competitors, many of the faculty and Dean Levitz alike wanted to emphasize the role of the curriculum and the students as "agents of change" in the marketing pieces, although it was not clear exactly how to do this. Professor Richardson felt that although the accelerated nature of degree completion did attract interest, it was married to a progressive curriculum that transformed people's lives. At a town hall meeting, many faculty became enthusiastic when talking about a marketing campaign that would emphasize student capstone projects as "audacious and exciting," because this demonstrated a "strategic attempt to change the world." They felt that these experiences in the classroom had transformed the lives of both the students and the communities and that sharing these personal stories with prospective students should be key to recruitment efforts. The meeting went on for a few hours more, with debates on everything from the definition of "applied scholarship" to marketing incentives ("why don't we offer a $3,000 discount to anyone who brings in a pink slip?"). Dean Levitz remained at the town hall meeting facilitating such conversations, but many of the admission counselors disappeared after a short time. Many of them felt that the town hall meetings were mainly for faculty, and administrators were far too busy "working" to spend the day in such debates.

The August 2009 marketing report prepared by an outside research group made a number of specific recommendations, but many administrators with whom I spoke found them to be either commonsensical or impractical, or they argued that the recommendations demonstrated that the research group had not "gotten" Ravenwood. For example, the report suggested that Ravenwood should expand beyond serving people of color and instead market programs to professional, White women. Dean Levitz actually laughed out loud at this recommendation, saying that White people rode the busses, listened to the radio stations, and saw the billboards. They also came to the campus, and although "twenty-nine-year-old, professional women from the suburbs have always been welcome," they tended to come in, look around, and leave. Professor Bhatt, chair of the Business Programs, likewise felt it would be unrealistic to make inroads into that market and rather felt that the college should just be comfortable with the fact that it served students of color.

Shifts and changes in the core market segment for Ravenwood were thus problematic for multiple reasons. Such shifts could be seen as a betrayal of the institution's mission but also deeply impractical, unrealistic, or risky. As institutions gain momentum in their particular niche or with a particular profile of prospect, it can become more and more difficult to break into new markets. Despite how much one spent on marketing, only a few White women would ever enroll.

Standing Out: Deploying Scripts and Cultivating a Niche

Every day, Ravenwood admissions counselors needed to articulate why Ravenwood was the best option for particular applicants. According to the staff at Ravenwood, a nearby selective, private institution had all of the selling points needed to recruit potential students; it held all the cards. Selling points included options: the university had hundreds of undergraduate majors, various specialized programs, and diverse sets of graduate programs. It had renowned faculty, large endowments to cushion them from the economic downturn, an extensive library, and the prestige of the name. Admission was highly selective, cost was astronomical, and a line of young people were waiting to get in. The admissions counselors were likely deeply fluent in all sorts of relevant metrics that elicited their selectivity, from average SAT scores to the number of volumes in the library. In recent years, this university had invested in capital projects to match the physical plant of the institution to its reputation. Thus, the university had not only manicured trails beneath a canopy of great oaks in the shadow of classical buildings but also dormitories that had grown to resemble luxury condominiums and a Starbucks in the library. Parking lots, vending machines, and a good view could not compete with that, and the admissions counselors at Ravenwood did not attempt to do so in any meaningful way.

The local public university system, in contrast, held a mixed position in the talk about higher education at Ravenwood; there was no consensus about its quality or its prestige. At times, the public university system was talked about with pride, but it was also talked about as having once been more prestigious. Some talked about it as the fallback option for locals, meaning that if admission applications were denied by more prestigious national institutions, local students could always go to one of the public colleges. Two of the defining characteristics of this public university system were its size and diversity; there were community colleges, four-year colleges, and honors colleges serving oceans of students. Although one flagship public institution that I visited had a more traditional, attractive physical plant, other institutions were decidedly less immaculate than elite universities and had the feel of a rather large and busy train station or bus terminal. The three traits of these public colleges or universities most often discussed at Ravenwood were their vast population, massive and complex bureaucracy for handling that population, and very low cost (sometimes less than a third the cost of attending Ravenwood). Also critical, some of these public institutions pursued the same mission of service and social justice for disadvantaged students that Ravenwood did. Ravenwood could and did compete for students with these public universities and colleges.

This was not an equal field, however. Many administrators that I encountered at the public universities had either never heard of Ravenwood College or confused it with other colleges or institutions. Ravenwood, however, constructed much of its marketing and recruitment with the assumption that if its prospective students were considering any other institution, it was most likely a public college. In fact, many students had attended other institutions before Ravenwood, and many of those students mentioned public ones. It seemed as if a number of smaller institutions with less prestige, like Ravenwood, spent a lot of time recruiting disaffected students from these public institutions. When discussing recruitment for new degree programs at a meeting in December 2008, Academic Dean Carla Martinez drummed the point home several times when speaking with the admissions staff: "I need colleges. Think about community colleges, [public college]. Those students are going to the [public university system]. I need to find out where those students are going." Public colleges were on everyone's mind.

If marketing campaigns were not successfully communicating Ravenwood's unique character and brand, than at least admissions counselors would be able to verbally deploy scripts that would.[4] Such scripts had been refined and revised in the face of economic crisis. Surviving a difficult fiscal moment in its recent history had highlighted how important it was that Ravenwood manage future risks. Persuasive recruitment scripts and marketing images were being deployed to suggest that students could cultivate and actualize a future at Ravenwood that would be prosperous, upwardly mobile, and, by implication, happy. Although grounded in a particular geographic space, and as with many other marketing campaigns (see Meneley 2007; Meneley 2004; Munn 1986; Wilk 2006; Wiley 2007), the selling of Ravenwood College included a distortion of time and space, with an emphasis on fantasies about the future. Failure to take such an approach with prospective students would have been risky for Ravenwood.

As such, in their everyday activity, admissions counselors did not need to deploy scripts that persuaded prospective students that Ravenwood was better than some selective research university, but they did need to persuade students that Ravenwood was a better option than local public institutions. Ravenwood knew the profile of its students and had cultivated marketing materials and scripts that spoke to them: the adult, working, female student of color. Even the ways that the curriculum was structured and courses were offered reflected the average undergraduate age of just over thirty-two, and this clearly differentiated Ravenwood from the public options.

In the fall of 2009, for example, Monday through Friday, there were only 126 undergraduate courses offered during the standard eight-hour work day

(9:00 a.m. to 5:00 p.m.), whereas on those same evenings, in the four hours from 6:00 to 10:00 p.m., there were 152 courses offered and an additional fifty-four courses on Saturday alone. This allowed students to attend courses wholly on evenings and weekends without ever needing to attend during typical working hours. This option was thus a powerful selling point for those adult students who had full-time day jobs. Another practical selling point was that because the summer included a full complement of courses, it was possible to complete a four-year undergraduate degree in under four years, while attending courses exclusively in the evenings and weekends.

The selling of Ravenwood College combined talk about the possibility of future success and economic mobility, practical advantages, and the unique character of the curriculum, which were crafted into progressive Learning Community (LC) Clusters. Students enrolled not for a single course but for a cluster of courses that integrated material from a variety of disciplines into a single theme for the semester. The capstone project for the semester explicitly linked the coursework for that cluster. The founders had designed this curriculum to speak to the needs of adult, working-class women, feeling that it better modeled the integrated nature of human learning. This curriculum design limited choices; there were no elective courses in the degree programs at Ravenwood, and although one had some choice in terms of which LC Cluster to take, one was unable to opt out of any courses within that cluster. One would think that this lack of choice could potentially be a disadvantage to recruitment, but, in fact, it was often positioned as a selling point; speakers at recruitment events (faculty and administrators alike) often explained that one need not worry about taking irrelevant courses (such as art history) or about which course to take or when. This lack of choice contrasted sharply with the larger institutions, where there were hundreds of majors, hundreds of potential courses to take in any given semester, and highly flexible programs of study. Furthermore, the structured program of study, close-knit cohorts, and accelerated speed contrasted sharply with the perceived weaknesses of the public university system in particular. It also meant that every alumnus of a given degree program had completed precisely the same courses (although likely with different instructors). Admissions counselor Nadira, an alumna, was very effective at crafting these broad strands into a cohesive script about attending Ravenwood.

Nadira frequently shared with students the story of how she had attended a local community college for a year before coming to Ravenwood. She excelled in Ravenwood's programs, completed her bachelor's degree, and then went on for her master's degree at Ravenwood (which followed a similar structure). After three and a half years of study at Ravenwood, she had earned a new master's degree and started a new business. She then ran into an old classmate she had known back in the community college, and she learned that he had not yet finished his associate's degree. She had been astonished. She thus argued that although Ravenwood College was much more expensive than the community college, students in the public system had to contend with limited and arbitrary course offerings and inconvenient schedules, and consequently, an associate degree could take five years to complete. Nadira also felt that public institutions were rife with bureaucratic confusion: huge course bulletins, headaches related to closed courses, complex systems of prerequisites, opaque degree requirements, and a massive, confusing bureaucracy that made you feel like you "were in high school again." She was clear that it was not that Ravenwood students were not savvy enough to handle such bureaucracy but rather that they "should not have to." Nadira's assumptions about the public university were anecdotal but very much informed the arguments she would make for attending Ravenwood. Public institutions were painted as being massive, bureaucratic, intimidating, and rigid, in contrast to Ravenwood's small cohort and a human-faced, student-centered curriculum that would lead to faster completion. Of course, the cost was much higher.

As an admissions counselor and alumna, Nadira often drew on her own life story as a woman of color who had struggled with, but cherished, her schooling. She felt that many "poor" and "ethnic" students were hesitant to take out loans, which largely meant that they would limit themselves to only public institutions. Loans, according to Nadira, were practically required for attending a private college, which was a shame because she felt that private colleges offered a lot of "nifty benefits," such as the accelerated programs and alternative curricula of Ravenwood. Ravenwood was thus positioned as better meeting the needs of particular kinds of students but only being able to do so as a private institution that would cost more.

Cole was hired as a tuition planner working in the Office of Admissions in order to fulfill many applicant needs, including teaching financial literacy, helping prospects through the financial planning process, and recruitment. During the application and recruitment process, Cole would meet with students to attempt to demonstrate how and why Ravenwood was such a good investment. This was further necessary because Ravenwood College had nearly no endowments, was completely reliant on tuition to cover its expenses, and was much more expensive than the public institutions with which it was competing. Ravenwood's tuition rate was between $450 and $800 per credit, which translated into between $15,000 and $26,000 per year for most students (program dependent).

Like Nadira, Cole informed prospects that at most colleges one would be unable to both work full-time and go to class full-time, as you were able to at Ravenwood. Therefore, in a four-year, liberal arts college where students were graduating on average after five or six years, they were not only paying for five years of tuition but also forgoing a full-time salary that could be as high as $30,000 a year. At a college with similar tuition rates, the cost of attendance might therefore be $50,000 in tuition + $150,000 that they would not have earned in wages because they could not work a full-time job. Although Ravenwood College was expensive, it allowed students to earn a full salary while they attended and made it easier for them to graduate more quickly. According to Cole, this helped some students to "get past the sticker shock." Cole was therefore positioning the college not only as meeting the needs of particular students but also as being the wiser fiscal investment.

Although not literally scripted, there were a number of such lines of argument that had been crafted for the adult student that seemed to work less effectively for more traditionally aged prospects. After years of recruitment for Ravenwood, Dean Levitz was fairly adamant that the college's student population was the working adult; he was not interested in targeting high school students. A couple of admissions counselors, such as Maggie, disagreed and spent some time nurturing relationships with high school counselors, looking for younger, "focused" students. Maggie, who had worked with Madelyn at a competitor before coming to Ravenwood College, had experience and connections with more traditionally aged, college-going students. Maggie said that at her previous employment, she was part of a strong, organized team, where all student contact, from tours to telephone calls, were literally scripted and monitored—whereas Ravenwood was looser and more informal. At Ravenwood College, admissions counselors worked independently and needed to structure their own time and experiences, but like anywhere else, at its heart it was a sales position, and so, according to Maggie, "our job is to paint a pretty picture."

In her former job, Maggie had the chance to develop relationships with young kids as early as their junior year, reaching out with scholarships or special summer programs to entice them. At a private college in the region, one admissions officer I interviewed described the institution's "in-depth communication plans" to engage even high school freshmen:

> The name studies have shown that if you are not on a student's list, college list, going into their sophomore year you have no shot at them—you have minimal shot at them . . . [and so some programs begin] very very early on. I do programs in [local community] for eighth-grade parents, for going to there and planning things for college for high school. And I do a presentation on college, and it's just so they can start thinking about it.

Unlike Ravenwood, this other institution was engaging students at much earlier ages, so that its name would be thought of as an option. Maggie's former job was at a proprietary college, which was both similar to and different from Ravenwood; she said that they both were "opportunity schools," by which she meant that they targeted prospective students wherever there was opportunity: particularly those who were rejected by or had dropped out from other colleges. Her previous employer, however, had a lot more resources and had both admission counselors (who assisted prospects through the admissions process) and an "outreach team," which spent all of its time on the road at college fairs and high schools "generating leads." As an admissions counselor, she had only to follow up on inquiries from students who had already expressed an interest in the college, whereas at Ravenwood she had to find those leads, follow up with them, guide them through applications, and so on. Still, she felt that her job mostly involved being pleasant and following up with people, admitting, "This is not a good thing to say, but Admissions is a job that a monkey can do if it's taught how to do it, know what I mean?" And yet, it also required articulating, elaborating, and deploying these persuasive scripts, as demonstrated at the *Cambia Tu Vida* event.

Ravenwood's *Cambia Tu Vida* recruitment event had all of the most obvious and essentialized markers of Latino culture, including a live Latin band and delicious Latin food. In fact, the food was so delicious and staff members were so busy snacking and chatting around the catered meal that even when prospective students arrived, staff practically ignored them, leaving them to wait awkwardly for the open house to begin. Sometimes the messaging at Ravenwood was not well scripted.

After a particularly prolonged moment of anxiety where several admission representatives argued among themselves about who would initiate the session, faculty from the two major schools were introduced. Although they overlapped in their messaging in many ways, each of them drew on different primary strategies for connecting to students and for provoking aspirations in attendees.

Dean Martinez of the School for Social Work began. She spoke in broad generalities about the available programs in a way that emphasized a few features. First, she emphasized the tight cohort nature of the programs along with a few catch phrases from the college marketing literature. She then referenced and deployed identity politics scripts as a successful woman of Puerto Rican descent. She mentioned that the college had "people like yourself," and she explained how proud she was at graduation when she saw "people like us" getting their degrees. She specifically mentioned President Obama and Supreme Court Justice Sotomayor several times. Finally, she emphasized that the goal of the college was to help students "move up and move on." To my ear, her tone and manner were somewhat flat and the themes became repetitive. She did not describe courses, programs of study, career opportunities, or alumni stories.

In contrast, Professor Bhatt of the School for Business and Technology was a dynamic and entertaining speaker. He began with a brief statement about the current state of the economy layered in the jargon of economics and business management and then said evenly, "If you understand what I just said, then you don't need to come to Ravenwood." He then asked the audience what percentage of businesses failed in their first year, which, of course, they underestimated. He then asked why it was that such businesses failed. His answer was that individual business owners did not have the core skills and knowledge sets required to let those businesses succeed. These were among the skills and knowledge sets that Ravenwood would offer; and Bhatt went on with examples. Water, he suggested, was essentially all the same. Whether it came from a tap or from a bottle, it was H_2O. And yet, business professionals had successfully utilized marketing and branding techniques to persuade various markets that there was a substantial difference between one bottle of water and another and, of course, that different prices were thus warranted. This was genius, he felt, and was representative of the skills and knowledge sets they would acquire as business students in Ravenwood.

Professor Bhatt's talk was far more persuasive. In fact, during the question and answer portion of the open house, a number of students said that they had arrived planning to study social work, but after the talks, they were considering studying business. During the event, both Dean Martinez and Professor Bhatt suggested that it was important not to decide on a major at that moment but rather to resolve to go to college. Nonetheless, Professor Bhatt whispered to me later as we left the open house that Dean Martinez was going to "kill" him, indicating that he also perceived his talk as having been far more persuasive. To a certain extent, the attractiveness of business over social work reflects the particular strengths of the programs and speakers involved, but several features of the talks given the responses of the prospective students are also suggestive of how race and ethnicity are spoken of in the context of aspiration and education.

Like the prospective students and Dean Martinez, Professor Bhatt was a person of color, with descent from the South Asian diaspora of the Caribbean, but he did not explicitly talk about his ethnic subjectivity. He emphasized instead market-based notions of skill, knowledge, and self (see Urciuoli 2008). Like Dean Martinez, his talk suggested the possibility of movement and success, but he never explicitly identified this possibility as connected to a particular class of person although the recruitment event was designed to target Latino/a applicants.

Although he also did not describe courses, programs of study, or alumni stories, Professor Bhatt did deploy a number of scripts that cultivated a subject in Ravenwood aligned with meritocratic-individualist models for achievement and engagement that were also seen in the marketing literature. The students were encouraged to embrace risk and risk-taking as a fundamental aspect of self not only in the present but as a way to "colonize the future." Demerath (2009) explained self-ascribed authority "as a kind of reflexive feedback mechanism that justified and reinforced students' identities and practices, including their aspirations and achievement orientations" (87). Subjects are required to control and discipline themselves as they take authority of their lives. The myth of a color-blind, modern America[5] is tied up with understandings of the competitive, objective marketplace as the only meaningful context in which agents make choices. Race and ethnicity may be ever present but may be deployed only in very particular conditions and in strategic ways that do not contradict the supposedly meritocratic market-place. Professor Bhatt was seemingly familiar with the delicate social terrain in which the discourse of race and ethnicity could be deployed effectively.

Ravenwood also struggled with finding ways both to recruit more students and to do so in a way that resonated and aligned with its educational mission. Dean Martinez shared with me a "Recruitment Strategies Report for the School for Social Work" that identified several areas for recruitment to Ravenwood, many of which most typical colleges and universities most likely never consider. Among these were an Ex-Offender Recruitment Initiative (never initiated) that worked to identify individuals serving time who required "educational opportunities as a condition of release." Another included recommendations for the Welfare-to-Careers Program for those receiving public assistance, which had been implemented. The Welfare-to-Careers Program was not advertised or pulled into the public brand, although there was information about it made available discreetly on the Ravenwood website. There were also a variety of initiatives that utilized the connections of existing faculty or staff, faculty phone-a-thons, and the development of articulation agreements, which would make transferring credits from other institutions far easier. Certain programs or aspects of the college that did not align with traditional notions of merit were not emphasized and would be recruited for quietly. Another example was the Ability-to-Benefit Program, which permitted students without a general equivalency diploma to obtain one while attending college-level courses. Dean Levitz once noted that another college openly advertised a similar program on its website, whereas at Ravenwood it was positioned more discreetly. Dean Levitz wondered if Ravenwood College should follow suit but later dismissed the idea as it did not align with the desired brand. This was the paradox for Ravenwood; such efforts resonated with the mission of the college to reach out to and support marginalized persons, but it contradicted the deeply entrenched, Jeffersonian paradigm of higher education as identifying the "best." It was thus unclear how to reconcile such contradictions.

Such contradictions would often arise when the contrast between one's current position in the social structure and the aspirational scripts used in recruitment were stark, such as at another recruitment event I attended with a local community organization that served the homeless. There were about five employees from the small organization and about thirty clients, and the discussion centered on a specific scholarship that would cover all expenses for those who completed the community organization's program successfully. Professor Stubbs and Professor Bhatt were the primary speakers along with the tuition planner (Cole) and a current student; admissions staff largely held peripheral roles, such as welcoming guests and introducing speakers.

Professor Stubbs effectively engaged the audience by suggesting that the program allowed students to both "improve the world" and pursue a career at the same time. He said, "helping others is transformative for yourself." He spoke mostly through vignettes about students he had known and said there was a "special spirit" in Ravenwood. He recalled former students as old as sixty successfully completing the program, which acknowledged "their life experiences," and respected them as adults. He also briefly mentioned Obama and Sotomayor before moving on to talk about the Ravenwood literature and sample course schedules in the participants' folders. Professor Stubbs described Ravenwood as a "special" place outside of the established social order—a place where the possibilities for college even extended to the homeless. He drew connections between his audience of prospective students (who were adults and mostly people of color) and individual models of success, through both local anecdotes (former sixty-year-old students) and through successful people of color who had national prestige (Obama and Sotomayor). Because poverty and race and ethnicity are often conflated in American contexts, Stubbs was able to draw parallels between prospective students and President Obama by erasing important differences, such as Obama's highly educated, international, and credentialed preparation. In so doing, he engaged his audience and opened up the possibilities of success, achievement, and mobility, in ways that seemed to me to be more effective than those of Dean Martinez.

Professor Bhatt spoke next about the economy with optimism. He suggested that there were always "dips" in the economy and that "we always manage to come out of it." The business program, he suggested, would teach them how to take advantage of the boom that would inevitably come. As in *Cambia Tu Vida*, he drew on some of the same scripts about the number of new businesses that succeeded. The answer was two out of ten, but this time he pointed to the individuals' inability to manage themselves as the source of that failure.[6] Just as Professor Stubbs had called on possibilities, Professor Bhatt stoked aspirations by opening up inclusive, professional possibilities through schooling. "Money will come," he said to a group of homeless persons in a program potentially offering a scholarship to some of them. "There will always be someone willing to take a chance on you," he continued, drawing parallels between both the possibility of the college granting access and a future investor offering money. Ravenwood was bundled up with representations of possibility, aspiration, and success in which even the fact of homelessness was considered assailable. This is particularly stark if one considers the structural challenges and risks that one faces as a homeless person. Ethnographic works from Liebow (1995) to Bourgois and Schonberg (2009) demonstrate the brutal, isolating, and demeaning conditions of living on the streets in the United Sates, and for the homeless, it is far less likely that there will always be someone willing to "take a chance on them."

Cole, the tuition planner, spoke next about "how to make it work for you." He described his job as one that empowered prospects to take control of their futures and to ease anxiety about paying for a private college. He then took a number of questions from the audience. For example, he reassured one person that bad credit history would not affect their ability to get a student loan and that financial aid had not been cut because of the economic crisis; this was then followed by more specific questions about the financial aid process.

Finally, a young woman who had completed the program from the community organization and received a full scholarship to Ravenwood spoke about her personal experience. She talked about her understanding of what it was like to be homeless, her fear in going to college, and her stubbornness to keep working at it until she got it right. She said that she eventually realized that she was not "dumb," and she told the audience that after some time, they would "fit in" like she had. She talked about her willingness to use the tutoring center and referred specifically back to Stubbs's speech by agreeing that there was a "special spirit" to the place, that she had grown, and that the audience would learn to feel good about themselves. The student seemingly embraced the inclusive message of the previous speakers and spoke to the personal transformation that she had experienced; she was the embodiment of these possibilities. She acknowledged that she had not had the symbolic markers associated with college when she had begun. She had not fit in, but over time and with assistance, she had acquired those markers. The dean of admissions then offered thanks and discussed deadlines and exams to great applause, after which there was mingling, eating, and laughter. The promise of success and personal change was in the air.

In many ways, it is admirable and extraordinary that these two institutions (Ravenwood and the nonprofit community organization serving the homeless) would work to provide a postsecondary credential for those struggling with the reality of homelessness. However, these sorts of representations of possibility were still meritocratic American Dream sorts of stories available for the few through competition. They did not question the structures that allowed the attendees to become homeless in the first place or that might keep them that way. Rather, the speakers fully embraced the notion that a few of them could be provided the opportunity (as individuals) to follow traditional paths to economic security (a college degree) with a little support from all sides. The American status quo remained unexamined. However, it is important to remember that this was not some philosophical dialogue about mobility in the United States but rather an attempt to persuade persons to invest significant time and money in the institution. Ravenwood College was not inexpensive. Although this open house focused on a scholarship that would cover expenses for these homeless, prospective students, I had heard these same arguments before. They were part of the persuasive scripts that Ravenwood staff and faculty drew on regularly to recruit students. About 80 percent of students were willing to take out student loans to finance their education at Ravenwood College. These facts lead to an inescapable question: did the "special spirit" of Ravenwood merit the cost of attendance? The admissions team needed students to feel that the answer to that question was yes.

But one of the big questions for Ravenwood was where to locate these prospective students. The vast majority of colleges and universities knew this answer: in high schools. As such, a good deal of undergraduate admissions work at most universities included developing strong relationships with local high schools and high school counselors. As we have seen already, however, there was not a single catchment area for Ravenwood, and more creative strategies need to be identified. Everyone was aware of this, as when during a town hall meeting a professor responded to the president's great optimism about the new veterans bill going through Congress at that time: "Where do you think the vets are? They're not in [the trendy neighborhood of Ravenwood]." So where could you find the vets? Where could you find any working adult with a high school diploma who was hitting a ceiling in career advancement?

As senior admissions counselor, Bernard actively organized and managed the various recruitment events that the college had participated in or was considering participating in; a large binder labeled "outreach" was an attempt to document where the prospective students were. He said that the events were really a result of trial and error: if attending an event or college fair yielded students, then they continued; if not, they didn't. This approach was logical, flexible, and easy to manage. The information cards and sign-in sheets were coded for event, and when the inquiry's information was entered into the computer systems, that code went with it, although Bernard did not know which codes went with which event, as that was controlled by the director of student records. Admissions counselors also engaged in what they called "drop-offs," some of which were described as terribly awkward. Essentially, the admissions counselor identified an organization of any kind in which prospective students might be found. These ranged from community colleges and high schools to libraries, private companies, and community organizations of all kinds. They preferred that there were already established links in the organization (for example, current students or alumni might be employed there), but at other times such links would have to be forged through a cold call to the human resources department. Admissions counselors would then gather all kinds of materials from their private hidden "stash," the supply room and literature dispensers to bring with them. They would then visit the organization (always within commuting distance of Ravenwood) and drop off the materials for display. Whether holding an event on campus or off campus, however, it was necessary for admissions counselors to engage in a good deal of impression management.

Stevens's (2007) ethnographic depiction of a selective college highlights how the institution's image was carefully cultivated, refined, and managed by the Office of Admissions. At different points, the director of admissions described both the receptionist and the man who mowed the lawn as some of the most important people in the college because they had such a powerful impact on prospective students' first impressions (Stevens 2007, 30). Although staff members at Ravenwood were sensitive to their image and impression, far less time was taken to script or polish the messages. As someone who has worked in higher education administration (and is frankly a little neurotic), I was often aware of or thinking about what students or prospects would see. As a participant observer, I would sometimes engage in simple image refinement; throughout the day, I would find myself straightening up brochures, files, stacks of paper, and literature that had been left in uneven piles. I would straighten out chairs and move the bag of promotional materials out of the view of the reception area. The receptionists, many of whom spent the day browsing the Internet at the front desk, were largely work-study students with only a vague sense of the academic programs and were not frequently active in polishing appearances. In fact, Ravenwood's limited resources, staffing, and constant pressure affected the degree to which moments were scripted.

I accompanied Aaron, Maggie, and Professor Kucharski to a large, local community organization with over five hundred employees to make a presentation about the college, which was a somewhat frequent strategy. In this particular organization, an executive had gotten a poor impression of Ravenwood graduates through a bad experience with one alumnus, and so Maggie had worked hard to mend relations and to make a presentation emphasizing graduate-level study for the unit that this executive supervised. With Maggie in the lead, we were led into a large boardroom where we set up the event. Food and refreshments were brought in, and we put an information packet filled with Ravenwood literature and promotional items (pens and highlighters) at each seat. Certain promotional items (such as the pens) were very popular, and admissions counselors hid private stashes both in their offices and at home, which was where Maggie's had come from.

When the employees came in, Maggie spoke very smoothly and capably, seeming to work from an internal script that she had used many times before. She talked extensively about the founders as "pioneers, reformers, and revolutionaries dedicated to women's education." She briefly described the history of the college (I noted a few minor errors in benchmark years and names) and then read off the names and credentials of certain faculty.

Maggie's speech specifically drew on specific arguments for education: she suggested first off that the economy was being "trashed," that we were moving toward a depression, and that there was little job security, thus implying that education was a means to mitigate economic risk. She also suggested that work for the public good was not only productive but also personally fulfilling and that with President Obama coming into office soon, there would be a lot of opportunity for those dedicated to communities and the public good.[7] By this point, she was speaking a little quickly and went on to say that the application fee would be waived for "today only" before introducing Professor Kucharski, who spoke briefly about the graduate programs at Ravenwood. Aaron, who by that point had been working as an admissions counselor for only a few weeks, gave a brief, nervous presentation before the floor was opened to questions and the food was served. There was a good deal of conversation and discussion, and a number of the roughly forty guests had questions for the admissions counselors, although very few talked to Professor Kucharski. All the questions asked were about admissions requirements: financial aid, deadlines, needed documents, transfer credits, and so on; no one asked about the size of the programs, academic content, curricula, faculty, or course design.

At a small, graduate open house on campus in June (with three attendees), Dean Levitz spoke about his close connection to the graduate programs from his work at Ravenwood in the 1980s. Many administrators, like the dean, had a personal connection to the institution and shared that connection by drawing on personal narratives with prospective students. Dean Levitz had a very soft speaking voice that required you to lean in to hear him carefully, but his messages were clear, concise, and articulate. He did make it clear that low grade point averages would not preclude admission, describing this not as an open admissions policy but as a sensitivity to the needs and expertise of the adult student and the understanding that people mature in different ways.

All of these various scripts were deployed in different times with different persons to persuade individuals to apply. Although the context was certainly precarious and uncertain, the scripts had been cultivated over time by the staff and seemingly worked well enough to ensure that Ravenwood had enough students to continue to exist.

Finding a Niche within the Niche

Maggie often spoke fondly about the support and resources of her former position, particularly when we would see entire strings of buses plastered with the advertisements for her former employer. Maggie was also clear, however, that some of her experiences in Ravenwood were far more rewarding; she had been there long enough to see some of the students she had recruited graduate from Ravenwood and then come back to thank her and praise their academic programs. That was something that she had never seen while she was working for the proprietary college. In fact, she said, there had been a lot more of a "give-me-all-your-money and we're going to claim-we-have-all-this-but-we-don't" attitude at her previous job, although from what she had heard through the grapevine, that was starting to change. In contrast, she felt more secure that Ravenwood was offering a positive educational experience.

Regardless, Maggie felt that some focused high school students could potentially be a great market for the college, and although the dean disagreed, she tried to "sneak" them in from time to time. These students were outside of Ravenwood's niche, and the dean would not allocate resources to their cultivation. From the point of view of Dean Levitz, spending resources on reaching new, unproven markets was too risky. Although it did not actively target a high school population, Ravenwood College would occasionally prepare recruitment tables for large college fairs or specific events where other colleges and prospective students were attending. Many of the admissions counselors reported dreading the questions that younger prospects would ask: "Do you have nursing?" "Do you have a basketball team?" "Is there a gym?" "What are the dorms like?" Despite its low academic ranking and prestige, admissions counselors reported that some parents were interested because Ravenwood lacked so much of the extracurricular student life that might be a distraction for their child; the children, however, often proved to be intractable.

Maggie knew that they were playing a high stakes game. One student who enrolled and graduated from the college would bring in $50,000 over the course of his or her studies, so if she spent a few thousand dollars and was able to recruit just one high school student, it was enough to cover all of the expenses. She wanted to develop the high school student as her niche within the niche. This approach was not without precedent.

Assistant Director Madelyn, Maggie's friend and former colleague, had successfully carved out her own niche within the niche: she was the resident expert on international students. Madelyn, who herself was a European national residing in the United States, had been trained on international student advisement and saw potential for Ravenwood to expand. Curriculum was a critical aspect of recruitment, including for international students. For example, international students (F1 status) were restricted from working while in the United States, unless work experience was built directly into the curriculum. The LC Clusters of Ravenwood included different levels of clinical and internship curricula, theoretically creating a way through which an F1 student could be authorized to work nearly every semester of his or her study. Madelyn had carefully crafted an argument to the administration for expanding international student populations while developing specific recruitment strategies and persuasive scripts to applicants, leading to an increase in international student enrollment from twenty-two in 2007 to seventy-five in the fall of 2009. As Madelyn was the expert on international students, she was not only expanding a niche for the college but establishing an irreplaceable role for herself within the office. More and more she was able to dedicate herself nearly entirely to developing the international marketing and recruitment activities, which culminated in a March 2009 recruitment trip to China. The trip was organized through an American company that had been arranging admissions counselors' travel on recruitment events throughout the world for about twenty-five years. Madelyn's trip included events in Shenzhen, Nanjing, Shanghai, and Beijing and cost about $9,000.00. Her report about the trip made a series of recommendations on "strengthening relationships" with key institutions, continued participation in international recruitment events, developing of relationships with international recruitment "agents," increasing "visibility and presence" in China, and expanding recruitment to include the Middle East, Turkey, and India. She offered city-by-city, institution-by-institution breakdowns of which potential students attended the events, which were largely set in various Chinese high schools and colleges. Once again, each recruited student could potentially yield $50,000 for the institution, and so she argued the cost of such recruitment trips more than paid for themselves.[8] Madelyn found that the highest interest in Ravenwood College came from its MBA programs, rather than any undergraduate degree; her taking on the role of "international expert" and familiarity with the MBA program led directly to her chaperoning an MBA student trip to London and Paris in July of 2009. For two years, Madelyn and Dean Levitz had also been attempting to break into the large, local Russian community and had finally worked into some local Russian Orthodox churches and Russian community centers. There were some ads for Ravenwood in local Russian newspapers and an event in August, but very few Russians actually enrolled in Ravenwood. Regardless, Madelyn was able to position herself as an authority for a particular niche within the institution.

Other admissions counselors had also been able to position themselves as experts in particular segments or niches of the student population, either purposefully or accidentally. At a staff meeting in January 2009, Dean Levitz announced that the president of Ravenwood had gone down to Washington, DC, for an orientation about the new veterans bill that was working its way through Congress. This bill would grant recent veterans an amount equal to the most expensive public institution in the state; thus, if the most expensive public institution cost $15,000 per year, veterans would receive a benefit of $15,000 to attend any institution in that state. Ravenwood's president, thrilled by the bill, decided to equalize the playing field with the local public university rates through internal funds, by waiving the difference between Ravenwood College's tuition and that of the public ones so that Ravenwood could offer an essentially competitive rate. At this meeting, Dean Levitz asked his staff to begin brainstorming other ways to recruit and serve veterans because every college in the region would attempt to recruit these same students.

A short time later, Aaron was surprised when he was identified as the person responsible for all veterans admissions issues and was required to train himself on all aspects of veteran recruitment, affairs, and benefits. Dean Levitz had selected Aaron because he had been in the Peace Corps, and that was the closest thing that they had to a veteran in the Office of Admissions. By May, Aaron was appearing in flyers and advertisements on bus stops, wearing a crisp clean suit and standing in front of an American flag. When he asked my opinion, I suggested that the materials gave me the impression of an election ad for a young congressman and also the impression that Aaron himself was a veteran. His direct e-mail and telephone number were listed on the materials, and his title was listed as "Veteran Advocate" for Ravenwood College, which made him very nervous. Over the summer, the college would spend over six figures on marketing to veterans; by that point, Aaron had still not mastered veterans issues and was worried about receiving phone calls about benefits or programs that he did not fully understand.

Aaron organized and ran an open house specifically for veterans in July 2009, in which professors, deans, and cheese and crackers were readily available. At first, it seemed as though there was a strong turnout, but as time passed it became clear that many were there to see a visiting nurse providing immunization shots,[9] and many of the students waiting for her were enjoying the refreshments for the open house for vets. In the end, only two veterans attended, whom Aaron met with one-on-one instead of in the open house format. As the veterans bill covered only post-9/11 veterans, and the two prospects were Vietnam War veterans, they were not even eligible for the benefits advertised. The various professors and deans who had come to speak were not pleased. In a tight economic climate, Dean Levitz was building arguments for his staff by encouraging these specializations within the Ravenwood niche, even if they did not always work out as intended. It takes a degree of foresight and political savvy to mediate bureaucratic systems in this way, and the dean was able to do so effectively.

Like Aaron, Louisa was under a great deal of pressure as an admissions counselor to recruit from her particular niche and also to achieve clarity in her role. Seventy-five percent of Louisa's salary was from a Title V grant, giving her a unique position in the Office of Admissions to increase the enrollment of Latino/a students.[10] When I first began my time in Ravenwood, I had noticed mysterious brochures and literature on something called "Pathways" that always confused me: sometimes it appeared to be a program, but the text never described exactly what it was about. When I asked, most admission counselors could not tell me about it and would direct me to Louisa. Louisa herself did not seem to know what the Pathways program was and would direct me to Dean Levitz, who vaguely sketched out the program as a collaboration with another college. I also had heard that there was a Title V grant used for a computer lab and a Title V committee, but I was unsure what the connections were between all these pieces—neither was Louisa. One day, Dean Levitz was unable to attend a meeting with the director of admissions with the college that was jointly operating Pathways, and Louisa did so in his place; she was asked for a recruitment plan and brochures about mathematics education. Mathematics education? She was confused about what her role should be and afterward went to find the original grant itself and read it, only to discover that "I was doing the job completely wrong—I was not doing what I was supposed to be doing."

Apparently, the college had received a joint grant with another college to develop a master's degree in mathematics education, through which both institutions were supposed to enroll ten to fifteen students in 2010. The partner college, which had no graduate degrees, was supposed to "funnel" some of its mathematics students into education rather than technical or engineering careers. Ravenwood was supposed to hire the faculty, organize the program, recruit students, and prepare a website about the program, which would allow students to move seamlessly from undergraduate programs (either at the partner college or Ravenwood) into the mathematics education program; this was the topic of the literature and brochures I had found titled "Pathways." Ravenwood had already spent grant money on a state-of-the-art mathematics computer laboratory for this program, while Student Services was supposed to be developing a bridge program for Ravenwood students who did not have the proper mathematics prerequisites to enter the program. As a condition of this grant, Ravenwood had to demonstrate that it had a Hispanic population totaling 25 percent of total student enrollment, which was why Louisa had been asked to recruit in the Latino/a community. Louisa had known none of this.

Louisa had spent her first year on the job working on recruiting Latino/a students (through events like the *Cambia Tu Vida* event) and "brand awareness" in the community, without ever realizing that the mathematics education program even existed. Throughout July she had worked tirelessly on organizing a role for Ravenwood College in the local Hispanic Heritage Festival, while also taking three courses a week in her own graduate studies (at a local, selective institution), recruiting students, and (literally) sleeping at her desk on her lunch hour. In the summer of 2009, Ravenwood was just over 21 percent Hispanic, and Louisa knew that although she had a different role than some others, she was consistently the recruiter with the lowest number of students. Louisa found herself cultivating specific niches but without a full sense of why. Dean Levitz was able to quite skillfully manage the bureaucracy by encouraging the niche specialization described above, which would help him to retain vital salary lines. Operating in this way was simply practical given the precarious position of the college.

The Provocative Space between Counseling and Sales

Implicit in college recruitment is the assemblage of ideas and ways of knowing that can be learned and the fluidity of professional aspirations connected to these assemblages. As previously suggested, Ravenwood College is a progressive institution with a mission and history dedicated to promoting social change and empowerment for communities traditionally living in poverty. Because Ravenwood offered only a few, largely vocational majors for undergraduates, the question of fit for prospective students became far more consequential than in an institution with hundreds of majors. For me, some of the programs seemed to resonate very closely with the mission (as in education, social work, and so forth) while others did not (as in business). My own training and values suggested that there was a contradiction between this mission and such academic programs, and I was not sure why an open house would target both areas of study at the same time. Both *Cambia Tu Vida* and the homeless outreach events demonstrated for me that prospective students could imagine themselves in a variety of professions—that is, they could imagine a variety of selves populating the future. For many of these prospective students, there seemed to be little contradiction between a self who was dedicated to providing counseling and services for poor families and a self who found an innovative way to persuade people to purchase bottles of water in bright packaging.

One way to interpret these findings would be that, as marginalized people of color, prospective students were susceptible to well-crafted arguments— that a smooth and interesting talker would be able to sway them easily from one way of thinking to another. This was important because there were few majors available, and thus someone may approach the college with an interest that did not align neatly with one of these. On occasion, admissions counselors spoke about these processes in just this way, but I find it *unlikely* that being susceptible to persuasive arguments is unique to marginalized people of color. Rather, I would argue that different persuasive scripts are deployed by all Offices of Admissions across the United States as tailored to their particular market segment or niche and thus represent a critically important aspect of college recruitment.

At Ravenwood, the ability to persuade prospects and students into different majors or programs was something that all admissions counselors reported struggling with on an ethical level. Essentially, they all aligned the work they did and liked doing with "counseling" and distanced it from "sales"; this binary was articulated again and again. Nadira, for example, was adamant that she could but would not do whatever was necessary to "make the sale." She would not "convince someone interested in interior design that she should go into the business program because it's the same thing" or that in order to "succeed" in interior design you needed to have a background in business and thus persuade a prospect to enroll therein. She would be clear to her students that there were no interior design programs. In her own words, she was not going to "turn rice into potatoes," which was something that she associated with proprietary colleges.

Again, Nadira herself was a graduate of Ravenwood, who had completed studies in the School for Social Work and gone on to start a somewhat successful business. She had taken the position in the Office of Admissions because as a Ravenwood alumna, she wanted to "give back." She reported that if she had felt the pressure to persuade students like that, she would have just "walked away" because she did not "need" this job. She would not mislead or "sucker" students into Ravenwood, and she did not feel pressure to do so, although she could not say how other admissions counselors felt. She saw her role as primarily career counseling, and what her students did was to "allow me to dream with them."

Aaron agreed. He suggested that he was not afraid to tell someone to apply somewhere else if he felt the applicant and Ravenwood College were not right for each other. He thought his priority was to be a counselor and not to worry about numbers, although he also was not sure that other admissions counselors agreed and so never told anyone else that. Louisa agreed. She stated that if she worked with a student interested in nursing,

> Potentially, I could persuade that student to still apply here and do a bachelor's in social work, because I can sell it, right? Because there is a sales piece, I can sell it, you know. "With this (degree program) you can do this," and "you can do that (academic program) and go on to do this (career path)."

She insisted, however, that none of it would be right for someone interested in nursing. She felt that she encountered many prospects who were "right on the edge" and that it would be easy to "push them over," but it would not be right for them. Maggie contrasted her experiences at her previous proprietary employer with her current job, indicating that at Ravenwood she was not as required to "sell." Another counselor, Jaleel, had previous admissions experience at yet another proprietary college and resigned because he felt it was too "sales-y." These exchanges highlighted that all of the admissions counselors seemed to feel that persuading too effectively would have been ethically questionable, and each found her or his own way to demarcate ethical boundaries, despite a lack of consensus on exactly where those boundaries lay. Still, all of these voices seemed to reinforce the notion that the prospective students were easily persuaded—that they were either unclear of their own aspirations or unclear as to how to pursue them.

When admissions counselors provoked aspiration in their prospective students, it was for a future self that was "successful"—but successful in what seemed less relevant. In this, Ravenwood's students do not seem that different from the masses of college students thinking about their investment and their own futures in uncertain economic times. Ravenwood's prospective students, fueled by popular discourses on mobility and success, were seemingly seeking a vehicle to take them "there"—and Ravenwood College was just such a vehicle. The "there," however, was a fluid destination.

Urciuoli (2008) described the ways that disparate and diverse skills are made commensurable within the market logic, both in terms of their market value and in the ability to acquire them as commodities. Further, the skills discourse is also penetrated by the logic of quantification, which fits in neatly with an understanding of education in the marketplace:

> The deployment of quantification rhetoric becomes part of the loose association of terms in this register, suggesting that all these disparate skills are commensurable. Their commensurability lies not in explicitly comparable qualities but implicitly in the notion that they can be assessed and inculcated in the same ways. This presupposition of workers as a set of measurable capacities is, in effect, an update of the Enlightenment notion of an abstract human that can be segmented into pieces. (217)

I am concerned here with how disparate personhoods and futures are made commensurable vis-à-vis the recruitment activities in which institutions of higher education engage. Nursing is then potentially like social work, interior design is like business, and even social work is like business in the sense that they each require the acquisition of unique skill sets and the investment of time and money, and they will eventually yield a dollar amount in future income. Therefore, all of these arguments resonate with the understanding of the self as a future project constructed to manage risky markets. In order to be successful, institutions of higher education need to lay out arguments that fold themselves into the self as future project. For institutions with national recognition and prestige, there is less need to articulate those arguments; they are implicit (almost ingrained) in the American mythology about success. For institutions that lack the symbolic capital, these arguments need to be laid out clearly to prospective students. Staff and faculty must be able to cultivate a space for the institution in prospective students' imagination. As Ravenwood had learned, failure to do so could yield enrollment disasters.

Conclusions: Caveat Emptor

Circulation into and through Ravenwood was both premised on and shaped by deep and powerful meanings that the institution sought to cultivate. In Moore's (2003) examination of a marketing firm, he describes the notion of "brand as promise" through the following "parable":

> "Imagine you are going to a party," began the marketing chief, "and you want the people you meet at the party to think you are beautiful. How to create that impression? You could go around at the party, and tell everyone you meet that you're beautiful—but that would be a strange approach," she began. Instead, fashioning the (external) brand means "Working out the logic, the story, finding the words that will elicit this [impression] from our customers, that will create this impression about us in the minds of others." The "method," she explained, was storytelling: construct a story, but leave it unfinished, "so that people reach this impression about us, and think of it as their own." (p. 340)

The faculty and administration at Ravenwood College seemed to be serious about providing individual students with pathways to economic mobility, but at least in the recruitment activities I observed, they told these sorts of unfinished stories about meritocratic individualism. The desire for success and the drive of aspirations are not unique to the prospective students of Ravenwood College, nor is it only under the guise of the market that educational desire is enacted.[11] Ravenwood's marketing materials and persuasive scripts told stories about the lives and futures of prospective students that were meant to suggest that success was at hand, and these stories tied up the colonized future and sense of self with market logics, brand, college recruitment materials, and activities.

As Nakassis (2012, 629) noted, "Brand offer themselves up to us as tools for self-actualization and, thus, as the very context of sociality and community" (Nakassis 2012). The analysis of brand requires an interrogation of classificatory schema whereby particular instantiations or tokens of brand (e.g., a particular pair of shoes) come to be associated with the desired identity or type (e.g., the notion that consumers of these shoes "just do it"). But this only makes sense given the cultural ontology and juridical structures in place that can recognize and enforce things like intellectual property, trademark, and copyright, respectively. The application of brand to higher education is far more complex.

In traditional, industrial corporations, a tangible product (token) is fashioned and consumed in ways that ideally align the product itself with the desired corporate identity. People purchase the tokens, which are then folded into their narratives about who they are, even if only in a very superficial way. Unlike in such contexts, I would argue that the token of higher education is not some material product, nor even commoditized forms of knowledge that are imagined as material, but rather a future version of the student him- or herself; the consumer is the token or rather will be. Thus, a particular instantiation of the "Harvard" brand is the "Harvard" alumnus. Although any brand engages in fashioning a particular fantasy about one's self, the brands of college and universities are fundamentally more powerful and deeply penetrative in that through the process of consumption a student literally becomes a token of that university. These tokens then become a part of the recruitment effort and are folded into persuasive scripts about success and achievement to bring in future generations of students. It is no surprise that institutions are able to charge so much in tuition as what they are selling is a fantasy of one's self and one's future to begin postgraduation.

The question, therefore, of admissions becomes all the more complex because in evaluating a particular applicant, the representative of the college or university must ask whether this particular person will become a suitable token for the brand. This is yet another way to think about the "niches" and "market segments" described earlier in this chapter. It is true that these questions relate to both whom these arguments can be cleanly and persuasively laid out to and who is likely to enroll, but it is also about having students and alumni who are logically consistent with the college's brand. This suggests that although institutions of higher education have moved more toward the corporate, profit-making model, the broader ontology is fundamentally different from the logic whereby consumers purchase footwear and actually aligns precisely with the Jeffersonian paradigm of education. As schooling (as a system and network) largely acts to sort students into like piles, there are significant consequences to being admitted to a particular college and being affiliated with the students therein. Part of the challenge that a less selective college like Ravenwood faces is that the profile of student is largely being reproduced along lines determined by outside forces, often related to the use of persuasive scripts and institutional momentum with certain populations. Because every student was needed, however, I observed no questions about applicants aligning with brand or institutional identity during the admissions process—which meant that such brand identities needed to be crafted after the fact. The result was a sense that the institution had less control over what the brand was; every applicant who met the minimum requirements would be accepted, and thus those stories needed to be folded into institutional ones, even if they were not logically consistent with these stories. Of course, this was a challenge that any college or university might struggle with, but there were stronger mechanisms in place for controlling this process in institutions that were more selective. Thus, by virtue of this process, the more selective an institution was, the more carefully it could craft a brand. Ravenwood's lack of brand recognition made it less selective, less prestigious, and tuition driven, which in turn prevented it from crafting a brand that could gain wide recognition.

Ravenwood was selling itself as the means for students to change their lives through their own initiative as reflected in titles like *Cambia Tu Vida* and "Making Your New Year Resolution Come True." Each of these reinforced the meritocratic individualism found throughout the public discourse about colleges in America, that with hard work and as the result of specific choices one would be able to secure a more stable and profitable personal future. The college was selling mobility and the American Dream. Furthermore, admissions counselors had elaborated persuasive scripts that seemed to work with those who matched the profile and which might not work as well with others. This was critical because the verbal repertoires deployed by admissions counselors and faculty at Admissions events needed to align with the brand that was being circulated in the media. Admissions staff thus encountered challenges in their everyday activity that paralleled some of what could be seen in the media.

Furthermore, the possibility of mobility resonated closely with the mission of the institution but was fundamentally at odds with the privilege-making culture of higher education. Admissions counselors at Ravenwood were not fluent in the various metrics and rankings that marked privilege in higher education and did not incorporate such numbers into their persuasive scripts. Although some were well practiced in crafting inclusive messages that encouraged aspirations for mobility and achievement through schooling, others were less so. The fact that they were willing to pursue any prospective student further reflected that Ravenwood had been unsuccessful in gaining name recognition, the ongoing anxiety over financial stability, and the institutional mission to reach nontraditional students. The nontraditional, potentially controversial, potentially embarrassing efforts (such as recruiting homeless or incarcerated persons) were to be found exclusively in spoken scripts and internal documents for particular audiences; they were not part of the brand of Ravenwood.

Individuals make choices, but a culture of meritocracy highlights these individual choices above and beyond any other contextual factors, which are rendered irrelevant or meaningless. The world we inhabit in which people can be transformed into bundles of numbers that are meaningful to the infrastructure is only made possible given this worldview. Colleges and universities invented neither aspiration nor market conditions. In the current marketplace, they prosper when potential students entwine market logic with aspiration vis-à-vis their institution. Ravenwood College actively highlighted this connection for its potential students in both its recruitment materials and activity, while erasing meaningful economic, political, social, and cultural contexts. This was necessary to managing future institutional risk.

Although I do argue that the particularities of Ravenwood mediate the ways that these activities are enacted, I resist here a conclusion that positions Ravenwood as either exceptional or an aberration. For example, other institutions may not have entwined Barack Obama's political discourse of hope with recruitment scripts, but I imagine that other institutions drew on other discourses relevant to their history, student population, and so on. Likewise, when working with a prospective student that is likely to attend college, it is important to persuade an applicant to attend this or that particular one, and the finest mark of distinction is to be an applicant's first choice. The "early decision" policies of many institutions serves to guarantee a seat in an incoming class at the applicant's supposed top choice. If such applicants are accepted, they are, however, required to withdraw their applications from any other colleges and universities. Thus, within the framework of fetishized, competitive individualism, for an institution to be someone's first choice serves as a point of pride, but it is also a way to manage the risk of future enrollments. At Ravenwood, the scripts that needed to be deployed were less about becoming the first choice among many institutions but rather about the decision to attend college at all. The project of intertwining aspiration and personhood with institutional narratives appears to be a key aspect of this process.

Attending to how these local persuasive scripts emerge from bureaucracies in relation to a historical moment is one way that ethnographic investigations can contribute to understanding how aspiration and identity become mutually entangled in institutions of higher education. Thus, individual students are encouraged to see their future in terms of their relationship with Ravenwood, and administrative staff see the future of Ravenwood as being closely tied to its student profile. Institutions (including faculty and staff) become deeply entwined with their students (including prospects, current students, and alumni) in an intimate dance to the tune of a future fantasy. It is a precarious dance, and with consequential missteps, but it is one that applicants and institutions must learn.

Other institutions of higher education that are equally subject to the vicissitudes of the marketplace must perceive their economic position as risky and thus must craft persuasive scripts that emerge from their own circumstances and an awareness of their brand. As such, other institutions engage in similarly persuasive arguments in which prospective students are folded into an imagined, future, successful self, and the case of Ravenwood represents a detailed analysis of how one institution struggles with making the argument that most colleges need to make: that future risk can be managed and that success is the result of individual choices, first to attend college and second to attend this college in particular. But when prospective students are persuaded to apply to Ravenwood College, it is only the first step toward becoming a college student; after the persuasive arguments are deployed is when the sorting machine in the educational infrastructure is truly activated.

Chapter 3

It's All about the Numbers

Be more selective at the time to enroll prospective students. The majority of
the students I interacted with at Ravenwood were not the kind of students
I expected to meet. I have a Master's degree from [institution], therefore
I was used to having classmates with different attitudes, and behavior
than the ones I met at Ravenwood College.

[Do] Not charge students that have passed classes, then change the
requirements, then have them do it over again. Have staff that are competent
and know what they are supposed to do. And most importantly get rid
of [employee] who is not approachable and not very friendly!

They should be more organized at the administrative level. Things should
be resolved easier over the phone and have less bureaucracy involved.
Regulations that make no sense should be revised.

ANONYMOUS COMMENTS, RAVENWOOD GRADUATION SURVEY 2007–2008

Once a prospective student has been persuaded and taken steps toward
joining the Ravenwood community, the institution's locus as a node for cir-
culating information in a massive educational infrastructure becomes readily
apparent. Massive bureaucracies are in place that require applicants to package themselves as a series of documents and institutionally acknowledged
bits of information. A glint of individual personality may filter through in
the form of personal statements or recommendation letters, but these are
limited in depth and mediated through institutionalized systems. This infrastructure is fundamentally (and intentionally) dehumanizing, as it turns
applicants into numbers that are theoretically commensurable with one another. Moving through the infrastructure is clearly of consequence, however,
as it allows students access to greater resources, opportunities, and social
capital vis-à-vis higher education.

But despite the dehumanizing exigencies of the infrastructure, it remains one that is built and navigated by human actors. Thus, in this chapter, I focus attention on how applicants are converted into numbers and made meaningful in the infrastructure and the ways that local cultures, agendas, and politics are layered into these processes.

The Life of Numbers

At Ravenwood College, there were great lulls in admissions work, giving staff ample time for discussion and debate with an anthropologist. Late August 2009, however, was not such a time, and I had made myself somewhat scarce in the Office of Admissions. I had been embedded in the setting for many months by that point and knew that during the height of recruitment work I would be little more than a distraction, and so I would only stop in from time to time to check on the team. At more elite or selective institutions, early admissions and deposits transformed August into a waiting game; at that point, the work of recruiting and enrolling students would be largely done, and admissions staff would be waiting to see who actually turned up in September. At Ravenwood, however, enrollment was far from over; in fact, recruitment would continue nearly two weeks into the fall semester, when enrollment would finally edge a hair over budget goals. That meant that some students would first attend a class in the third week, a two full weeks behind the rest of their classmates and without an orientation. In August, admissions counselors at Ravenwood were busy juggling several different aspects of prospective students' applications via telephone, voice mail, e-mail, and paper. On one such afternoon, I caught admissions counselor Louisa just outside her office, her harried pace and hoarse voice signaling the intensity of the season. I asked how she was holding up. Louisa said that the pressure was on more than ever and that the dean was requesting an update on prospects every Monday, Wednesday, and Friday. Each admissions counselor had an enrollment goal set by Dean Levitz and the assistant director, Madelyn,[1] and Louisa knew that she was consistently the lowest producer of new students on the team. Dean Levitz, Madelyn, and Louisa all accounted for these low numbers as acceptable for the circumstances, but it seemed to me that Louisa's harried appearance was partly a result of those numbers. On this afternoon, Louisa told me that her students were increasingly concerned with the cost and were deferring attendance. Some students reported that they were heading to a large, public college in the region, where tuition was less than half the cost of Ravenwood.

As we spoke, Bernard came in to talk business with Louisa, and in college admissions, "business" is always about numbers. Bernard, who also happened to be studying for his MBA at Ravenwood, was consistently one of the top producers of new students in the office. They were playfully antagonistic with each other—one generally considered an extraordinary recruiter, the other not so much. I asked Bernard whether he had observed the same trend among inquiries and applicants as Louisa had. He agreed and estimated that five or six of every ten students he met were unemployed and needed a bit more convincing when it came to costs and taking out loans in particular. He said that he explained to applicants that this was just the way higher education was today; everyone needed to take a loan to attend college. Louisa had reservations about whether unemployed applicants should be taking loans, but Bernard retorted that it was far better for them to be "productive" than to just "sit around at home." Furthermore, he added, unemployment might be bad for them, but it was good for the college. Louisa had an edge in her voice when she asserted that these were "people," not just "numbers."

Bernard responded quietly but with a smile, "They're people *and* they're numbers."

"*Business* student," Louisa spat at him. Of course, within the context of admission to institutions of higher education, Bernard was right. Although it might not have been as true for the classroom experience, the bureaucratic network of relations in the institution was predicated on converting people into numbers. Some found it difficult to reconcile contradictions that emerged from this process. Like Bernard, Louisa was a graduate student, but studying industrial psychology at an elite university in her spare nights and weekends. About a month after this conversation, Louisa came into the office, explained to everyone that she needed to focus on her studies, and resigned. She cleaned out her office and left the same day.

College admissions is a high-pressure part of higher education administration, and turnover can be high. Admissions counselors needed to be part salesperson, part career counselor, and part bureaucrat, and not everyone could handle such disparate pressures. Both Jaleel and Aaron were hired in November 2008, Nadira resigned and Kenya was hired in March 2009, and

Louisa resigned in September 2009. Unlike at elite institutions, these admissions counselors did not have the luxury of waiting around for prospective students to ask for access or for long negotiations with privileged families. Rather, they faced high-tension activities daily: recruiting students, competing with other counselors, competing with other colleges, dealing with endless phone inquiries, putting up with unreturned calls, explaining curricula that they did not know intimately, guiding students through processes that they did not fully understand, wearing a constant smile, and the striving—always striving—to hit their numbers. A cornucopia of numbers confronted the admissions counselors every day: there were test scores, years of birth, deadlines, financial costs, grade point averages (GPAs), transfer credits, and numbers of applicants. Although no one was terminated during this study for not achieving his or her enrollment goal (or for any other reason), annual professional evaluations of admissions counselors were reportedly very closely tied to the goals set by the dean and the assistant director. Likewise, the dean was being evaluated on those same numbers in aggregate and would be held accountable by nearly everyone in the institution: from faculty decrying the low academic standards to the Board of Trustees worrying about breaking even.

The admissions counselors were keenly aware of the numbers. Not only did they know the number of students they had recruited, but they knew the number necessary to keep the college in business. They also knew that they were partly responsible for the continued employment of others in the institution. As mentioned, after the sharp declines in enrollments in 2006–2007, the college had gone through a drastic series of layoffs and budget cuts; the consequences of numbers were both clear and real. "It's all about the numbers," Aaron lamented, after having heard this same axiom repeated for the fourth time in one day.

One might wonder—as did some of the admissions counselors themselves—why all of the recruitment happened in such concentrated bursts right around the start dates for a semester. By this point at many other colleges, admissions counselors would have already recruited their entire class and would be waiting with baited breath to see how many would actually enroll; in such sites, these bursts of activity happened around deadlines that took place months before the actual start of the semester. As the summer passed at Ravenwood, and the numbers only jiggled, the heads in the Office of Admissions remained calm. They had been through such cycles many times before and were familiar with the axioms of the job, such as knowing that if it rained or snowed on the day of an open house, no one would attend. The relevant axiom here was "everyone waits until the last minute."

Much of the work of admissions at Ravenwood was infused with urgency and immediacy that might well be unrecognizable to admissions counselors at selective institutions. The prospective students were not high school students in their junior year who had taken the SATs (after having cut their teeth on the PSATs), and recruitment did not involve long conversations with parents and family members. Work did not involve cultivating long-term relationships with potential students, pushing for early admission, negotiating the best financial aid offer, or coming to an agreement on academic standards with the coach about the new star football prospect. The college's financial position made every student a necessity, and so prospective students were rarely encouraged to defer to some distant semester. The college needed to make its budget number, and the admissions counselors needed to make their enrollment goals, so every applicant was encouraged to enroll quickly; it was possible (although atypical) for a prospect to apply, test, be admitted, and enroll in classes in a single day. Admissions counselors in part created this sense of urgency for their prospects, who then had to provide the documents upon which their entry would be contingent. All of those students applying had their own life histories and experiences that were far too nuanced to compare. Nonetheless, they needed to be made commensurable. Numbers served this function.

The Rhetoric of Numbers

Numbers weave their way around life in college admissions and in higher education more broadly. Applicant narratives are woven with a variety of numbers that supposedly capture their "merit" or their "essence." Numbers are equally central to institutional narratives. In Stevens's (2007) *Crafting a Class*, we get a window into the ways that admissions is configured at an elite, selective institution: at one point, admissions officers learn that their acceptance rate was actually 33.54 percent and not 33 percent, and this is met with "surprise" and "dismay" (Stevens 2007, 48). Such admissions counselors displayed an amazing fluency in relevant numbers down to the decimal point

and could name the number of volumes in the library, number of fraterni-
ties, number of acres of campus, important dates in the college's history, and
number of endowment funds per student. They would draw on these numbers to impress inquiries and applicants throughout the recruitment process. This process was designed to make institutions commensurable for the
prospective students, and the college described by Stevens had consistent reports of such numbers dating as far back as 1941. A number of admissions
officers I interviewed at other institutions confirmed that inquiring prospective students (and their parents) were very interested in these various
numbers that included number of faculty with terminal degrees, total enrollments, class size, average SAT/ACT scores, student to faculty ratios, and,
of course, "rank"—the distillation of all of these numbers into a single, commensurable number that allowed every institution to be compared with
every other institution. But these numbers were very fluid. Should student to
faculty ratios account for only full-time faculty or also include contingent
labor? Should total enrollment be counted from the beginning of the semester
or at the end, after significant dropout has occurred? At a "less-selective" college such as Ravenwood, these numbers were less flattering, but the admissions counselors also seemed far less fluent in them. The persuasive scripts
did not include these metrics, and prospective students and applicants seemed
less interested in them.

Admissions counselors at Ravenwood reported that they were occasionally asked about class size, but very few were ever asked about faculty—
how many there were, how many had PhDs, and so on. As they were
physically located in different parts of the building than faculty members,
admissions counselors would encounter only a handful of faculty members
who ventured down to them; indeed, they would occasionally attribute to
faculty the wrong titles (usually inflating ranks for those individuals who
interacted with them more often) and were not familiar with who had which
credentials. Admissions counselors' knowledge of such numbers was thus
inconsistent.

Various published college guides were also inconsistent in their descriptions of Ravenwood across all of its traits and numbers. Among four such
popular college guides, between twenty-nine and forty-eight full-time faculty were reported for Ravenwood, with as many as 250 adjunct faculty. According to those guides, student–faculty ratios varied from as few as eleven
to one to as many as twenty to one, whereas average class size was variously

reported to be between ten and twenty students. At Ravenwood, I separately interviewed admissions counselors about these metrics and numbers and found the range of responses interesting. Admissions counselors generally estimated between eighteen and twenty-two students per class, although some guessed more or less. Like the guides themselves, admissions counselors were not sure of these numbers and reported student–faculty ratios that varied from eighteen to one to thirty to one.

The college accepted SAT or ACT scores, but the majority of applicants did not take these exams; most applicants took an entrance exam called Accuplacer,[2] which was administered on campus. Admissions counselors thus did not know average scores for accepted students, nor did they even have a clear sense of one of the most treasured measures of academic merit and prestige for colleges: the percentage of applications rejected. Even Ravenwood's rank seemed to be mysterious to many Ravenwood admissions staff.

Selective colleges spend a tremendous amount of time demonstrating academic merit through numbers; they are keenly aware not only of their rankings in the major publications but also of all of the variables that go into calculating those rankings. Thus, for their freshmen classes, admissions counselors in other institutions are aware of how many students come from the top quartile of their secondary schools or how many scored in a certain range on the SATs (see Stevens 2007). Selectivity, the number of applicants who were rejected, is likewise one of the most important such numbers. In contrast, many Ravenwood admissions counselors seemed surprised to hear that their institution was even listed in guides or rankings at all. What accounts for these differences?

Even the institutional research officer, Gary, was not quite concerned with where the college placed in the *U.S. News & World Report* rankings; within the past few years, Ravenwood had been both fourth tier and "unranked." *U.S. News & World Report* generates its rankings based on self-reported surveys that it mails out to institutions annually. Gary had neglected it entirely, not because he agreed with a recent boycott of the ranking system by around ninety colleges that deemed it reductionist, but just because he had been too busy. It remained on his desk, unfilled. It would be hard to imagine those in selective colleges being so dismissive of what was considered the most influential college ranking system available in the United States. In fact, all admissions officers I interviewed at other institutions in the region felt that even though *U.S. News & World Report* inaccurately measured their institutional merit, they were compelled to consider these rankings because parents and trustees would walk in with the magazine in hand. Boards of Trustees and presidents would reportedly attempt to push the institution to address those variables that directly affected the metrics in the rankings.

Aside from the occasional student in the MBA program, admissions counselors reported that virtually no applicants asked about rankings. When the subject came up, many admissions counselors asked me where Ravenwood ranked. Occasionally, students asked about selectivity (i.e., how hard it was to get in), and admissions counselors would allay their fears. Having asked a number of admissions counselors about these systems, I found that every individual had his or her own understanding of how rankings were weighted and formulated. The admissions staff at Ravenwood College lacked both the fluency in numbers and a thorough understanding of ranking and classificatory systems that resulted from these numbers. Bourdieu's description of discrete categories and systems of knowledge suggest that those in marginalized or peripheral positions will have only imprecise understanding of these classificatory systems:

> But if, as has often been observed, respondents do not agree either on the number of divisions they make within the group, or on the limits of the "strata" and the criteria used to define them, this is not simply due to the fuzziness inherent in all practical logics. It is also because people's image of the classification is a function of their position within it. (Bourdieu 1984, 473)

As such, fluency in numbers may, in fact, be a function of an elite institution's position in the social order; the inverse was true for Ravenwood.

There were, however, certain numbers that Ravenwood staff were fluent in: most notably, enrollment goals. When it came to enrollments, most admissions staff described the Board of Trustees as a source of stress and anxiety for setting goals that they thought beyond the scope of the college. For example, for the Spring 2009 semester, the board set a goal of 393 new students, although only 262 actually enrolled. There were often comments about the board being "unrealistic," "ridiculous," or "crazy." Both board members that I interviewed, however, reported that the board did not set the enrollment goals but only approved the number that came from the chief financial officer. The chief financial officer, however, claimed only to collect and present financial data to the board from which they could make decisions. During periods of heavy enrollment, Dean Levitz would send out applicant reports to the entire Ravenwood staff and faculty, which detailed the number of people who applied, were accepted, had incomplete applications, canceled their applications, and enrolled as students; it also included the total enrollment figures for the same date of the previous year. These reports documented how close Ravenwood was to achieving its enrollment goals. When I brought up such reports outside of the Office of Admissions, I was often met with a roll of eyes, a shrug, a dismissive grunt, or even blunt skepticism. Everyone seemed to feel that numbers were a very fluid medium; given the varied numbers about Ravenwood in different college guides, they may have been on to something. Even a number as seemingly straightforward as "enrollment" was complex, fluid, and rhetorical and as such difficult to trust.

Gary, in institutional research (who was too busy for the *U.S. News & World Report* survey), explained for me just how fluid such numbers were. Every year, Gary completed between thirty and forty institutional surveys that were mandated by the state. Each required reporting certain kinds of data—but as defined by those various state agencies. A simple number such as how many students there were in the college had multiple possible answers. On occasion, it could mean the literal student headcount, but other times it indicated how many had paid their bills or how many had actually registered (whether or not they ever attended a class), whereas others wanted to discount "no-shows" who had never attended a class. Most of these reports looked only at the number of students in the fall semester, but even this could indicate how many were enrolled in September when classes began or how many completed the semester in December (after an often significant freshmen dropout rate). Others looked for an annual enrollment, which introduced the complication of duplicates. For example, if one simply added up how many students attended in the fall, spring, and summer, one would encounter a large number of duplications: a student who was enrolled in all three semesters would get counted three times, seriously inflating the size of the institution. For this reason, some reports specifically asked for unduplicated headcounts, which required the institution to take into account duplications before providing enrollment figures. Some counted part-time students; some did not. This required constant work of translation from one policy to another. Most outside college guides and ranking systems would rely on self-reported

Table 3-1. Ravenwood Semester-Start Enrollments, Fall 2002 to Fall 2009 (with semester breakdown for the semesters in which this study took place)

	Historical						During This Study			
	2002	2003	2004	2005	2006	2007	2008	2009	2009	2009
	Fall	Fall	Fall	Fall	Fall	Fall	Fall	Spring	Summer	Fall
Total Enrollment	2,365	2,311	2,313	1,969	1,768	1,414	1,348	1,507	1,399	1,687

data, and in theory Gary was to receive and (at his discretion) complete these reports. In fact, Gary told me that he did not have time to complete these "optional" reports and generally did not do so. Occasionally, these requests for data would end up in different places and would be completed (or not) by different individuals; even admissions counselors might end up completing reports upon which college guides based their figures and rankings. Although Gary was sensitive to these complex variations of numbers, most staff were not, and it was therefore relatively easy to hear many people truthfully cite different numbers for the same trait and each be correct. For this reason, reported numbers of all kinds were received very skeptically.

Therefore, because of both fluctuations and different ways of counting, admissions counselors would give only estimates and rarely had a specific number ready when asked; a strict, single number would have been inaccurate. According to the various college guides I examined, Ravenwood enrolled from as few as 873 to as many as 1,640 students. In fact, at its highest point, there were almost 2,400 students enrolling in classes in the fall of 2002, but by 2009 the number seemed to hover around 1,500 at the beginning of each semester. When I began this research in Fall 2008 (see table 3-1), the college was celebrating the stabilization of enrollments for the first time since the steady decline of the previous years, an achievement Dean Levitz was enormously proud of. He was also pleased to have reduced the acceptance rate, which likewise varied dramatically.

In 2008, only about 40 percent of applicants were accepted, although as we will see, the precise meaning of this number was also flexible. Still, this was markedly different from 2005, when the acceptance rate had been about 97 percent (see table 3-2).

Table 3-2. Ravenwood Acceptance Rate, 1999–2007

	1999	2000	2001	2002	2003	2004	2005	2006	2007
Applicants	717	645	762	1020	618	570	309	470	587
Applicants accepted	531	440	465	536	438	524	299	152	236
Acceptance rate	74%	68%	61%	53%	71%	92%	97%	32%	40%

Of course, even these numbers are fluid. The acceptance rate of an institution is another key metric in determining rank and as such is one that might be played with in various ways. For example, each semester there would be a large number of applications that were never completed; if all incomplete applications were formally rejected, it would noticeably lower any college's acceptance rate.

Even presuming its accuracy, the acceptance rate at Ravenwood varied wildly and reflected its recent history. Regardless of the institutional narrative, the practice was that Ravenwood had open admissions. Anyone who had the correct documentation and the right score on the entrance exam (again, usually Accuplacer) would be admitted. It was not that Ravenwood refused to play the rankings games that drove so much of admissions in other campuses; rather, it seemed that Ravenwood was hardly aware that such a game was taking place. Admissions at Ravenwood was a formulaic checklist and lacked the complexity of distinguishing merit in elite institutions, where leadership, extracurricular activity, community service, and creative video-essays were weighed and evaluated.

Numbers mattered, but not in the same way as they did in other spaces. Perhaps this is best demonstrated in the number that mattered the most at Ravenwood College: the number of people sitting in seats or, as the tuition planner Cole liked to say, "asses in classes." Tuition-driven institutions such as Ravenwood often discussed a variation of this number that was nearly absent from Stevens's (2007) ethnographic description of a selective institution: the budget number, or the number of new students that the college would have to recruit in order to pay its bills.[3]

Because the enrollment of new students is consequential, Offices of Admissions in every college or university require an elaborate machinery for clearly defining, documenting, and monitoring persons as they moved toward membership in the community. The entire universe of people was portioned into different segments in terms of their relationship with Ravenwood College, and in many ways, the conversion from one segment to the next mapped out their trajectories. And this conversion required work.

Conversions: Persons–Applicants–Students

If we imagine Ravenwood as a node of activity, we can see that various individuals and institutions are implicated in it—in other words, they have a stake in how the activity takes place and in the consequences of that activity. Each of these constituents shapes the ways that others act. For example, in order to become a student, an applicant must first take certain exams, report those exams, fill out applications, and so on. Although Ravenwood College required and administered an entrance exam, it did not design it. Likewise, although students were required to complete certain financial aid applications, these were likewise produced not by Ravenwood but by a variety of governmental and private institutions. Thus, for the prospective student and Ravenwood to meet, all sorts of activities, bureaucracies, and networks must be assembled and activated; a whole universe of institutional activities is mobilized by prospective students when they begin the process of becoming a student.

Although colleges often tout themselves as a space for personal transformation, the process of becoming is initiated far earlier, when the prospective student first takes steps toward participating in higher education. The admissions process, in many ways, is a very formal and carefully regulated process of becoming. It requires that the prospect, the interested person with no formal affiliation with Ravenwood, be converted through careful steps into a member of the Ravenwood community. Again, this process requires not only agents of the institution and the person requesting that membership but also a wide range of constituents, from regulators in Washington, DC, to the designers of exams at the College Boards, from private lenders to state officials. Indeed, from this point of view, the primary function of the Office of Admissions is to precisely oversee the conversion of persons from one category to another; "conversion" is a term that is regularly used both in Ravenwood admissions and among admissions professionals elsewhere.

Of course, at this stage, this is a bureaucratic becoming, not an embodied or social one. There is a flesh-and-blood person attached to the applications completed, but his or her personal transformation will have to wait (theoretically, anyway) for classroom experiences and faculty engagement. Applicants begin the process, and an engine of activity is initiated in which they only occasionally participate: a signature is required here, a request there, and so on. The admissions counselors are charged with overseeing, monitoring, and coordinating the multiple networks that will mark the conversion of this person into a student.

At a nearby first-tier university, an admissions officer I met with had perhaps the most elaborated, theoretical understanding of the process of becoming, with diagrams to go along with it. This admissions officer saw the universe of potential students as being made of different segments and defined by their movement toward enrollment. This view was essentially based on academic marketing and business administration models; in the field of enrollment management, it is known as the *admission funnel*. Although this was the only research participant to articulate and diagram the model explicitly, the logic of the admission funnel seemed to infiltrate the implicit understanding of the field that many admissions officers subscribed to (and can be found elaborated in higher education literature). Ravenwood College was no different. This model identifies the entire universe of persons in terms of relationship or potential relationship with the institution; every person fits in some segment of this funnel. It is a funnel in that it is widest at the top and narrows as individuals become more formally affiliated with the institution. This is a model for understanding the process of becoming that deeply infiltrated the local activities and understandings of participants. I thus bring it up here not as my own theoretical model for understanding admissions but rather as an object of inquiry—a point of data. The funnel is differently configured in different institutions, and so Ravenwood's funnel as I describe it will not exactly conform with others.

The broadest segment of the population is the *suspect,* which includes the entire potential universe of college-going adults, the vast majority of whom may never have even heard of the particular institution. *Prospects,* in contrast, are potential students in the sense that they may have heard of the institution and fit the likely profile of a potential student. As seen in chapter 2, institutions identify prospects largely through the history of enrollments at the institution in terms of demographics in gender, academics, geographic origin, race, and so on. Thus, at Ravenwood, women of color, living in the region, between the ages of twenty-five and fifty-five, were the majority of prospects. Prospects were often the target of marketing campaigns intended to spread a general awareness of the institution among likely potential students.[4] These two terms were not really actively used at Ravenwood to describe the population.

Inquiries are prospects who have in some way expressed an interest in the institution. Such an interest, however, is made meaningful only when attached to a particular activity that then generates some form of peripheral participation in the institution. An inquiry may have made a telephone call, requested a catalog, attended an information session, or stopped by a booth at a college fair. Their names and information are then added to a database, an act that then implicates them in Ravenwood; admissions counselors would now feel free to call, e-mail, or otherwise contact such people and encourage their continued conversion toward *applicant*. Although it was easy to get into this segment, and easy to move forward, it was difficult to back out of; individuals who expressed an interest could find themselves the subject of advertisements and calls for years, regardless of their continued interest.

Some inquiries would never take another step toward membership in Ravenwood. A few, however, would fill out an application and pay a fee—an activity that initiated them into a new relationship with Ravenwood. The applicant segment actually entailed at least three subsegments. The application process required both particular forms of activity: completion of forms and the obtaining of various other documents from other bureaucracies. At the early stages, therefore, after the application was filled out and the fee paid, the person was an *incomplete applicant*. Once all of the exam scores, transcripts, copies of high school diplomas, and immunization records were received, the applicant would be considered a *completed applicant*. A completed applicant, however, was a very brief category, as individuals in this segment were almost immediately recategorized as either an *admit* or a *reject*. In some institutions, individual applicants are admitted or rejected by a faculty member or admissions committee based upon their merits in relation to others in the pool. At Ravenwood, the decision was made at the institutional level; an admit was someone who had all the right documents and certain minimum scores; there really was no evaluation of the application.

Admits were admitted to the degree program of their choice but would not move forward into the next segment unless they registered for and began attending classes. After all, some persons would be admitted to Ravenwood but choose not to attend.

In many colleges or universities, a reject was the end of the road, when an applicant was deemed inadequate to the standards of the college and would be essentially pushed out of the funnel. Such persons could theoretically reapply during the next cycle but would be treated like new candidates. In Ravenwood, however, rejection was not really being pushed out of the funnel but being held up at a particular stage. Such applicants were stopped at a particular gate, and admissions counselors would continue to work with them until they could pass through it. In many ways, the rejected applicant was no different from an incomplete applicant; one applicant was considered incomplete because she did not have a piece of paper that indicated she graduated from high school. Once that piece of paper was obtained, she could move forward. A reject was simply a student who had not obtained a piece of paper that indicated that his or her score on an exam was high enough . . . yet. Many students were encouraged to continue taking exams until they passed.

From the admissions point of view, the final segment of the admissions funnel was *student*. Accepted applicants needed only register for and attend classes to complete the process of becoming a matriculated student at Ravenwood College and thus a full-fledged member of the community.

At Ravenwood, the admission funnel had an amorphous and liminal segment termed *conditional student*, which indicated that although a student had not met all requirements, they were officially but conditionally permitted to enroll. Conditional student status was conferred by admissions staff who made this offer on the basis of certain basic criteria. For example, state law required students to be immunized against certain ailments. If a student never received immunization shots, he or she could do so outside the college or with a visiting nurse who stopped by the college once a week during heavy enrollment periods. Immunization started with a single shot but required a second shot to be administered within two weeks. Such requirements were often waived, and these conditional students were required to sign a statement that they were aware that if they did not get the second shot they would be dismissed from the college. An incomplete applicant could be waived into conditional student-hood if he or she were lacking immunization records, official copies of transcripts, or official proof of a high school diploma or its equivalent.

Understanding this local model of college admissions uncovers certain logics in college admissions and recruitment more broadly. For example, a few renowned, selective institutions face an advantage in that nearly every suspect (i.e., college-going adult) is also a prospect, having heard of the institution and potentially wishing to attend.

This model also shapes the way that admissions staff members think about the pool of potential applicants. At Ravenwood, the emphasis was on conversion, which implied that the admissions counselors had a tremendous impact on how (or even if) one moved from one segment to the next. For some, this was not a process of "becoming" or "conversion" but rather one of "revelation" akin to the Jeffersonian paradigm of schooling. Those who embrace this paradigm would interpret such segments as if they were predetermined—in other words, among the whole universe of suspects, there were those who would only inquire and never start an application, some who would fill out an application but never bother to complete it (incomplete applicant), and some who, although admitted, would never enroll. Such an understanding suggested that the trick to admissions was in predicting which student fit into which segment as early as possible. This process allowed the institution to reveal which individuals fit into which category. Entire specialized industries were built around the premise that they could render these invisible categories visible with better business practices and research; they argued that with access to reams of demographic data they could identify, among the universe of suspects, which individuals would eventually become completed applicants or enroll. They would thus argue that they could reduce the cost involved with the culling of individuals by predicting who would become a student. This would save money, for example, because time and energy might be otherwise misused to cultivate relations with an inquiry who would never apply.

For Ravenwood College, whether or not such a thing was possible was not entirely relevant, as it did not have the resources to hire a large corporation to sift through its data and magically render Ravenwood students visible before they even applied. Indeed, at the time of this study, Ravenwood had no mechanism even for identifying *confirmed admits,* which was a segment used at other institutions but not Ravenwood. Confirmed admits were admits who accepted a college's offer through some official mechanism (such as paying a deposit) to hold a seat in the upcoming semester. At Ravenwood, one would not know if an admit would truly become a student until the first days of class rolled around.

The understanding of this admission funnel shaped the way business was carried out in the Office of Admissions. Different kinds of conversion became central at different times of the year; for example, early in the recruitment cycle, I would mostly hear of converting inquiries into applicants, whereas toward the start of the semester, the emphasis was on converting incomplete applicants to admits. There was an enormous cost attached to activities at each of these segments. The Office of Admissions needed to keep an eye on these numbers.

In December 2008, I asked about recruitment progress, and Jaleel told me that it was largely held up because applicants were no good at managing their time; they needed constant reminding. Aaron concurred, explaining how one applicant had just moved into the state and was still adjusting; one claimed she was waiting for a copy of her general equivalency diploma to arrive from the state capital, although her file indicated that Ravenwood had already received a copy; and another had hung up on him in midsentence because she was angry that, although she had failed only one part of the Accuplacer exam, she needed to retake the entire thing. Bernard thought that individuals stopped at particular segments because of anxiety and said that he tried to get people to take the exam in the first week of contact—or in the second week at latest. The longer they waited to take the exam, the more likely they were to develop test anxiety and cold feet. He said that most of "his" applicants were held up because of the exam itself. For Ravenwood, conversion from incomplete applicant to completed applicant took the most time and energy, and each sort of conversion took different persuasive scripts.

At a staff meeting in January 2009, Madelyn came in and began to hand out copies of a report. Bernard asked what it was, but when he saw the tables answered his own question: "numbers crap." Flipping through it, he saw that there were figures for the summer of 2009 and responded with "shit." He also flipped ahead to the second-to-last page and pointed out that by this point last year, there were twenty-seven accepted students for the summer of 2008, but right now there were only eight such accepted students. When Dean Levitz came in, everything became business.

According to Dean Levitz's records, the number of students converting from admit to student (i.e., registered) was extraordinary—nearly 90 percent, which he suggested was "impressive for any college." However, conversion from incomplete applicant to completed applicant was a problem, as although there were sixty-three new applications in the past week alone, only one had been completed. So as not to fall behind, they needed the widest pool of applicants available, and Dean Levitz therefore announced to everyone that in preparation for the summer semester, he wanted every admissions counselor to organize and run twenty recruitment events beyond the ones that had already been arranged; this would generate a larger pool of inquiries, with the assumption that each of the following segments would likewise be increased in size.

The admissions counselors were not happy with their each being individually responsible for running twenty events, but in the upcoming weeks they would think creatively about how to organize so many events with all of the other pressures and constraints of their job. Jaleel, for example, stopped by every occupant in the building in which Ravenwood leased floors and dropped off promotional materials about the college, counting each as a separate "recruiting event." Once, while chatting with a few admissions counselors in the hallway, I asked how their twenty events were coming; one counselor handed me some promotional literature and said, "there, that's another one," to much laughter. The admissions counselors needed to conform to the dean's understanding of the admission funnel under various constraints and did so in creative ways.

Documentation always drove the process of becoming in Ravenwood. Even the data management program used by the college, "CollegeNode," used a similar but simpler variation of the admission funnel for tracking prospective students. This system recognized *inquiries, applicants,* and *students.* The *inquiry* was exactly the same as in the model described above and is the first segment or stage of prospective student acknowledged by the system. The entire process of becoming (an applicant, a student, and so on) was defined by the circulation of documents, and in the eyes of the system, a person began to exist as an inquiry. Again, when a prospect came in and requested information, he or she would complete a walk-in sheet and meet with a counselor (or, alternatively, complete a sign-in sheet at an information session, an online request for a catalog, or a mailed-in postcard expressing interest). Regardless of the form of initial contact, that action would be documented and initiate the creation of a digital file for that person in CollegeNode, and then he or she would become an inquiry. Every inquiry would be assigned to an admissions counselor (either the one associated with the initial contact or equitably distributed for online inquiries) who would receive their contact information. The creation of the digital file as inquiry ensured that the individual would receive mail, e-mail, and telephone calls about the college from his or her new admissions counselor.

The CollegeNode software itself organized information that must be captured by staff through a set of screens called a "workflow" and that defined persons in terms of what actions they took and the documents on file, the latter of which were all put into the system by the "ladies in the back," who very carefully controlled and guarded their access to CollegeNode. Although admissions counselors could theoretically input information themselves, conflicts in the office had led to administrative support staff alone having the authority to do so. CollegeNode not only was a resource and a tool but both conformed with an admission funnel model and configured the ways that interactions unfolded in practice.

CollegeNode was designed to capture a tremendous amount of data but was notoriously incomplete; this was true of inquiries broadly—most of whom never converted to applicants. CollegeNode was entirely digital, but when an inquiry did complete an application, it would trigger the creation of a physical file. Transcripts, scores reports, and other relevant documents would find their way to this folder after being demarcated in CollegeNode. Occasionally, an inquiry (who never completed an application) would have transcripts (or other documents) sent in; this aberration of the workflow (i.e., an inquiry acting like an applicant) would disrupt the entire process for that applicant. When physical documents had no physical folder to house them, they made their way to the limbo of a large filing cabinet in Admissions. As this filing cabinet was not organized by folder, name, or date, admissions counselors described it as an "abyss" of documents. Many admissions counselors lamented the trek to this filing cabinet filled with unorganized papers because some applicant had informed him or her that a high school diploma had been submitted before an application was filled out. One had to either manually go through every page in the cabinet or simply ask the student to provide additional copies. For these reasons, admissions counselors would often attempt to act as intermediaries with their inquiries. They would inform their inquiries not to send any documents through the official channels but rather to bring or send them directly to the admissions counselors, who often operated their own parallel filing systems for those with whom they worked.

Although in many colleges applications were fully digital in 2008–2009, at Ravenwood one could still find applicants sitting in the Office of Admissions filling out paper applications. Online applications were available but, as I discuss later, posed other challenges. In CollegeNode an entirely new digital file would be triggered when moving from one segment to the next, migrating over the data from the inquiry file into a new-applicant digital file. As an "applicant," entirely new workflows would be activated that would allow the filing of GPA, test scores, immunization records received, and so on. The system could not accommodate persons who did not move through the admission funnel sequentially.

CollegeNode required that persons move through all of the segments of the admission funnel en route to student; the bureaucratic machine could not operate outside of this system of categorization. It was thus theoretically possible (although highly unlikely) for a student to walk into the Office of Admissions for the first time, sit and meet with a counselor, complete an application by hand, take the entrance exam, and submit a sealed transcript and immunization records, receive the passing exam scores, and register for classes all in the same day. Such a person, however, would not be able to simply appear as a "student." CollegeNode required that they be created as an "inquiry" before checking the box that indicated an application was filled out. The inquiry would then become an "incomplete applicant" until all the boxes were checked and he or she became a "completed applicant." Presuming that the applicant had passed the exam, the applicant would be "admitted" and, after registration, would become a "student." Each movement not only opened up new workflows for the person's file but activated screens in other departments. Only people who had been admitted would be able to register in Student Services or apply for a loan in Financial Aid; without that process being completed, administrators in these offices would be unable to act upon the student in any way. Thus, although the speed at which an individual could move through the process varied tremendously, the process itself was inviolate; there were no other paths to becoming a student of Ravenwood College.

Considering the vast amounts of information and relations that needed to be managed, Ravenwood admissions counselors were extremely adept at negotiating this complex system and producing enrolled students. Of course, some were more adept than others.

The Politics of Numbers

Only a few weeks into my fieldwork, as I was exploring the application process, Nadira bluntly asked whether I was aware of "applicant stealing." She told me that she had been a victim of it only the week before. I thus came to see very early how numbers were always politically textured.

Individual admissions counselors typically guided individual persons through the entire conversion process, from inquiry to enrolled student. They would develop relationships with them over time and thought of such applicants as "their" students. Such applicants were marked in CollegeNode as their students and were counted toward that admissions counselor's enrollment goals for the semester. But admissions counselors could not be at their desk twenty-four hours a day to help their applicants. Nadira described how other admissions counselors would attend to some prospective student to assist with whatever questions he or she had when "his" or "her" counselor was out of the office. A few admissions counselors would be particularly friendly and openly develop a rapport with that prospective student. Some would even cross off the name of the previous admissions counselor and write his or her own in the application folder—in essence, "stealing" the applicant to be counted toward their own enrollment goals. During the course of this study, three different admissions counselors independently told me about being the victims of applicant stealing, although none of them were willing to name the perpetrator(s). I was never able to deduce how the name of the admissions counselor was changed even in the CollegeNode system; none of the perpetrators (whoever they were) openly discussed the matter with me. It was possible that either the individual admissions counselor had figured out how to change it directly or a colleague in the administrative support area did it for them. On one occasion during the busy season, I observed one admissions counselor working with a prospect in his office. As the prospect left his office, Nadira swooped down on the prospect and playfully teased that she was "no longer talking to him," because he had gone to see the other counselor instead of her. Although I earlier described the various segments of the admission funnel through which persons moved, for most admissions counselors they were just "students," or rather they were "*my* students." There was thus a professional breach felt when they were "stolen."

At some colleges, there are two separate roles in the Office of Admissions: admissions counselors, who help applicants through the process on campus, and recruiters, who go into the field to generate "leads," or locate interested prospects (usually high school students) and direct them back to the college. Ravenwood College had too few staff for such an arrangement, and so admissions counselors both assisted applicants through the process and organized events outside of it to identify new inquiries. Admissions counselors did not get paid a commission for recruited students, which would have crossed an ethical and legal boundary, but meeting individual targets was an essential part of their annual review.

Other sorts of practices were considered unethical, if not exactly stealing. For example, a system had been created to ensure the equitable distribution of inquiries and applicants. The front desk of the Office of Admissions had a short list tacked to it with the names of the counselors. When a new inquiry walked in off the street, a student worker (who usually handled the front desk) would look at the next name on the list and call that admissions counselor. If he or she were busy, she would call the next, and the next, until a counselor was available to come and speak to the person, so that no single staff member would receive an unfair number of walk-in inquiries. Some admissions counselors, however, were far more proactive in handling such walk-ins. Such a counselor might have an applicant in his or her office working on some paperwork while keeping a close eye on the front entrance. If he or she ever saw a second person sitting there and waiting, the counselor would immediately ask if they were waiting for someone in particular. If not, the counselor would then turn on the charm and offer his or her services and suggest that there was no need to wait; the counselor would then lead the person to a different space to start completing paperwork. In this way, the counselor might be able to assist two or three prospects at the same time and completely circumvent the list at the front counter. Some admissions counselors would also cultivate strong relationships with the student workers, who might increase the flow of traffic in their direction. There was no way to substantiate such relationships, however; even if it was noticed that a student worker skipped someone in the list, it was easy to cover up through such excuses as "oh, I thought you were out to lunch," "you must have been on the other line, I tried to call," or "I thought there was a student in there with you." There were thus certain activities that were often reported as happening but about which staff members were unwilling to name names (at least to an anthropologist). The Office of Admissions was an office—a workplace—and as such was subject to the same political squabbles, backstabbing, alliance building, and gossip as any other workplace.

Staff members were always polite, professional, and articulate, and I never directly observed an open conflict among admissions counselors, but as the reports of applicant stealing indicate, there were tensions below the surface. There were certainly a good deal of friendships in the office as well. For example, Madelyn (assistant director) had worked with Maggie (admissions counselor) in the Office of Admissions at a less selective proprietary college in the region and had brought Maggie over to Ravenwood after she was hired. Louisa and Nadira, both of whom resigned during the course of this research, were close to each other, as were Bernard and Louisa, despite some playful antagonism. Jaleel mostly kept to himself.

In April, Kenya was hired after Nadira resigned, and during one of our earliest meetings she told me that she felt like one of the other admissions counselors hated her and she had no idea what she had done. As she did not want to tell me who it was, endless possibilities came to mind, even aside from personal dislike. For example, Kenya was very photogenic and in the first couple of weeks as an employee stumbled into a photo shoot for promotional literature on campus. The photographer liked Kenya so much that she almost immediately began appearing in brochures and other promotional literature for the college: was this "hatred" a result of envy? Another possibility was that someone who was close to Nadira might have resented Kenya taking her place. And then there was Jaleel. Often, staff would get paired with one another for the purpose of organizing an event and would be required to work with one another closely. Jaleel seemed to bristle at such moments, and I had heard him suggest that his peers did not produce work quite to his standards. I wondered whether this tension might be related to sharing inquiries; if an admissions counselor organized an event, anyone attending that event would automatically "go to" that admissions counselor as "their student." If two counselors were co-running the event, they had to divide the list. And yet, on an occasion when I was available and offered my assistance, Jaleel refused my help even in stuffing promotional materials into folders; he was an independent spirit in Ravenwood. Certainly, Kenya may have interpreted his behaviors as "hate." Admissions counselors were both largely competitive with and somewhat peripheral to each other; they were required to act independently and were rewarded independently. It seemed that numbers could be at the root of conflict.

Political conflicts also took place between offices or among power brokers in the college. At Ravenwood, Student Services had a role more expansive than at many colleges I have observed in the past. Beyond international student advisement, student life, commencement, and orientations, Student Services staff members at Ravenwood were responsible for the academic advisement and registration of current students (which in many colleges were the responsibility of faculty or a separate office). In Student Services, a great deal of energy was thus spent in making sure that continuing students were advised and registered for the following semester, giving the impression that Student Services was in some way accountable for retention. For example, when retention of continuing students fell, some people would point their fingers at Dean of Students Arriza and her team, just as when new student enrollments fell, they would point fingers at Dean Levitz and the admissions counselors working under him. Like Dean Levitz, Dean Arriza had been at the college for over twenty years; unlike Dean Levitz, she was also an alumna. Dean Arriza likewise found herself consumed by numbers, and her staff were often on the phone contacting current students to find out why they had not yet registered for the following semester. Dean Arriza oversaw the Testing Center, where applicants took the entrance exam. Although I never even saw the two deans in the same place at the same time, and all of the admissions counselors named Student Services as a department with which they worked the most often, there was palpable tension between the two.

Aaron related a story about an open admission day that had taken place on a Saturday. He had been waiting for two sisters to show up to take the entrance exam for the new semester but had received word that they had been delayed and might not make it in at all. He ended up helping other applicants, and as he was finishing up for the day and getting ready to leave, he saw the two applicants at the front desk. They made excuses for being late and said that they wanted to take the test. Aaron knew it was too late but also knew that the college needed students, and, of course, they were "his" students. He prepared them for the fact that they most likely would not be able to take the test that day but told them to go upstairs just to ask anyway. On Monday, there was an e-mail to him from someone in Student Services that copied in the assistant director, Dean Levitz, Dean Arriza, and various other important persons about Aaron's "unprofessional" behavior. The e-mail admonished Aaron for blatantly breaking policies and creating work for others by sending applicants on off-hours and inconveniencing the applicants who could not be serviced anyway. Aaron was clearly frustrated and hurt and said in exasperation that the whole thing was ridiculous. He felt that rather than simply "doing their job" or trying to help the admissions team do a better job, the Student Services staff seemed more concerned with highlighting and broadcasting their failures. Such e-mails were not uncommon, and I am certain that Student Services staff would find themselves on the receiving end of such e-mails on occasion. Some staff in Student Services reported that they wanted to go down to the first floor and offer some advice and tips on working with students, events, or activities but felt an enormous pressure not to help. Helping was a political act that implicated systems of alliances in the college, and therefore political considerations needed to be made before a coworker was helped. I was not sure of the origins of the political tension between the offices (or if the source of the conflict lay between the two deans that oversaw those units). Both were deeply implicated in the social world of numbers, which required explanation and, at times, finger-pointing.

Numbers needed to be explained; they signaled something to people in the network. The numbers for student retention came up while I spoke with Gary, director of institutional research. He had noted that there was a silver lining to the enrollment crisis; the freshman dropout rate had at its worst been about 70 percent and had since shrunk to about 60 percent. Despite these alarming figures, however, he proudly reported that student satisfaction was very high. His explanation was that students gained a more sophisticated appreciation for the curriculum as time passed. I found this puzzling. I offered an alternative explanation: if 60 to 70 percent of the students were leaving Ravenwood College, the remaining 30 to 40 percent would be the ones who were satisfied. I asked whether surveying the 30 to 40 percent who had not dropped out if they were satisfied was a form of invalid sampling method. Gary had not thought of this explanation and was quiet for a short time, thinking of how we might be able to substantiate that hypothesis. Different explanations for numbers were mobilized in different ways and at different times for different purposes, and there were always political implications. Although some were certainly sensitive to the nuances of meaning that one could find in these numbers, for others the metric became a simple indicator of one department's failures or another's successes. Numbers shifted, and even for relatively minor shifts, either positive or negative, there was a need to establish blame or credit that exacerbated interoffice tension.

Nadira had a theory about the difficulty that they had in converting incomplete applicants to applicants and brought this up at a meeting. The problem, she insisted, were two kinds of applications in use: express and online. These two applications were not the standard pen-and-paper application that the college used, which was made up of several pages of well-designed forms in a flashy folder. Express applications had been designed to simplify the entire application to a single page, which was available at the reception area. At the meeting, Dean Levitz said they might want to move away from express applications as they may have been little more than a "glorified inquiry form." Nadira insisted that she had complained about this express application from the first day she was hired; she had said it was "confusing and would create problems" because prospects filling out the simple page would not realize that they were actually applying to Ravenwood. Furthermore, she felt that student workers were not well prepared to be dispensing it and were themselves unclear that prospects were applying to the college through those forms. Although she was very friendly with the student workers, she did not feel that they should be giving out applications to someone when they came in for a brochure. Nadira was challenging the notion that these forms should even exist. Dean Levitz in turn insisted that it had to be the responsibility of the student workers; Nadira responded that it should not be and that it was inflating the number of applications. She then turned to complain about online applications, which did not require an application fee (as the traditional paper ones did), as she felt that many people who had no intention of enrolling at Ravenwood just filled out an application on a whim. People filled in the online applications with bogus information: telephone numbers with 555 area codes, fake mailing addresses, and so on. Nadira felt that the system needed to incorporate "required" fields or to charge an application fee to weed out all the whimsical applications, but Dean Levitz (with some reproach in his voice) declared that it was up to the individual admissions counselor to go through those applications and cancel the ones that were bogus. Tension rose about these two types of applications until voices were raised and Dean Levitz left the room, ending the meeting abruptly. Most of the admissions counselors had silently and awkwardly sat through the disagreement. Although students who completed these applications may not have intended to actually attend Ravenwood College, the three forms of applications (traditional paper, express, online) together generated lots of numbers. And lots of applications would make the Office of Admissions look good. Blame, credit, and other sorts of explanations for numbers infiltrated the campus culture and its historical narrative.

Although some numbers could easily be interpreted in very nuanced ways, there were some figures that were so stark that they could not be spun in a positive light. The most extreme example of this was the dramatic fall in enrollment numbers that took place between 2002 and 2008, the consequences of which were still being felt throughout the college. Many staff members were still talking about the layoffs of 2006–2007, as well as the poor benefit package available while I was conducting this research (there were no pensions of any kind and covering one's family for health insurance cost as much as $800 per month out of pocket). These changes to the lives of people were driven by numbers, and the staff members were very interested in explanations for them. Virtually every staff person I encountered who had been employed at the college during that period accounted for the rapid decline as tied to executive-level decision making. There were several troubling decisions that were made by various key figures in the institution, and those who had a hand in making those decisions were largely cast as the antagonist in the history of the college. When I sift through my field notes, several such decisions emerge:

- The Ravenwood mission and values statements were revised, and although they included many of the same concepts (social justice, empowerment, and so forth), I had heard complaints that the particular wording had implications that were disliked;
- Expensive renovation of a separate entrance to the building for Ravenwood;
- The decision to close the three extension campuses in the region;
- The decision to hire faculty on the basis of traditional research and publication tracks rather than emphasizing social justice and teaching;
- Lowering admission standards to pull in as many students as possible;
- A marketing campaign that dropped the "1-800 number" and seemed like every other competitor;
- A move away from the traditional curriculum, even possibly eliminating the capstone project entirely;

- The decision to hire new levels of executive administration, such as various deans and vice presidents; and
- Antagonism between the college and the local blues and jazz festival.

The chief antagonist, nearly universally disliked in the college in 2009, was former president Hartwick, who served until 2007. He was either directly credited with all of the decisions above or with hiring the inept or iniquitous staff who made those decisions. Hartwick himself openly embraced goals of institutional change and was more flexible in his interpretation of the activist history and mission as laid out by the founders. For many years, the college operated with a single vice president and two deans, but in the period under Hartwick's tenure, many layers of administration were added, with as many as six or seven vice presidents and an equal number of deans, as well as a provost who was determined, according to Professor Richardson (a longtime faculty member holding the faculty seat on the Board of Trustees when I interviewed him), to turn the college into "a Little Harvard." Professor Richardson suggested that faculty in particular were virulently dismissive of Hartwick as a lawyer and supposedly foresaw many of the bad decisions described above before they were made.

The college itself did not systematically record its history; there was only an oral history that shifted with both the storytellers and the audience at hand, and much of this constituted gossip—a considerable amount of which was about the staff persons that Hartwick brought in but who were no longer around. For example, some participants reported that former vice president Nate Smythe had had an affair with the then director of admissions; both were married, and illicit photographs were allegedly passed around among the staff members. After that director resigned, the vice president hired a director who apparently had never worked in a college before taking the position. Vice President Smythe then allegedly continued a campaign of sexual harassment against multiple young Latina women working in the college, all of whom resigned. One professor waited until after we had walked off of the campus one day to describe to me how many faculty of color felt targeted by the administration and likewise resigned. Stories likes these circulated about this period of Ravenwood's history and were difficult to substantiate because few of those individuals remained—and those who did remain painted themselves in a particular light.

Perhaps such gossip was only that, but this gossip also corresponded and was co-narrated with important stories about numbers. Although stories of sexual harassment and racism were told in whispers by water coolers or in back offices, the closing of Extension Campus I was openly brought up in nearly every conversation I heard about the decline in enrollment, the lay-offs, and the Hartwick administration. Ravenwood had once maintained these extension campuses across the region, offering a number of courses for students unwilling to travel to the main campus. Although the closing of Extension Campuses II and III was met with little surprise (they had been very low in enrollment), Extension Campus I had maintained a full enroll-ment that nearly rivaled the main campus, including nearly every course offering and degree program. Many of my interlocutors suggested that the administration assumed that when the extension campuses closed, all of the students would simply travel to the main campus—thus cutting the over-head costs while maintaining the same income from tuition. Instead, accord-ing to staff members, the majority of those students simply dropped out. After the largest declines in enrollment, I was told, the layoffs and closings began. The closing of Extension Campus I was a death knell, and even two years after his resignation, everyone agreed that the one who rang it was former president Hartwick.

In my experience, the blame for these sorts of decisions was always laid at the feet of staff who no longer worked in Ravenwood, and those who still remained from those times maintained narratives about themselves during these "dark years."[5] Dean Levitz, for example, had been the director of ad-missions up until about 2003, when he was "pushed" into marketing, after which Vice President Nate Smythe and his various directors of admission were causing so much trouble managing the Office of Admissions. On the first day that I met Dean Levitz, he told me that in the fall of 2007, someone had told him that he ought to go back to Admissions to "show them how it's done." He described himself as having taken up the challenge, returning to a difficult job that few wanted and which afforded little respect. He de-scribed himself as taking the reins and trying to "rebuild everything" that the former president had "destroyed." He had succeeded in stabilizing the new enrollments for the first time since those "dark years."

In general, I remain skeptical about the assigning of blame or credit for decisions made in the past. As with the setting of enrollment targets, not only did none of the key persons on campus take credit for decisions, but no one seemed to be able to determine where the decision really came from. It seems to me that, in such bureaucracies, decisions are brought forward by individuals who have already garnered some support for them. Just as with marketing materials (chapter 2) and with the setting of enrollment goals (as above), it can be difficult to assign decisions to particular decision-makers. As an idea moves forward, some support it and some oppose it; at each of these encounters, the policy decision may shift to meet the needs of various constituents. In many ways, no one person is responsible for most adminis-trative decisions I have seen; rather, numerous constituents in the bureau-cracy shape the decision as it moves toward implementation; once an idea gains momentum, the decision almost makes itself. President Hartwick re-signed before I ever came to campus, but it would surprise me if all of the decisions he made came only from him or his inner circle of allies who all resigned as well. Although I am certain that many of this president's deci-sions were controversial, I expect that individuals who continued to work at Ravenwood even after Hartwick's departure had a hand to play in those de-cisions, but these would contradict their narratives about those "dark years." I wanted to get some other perspectives about that time.

Roslyn Fordyce was employed by the Office of Admissions during Hart-wick's tenure, although she resigned well before my study began. I was able to track her down through some current Ravenwood employees with whom she had remained close and who recommended I speak with her. She painted a picture of Admissions at Ravenwood that was starkly different from what I encountered in 2008–2009. She told me frankly about the many question-able practices of individual counselors who were encouraged to do whatever was necessary to recruit students and credited her unwillingness to partici-pate as one of the primary reasons for her eventual resignation. There were admissions counselors for whom 50 percent of their incoming students had had a component waived and whose student status was thus conditional. There were others who would give $3,000 to $4,000 in merit scholarships to every one of their students, without regard to what the college could afford or students' qualities as candidates. She had been continuously shocked, because the college always honored those scholarships, even when it was clearly beyond the means of the institution. What upset her most was that the people who were laid off or fired were never the ones that she felt were acting unethically; those individuals were allowed to resign in their own time. Furthermore, at least according to Roslyn, there were still several people employed at the college in 2009 who had their hand in the decisions made in the "dark years."

Furthermore, Roslyn departed from nearly every story about this period of Ravenwood's history when she highlighted her opinion that the worst layoffs and campus closings came before the largest declines in enrollment; the figures and history I have reconstructed independently of her interviews substantiate this claim. The biggest layoffs came in the Spring 2006 semester, although other layoffs and resignations continued throughout all of 2006. Although the smaller Campus III was closed in Spring 2006, Campus I was not closed until Fall 2006 and Campus II until Spring 2007, a full year after the worst layoffs. In Spring 2006, when the layoffs occurred, Ravenwood was still holding a somewhat stable population of around 1,800. As such, despite what I had heard, low enrollments did not lead to layoffs, but rather layoffs may have contributed to low enrollments.

According to Roslyn, the enrollment crisis was actually twofold. First, the layoffs of staff and closing of campuses caused the decline of enrollment, not the other way around. Fewer staff resulted in poorer and more limited service, which led to student flight. Second, she felt that the numbers of students were seriously inflated and doubted that the college ever had 2,400 students as recorded.

During that period, another decision made was to create a "Student Central" during points of heaviest enrollment and the express applications that Nadira complained about. Admissions counselors invited all other key administrators to set up space downstairs in the Office of Admissions in order to create an efficient "student enrollment experience," which meant that offices such as Financial Aid, Student Services, and the Registrar would all be conveniently located in one space: a "Student Central." Roslyn argued that "it created numbers on paper, but it didn't create real students." She suggested that there was so much paperwork signing and activity that applicants were often unclear what they were doing. "When you filled out the application and the last page is an actual registration form for classes—am I registered? Am I not registered?" Roslyn asked. Although the college was clearly maintaining the differences in the technical segments of the admission funnel, at that time, the process for moving from one segment to another was radically blurred. At about the same time, Ravenwood College was changing to CollegeNode from an older computer system, and thus records themselves were also chaotic, being kept as much on paper as digitally. Roslyn said that in Student Services they started to note strange patterns on the paper attendance records and to call the large numbers of absentee students. Students were surprised to find out that not only had they registered for classes, but the college said that they had been absent and owed them money. According to Roslyn, the initial drop in enrollment that led to the layoffs was not a drop at all; it was a matter of artificially inflated numbers that never materialized. It was in this climate that Roslyn resigned. Much of what Roslyn told me is unsubstantiated in that the college recorded only the numbers and not the practices on paper, and the living stories about the past only hinted at some of these possibilities. To be clear, there was no evidence of any such unethical practices taking place during the course of this study, and Roslyn may have simply been a disgruntled former employee. Her perspective is still suggestive, however, that the rhetorical and fluid configuration of numbers itself may have contributed to the rapid declines in enrollment.

Conclusions: Running to Stand Still

Numbers are not the same everywhere. Although they themselves may be rational, numbers can be flexibly deployed by persons with particular agendas and then configured in particular ways. Ravenwood was not formally part of the public sector but was both closely regulated by government and financed by the public in the form of financial aid for its students; public and private spheres are blurred as quite varied institutions and agendas are pulled together into higher education. I have therefore attempted not just to demonstrate that numbers mattered but also to reconstruct how they infiltrate and are constitutive of a tremendous amount of work that Ravenwood needed to engage in. Rather than having discrete boundaries and acting in isolation, Ravenwood, as locus for activity, reveals how closely it is tied into multiple, highly distributed, stratified activities with regulators (federal and state agencies), voluntary associations (accreditation), or private evaluators (college ranking groups). Ravenwood's "mediocre" position deeply shaped the ways that numbers were understood, configured, and deployed in everyday life.

Hall (2005) has argued that current iterations of "evidence-based policy" and high-stakes testing in education are part of what Weber termed "rational bureaucratic authority," which aims at projects of standardization of quality, regulation of expertise, a modicum of predictability in fragmented times, and calls for accountability. The neoliberal character of recent accountability reforms in education are thus a particular variation of a modern phenomenon. However, although the aims of these reforms may be to "make government more open, transparent, consumer accountable, responsive, efficient and cost effective" (Hall 2005, 180), Hall also argues that the reliance on an instrumentalist, scientific rationality as applied to the public sector has had other unforeseen consequences, including shifting the conversation from one deliberating on educational challenges to the finding of discrete solutions to discrete problems. Although Hall was largely discussing the shifting character of educational research and funding opportunities, the accountability rationale that sees only particular sorts of numbers as meaningful has infiltrated many aspects of the educational infrastructure. Accountability in the new audit culture requires commensurability across contexts, and only numbers are qualified to satisfy this requirement. Thus, people and their ideas circulate through higher education only as mediated by transformation into certain sorts of numbers.

In this chapter, I have diagrammed out the trajectory of admission to Ravenwood, the work needed to maintain those trajectories, and the ways that numbers flowed into and were made meaningful at Ravenwood. There was a near constant flow of numbers in around the Office of Admissions, some strictly related to individuals, some reflecting aggregates, and others pointing to the institution itself. But those numbers also hid a tremendously complex, nuanced, and political landscape inhabited by human beings who were doing what they could to keep Ravenwood solvent.

Ravenwood's position in a meritocratic, educational infrastructure was precarious. There was a sense that the tremendous amount of activity was being enacted not only to keep the doors open but also to prevent its slide further down the meritocratic curve. The constant activity described here did not seem to be pushing Ravenwood ahead but rather was required just to keep it where it stood. There was never enough time for careful forethought or long-range planning; these were luxuries for different sorts of institutions. Ravenwood needed students, and the ad hoc nature of activity at Ravenwood produced them very quickly. This way of being led some members of the community to ask whether Ravenwood was even a "real" college at all—and reflects the very real battle for legitimacy that such institutions often face.

Chapter 4

Being a "Real" College in America

Continue to hire qualified faculty members. I experienced some
of the BEST while at Ravenwood.

I think the program should be more proactive in dismissing professors only
there for a paycheck! I also felt that professors that have pride in Ravenwood
College (and not Ivy League schools like [Institution, Institution]) should
teach. . . . Many professors at Ravenwood gave baby work because they
themselves did not think much of the school. Very disappointing.
They should be fired immediately.

I would recommend the school because it's only a one year program for a
[graduate degree]. However, I would tell them about the kind of students
they will encounter at Ravenwood, whom in the majority are the worst.

If possible could the school increase the numbers of computers and printers
available for students? The classrooms should be cleaner and the carpet
should be shampooed due to the smell. All classrooms should have windows
if possible and if not please do not have a 2.5 hour class in these rooms as it
becomes hard to pay attention after 1 hour.

Anonymous comments, Ravenwood Graduation Survey 2007–2008

Although universities are nodes within a massive network of activities, the ways that those strands are knotted together can differ radically
depending on the position of the institution, its history, its student profile,
and so forth. The ways that meaning gets layered into those different positions is precisely indicative of meritocracy—or the ways that merit moves
from a philosophical position to being codified and operationalized into
society.

This chapter therefore interrogates questions of merit that are central to
this book: How did those at Ravenwood recognize merit in the world around
them? How much of merit is connected to things like standardized scores,
and how much is related to how people carry themselves? What challenges

do those positioned in a particular place in the meritocratic curve have with legitimacy? These are questions that Ravenwood College struggled with as an institution and which many constituent members struggled with as well. Merit is constituted by a whole constellation of factors, including affiliation with particular groups (which resonates with earlier discussions of brand), scores on standardized tests, persistence and hard work, and even how choices are made.

Standardized Testing: Measuring Merit, Granting Legitimacy

Every day, regardless of bureaucratic machines or formal institutions, people process and integrate new information into their current understanding of the world. Schools within a Jeffersonian paradigm are concerned not only with learning but also with measuring, marking, and sorting people in the meritocratic curve in ways that will be meaningful to other institutions. This one is an "A student"; that one is "disabled"; this one is a "college graduate"; that one is a "high school dropout"; this one is "performing above state re-quired levels of competency," that one "below." In recent decades, there has been an explicit movement toward more powerful assessment tools in school-ing and greater consequence in testing. Scores and grades thus can be de-ployed as part of scripts to justify, explain, and mark individuals' (and, in the aggregate, institutions') position in the broader social structure; they are an important form of symbolic capital in the modern world. Whether in the form of No Child Left Behind reform (discussed in Koyama 2010; McDermott and Hall 2007) or broader accreditation standards (Varenne 2007), there is a movement to better document and control learning through formal assess-ment tools. Admission to college is far ahead of this trend. For better or worse, at Ravenwood College, as for most institutions of higher education in the United States, the basis for admission was primarily academic assess-ment through standardized testing.[1]

Because it is both noncompulsory and characterized by a range of public and private institutions, getting into college is a process in which prospective student and institution mutually assess one another. The SAT (Scholastic Assessment Test) and ACT (American College Test) are nearly universally recognized in the United States as the exams through which prospective col-lege students are legitimately assessed. The ACT is somewhat less well known on the East and West Coasts and is more popular throughout the Midwest. The SAT is a standardized test used by the College Board to assess a prospective student in the areas of reading, writing, and mathematics through a series of standardized, multiple choice questions and an essay, although it also has more specialized exams for specific subjects. Students are seeking the right-tiered bin in which to fit themselves; mean institutional scores published on websites supposedly give them a sense of how the aggregate of students perform academically at that institution and whether they are worthy to be "peers." Like Goldilocks and the three bears, University X has students who score too high on average (intimidating, a reach); College Y has students who score too low on average (not challenging enough, a fallback); but College Z is just right. For those who design and administer such assessments, the goal is often prediction: predict who will or will not succeed. Lemann (1999) described his own fascination with this dimension of testing:

> Testing touched upon the deepest, mythic themes: the ability to see the invisible (what was inside people's heads), the oracular ability to predict the future (what someone's grades would be in courses that they hadn't even chosen yet). (Lemann 1999, 18)

Once again, this emphasizes the Jeffersonian paradigm in which schooling broadly and testing in particular is revelatory. At the time of this study, the SAT was so much accepted by colleges across the United States that admissions counselors in most colleges knew the average SAT scores of their freshmen classes right off the top of their head. It is ironic that the test was devised in order to reduce bias based on socioeconomic background, despite the famous questions that required one to know that "runner" is to "marathon" as "oarsman" is to "regatta." Despite its having been endlessly refined, there had been a movement toward SAT-optional admission since the early 2000s; some institutions held that students' long-term performance as captured in transcripts and other academic activities would be a better indicator of academic aptitude than a single exam (Soares 2012). I interviewed admissions counselors at one such institution who found that dropping the SAT did not actually affect their enrollments. Indeed, it has been argued that the SAT is both expensive and time-consuming while privileging affluent applicants (as reviewed and explored, for example, by Dixon-Román, Everson, and McArdle

2013). At Ravenwood, SATs and ACTs were likewise optional but not for the same reasons.

Ravenwood used Accuplacer as an entrance exam, which like the SATs and ACTs was a standardized exam developed by Educational Testing Service. According to a number of students with whom I had spoken, one of the most important and nerve-racking parts of the admissions process was the entrance exam, and there were some who identified not having to take the SATs as an important reason for attending Ravenwood. Admissions counselors likewise often complained that getting prospects to take the Accuplacer exam was one of the most challenging parts of recruitment. The preference was to get prospects to take the exam as soon as possible—the longer they waited, the less likely that he or she would ever take the exam. It appears that prospective students knew that such assessments were touted in the public discourse as a means not only to reveal the whole of their intellectual capacity but to predict their futures. It was around this anxiety that the decision to not require the SAT or ACT was made.

In the middle of March, I took the Ravenwood Accuplacer entrance exam, as I wanted to experience the embodied act through which prospective students could gain access to the institution. Like many prospects, I was anxious. The mathematics sections of the exam included long division and factoring polynomial expressions; my learning in these areas seemed like distant memories at best. Gregoire, the professional proctor of the exam for Ravenwood, was the only one who knew I was taking the exam at that point, although I had casually picked up many of the study guides that the Office of Admissions prepared for prospects. I was cognizant that if the scores did not demonstrate my "doctoral-level" merit, then it could undermine my own legitimacy as a researcher in the site. Thus, I had wanted to study. The study guides were mostly photocopies of photocopies, grainy, fuzzy, and stapled in the corner. Although I had planned on taking the entrance exam earlier in the research, a number of distractions had surfaced, including back pain and marking midterm exams for a few evening courses I was teaching in another institution. That very same day I had also arranged to interview Dean Arizza, but just as we were about to begin, a fire alarm went off, and as fire warden she left me to do her duty in clearing the floor. Eventually all returned to normal, as did the interview; however, I found that I had almost no time to prepare myself for the exam as I had originally planned. Like an ancient Greek approaching the Oracle at Delphi, I walked into the Testing

Center wondering what the assessment would say about me. What would it predict?

The Accuplacer exam was a computer adaptive exam, which meant that if you took the exam and answered a question incorrectly, it would automatically follow up with an easier question. If you answered a question correctly, it would then ask you more difficult questions. Individual questions were thus weighted differently. At this time, the ACT, SAT, and the GRE (Graduate Record Examination) used such a system. Situated in a high-traffic location between the School for Social Work and the restrooms, the Testing Center had about fifteen computers and a sound-proof glass wall, and all sorts of people passed by and watched as I took the exam. Again, performance anxiety became an issue as I had come to know many members of the community and did not want to threaten my own legitimacy—or my pride. I came in with a pencil and notepad and nothing else, with the understanding that this was how prospects entered, although I was using the notepad both for math (which was typical) and for making notes about what I saw in the exam (which was not). I mentioned my anxiety to Gregoire about the polynomial equations, and he said that there were no such sections like that on the exam; he was correct—there was only arithmetic. The study materials I had acquired were prepared a long time before my study, and the staff had assumed that these handouts were still accurate. There was an indication of this as early as December 2008, when a student had complained that the material in the exam was not what was covered in the review materials. As within many bureaucracies, the first step is to deflect blame even before someone suggests it, and thus Dean Levitz had responded, "I think the exam changed and no one bothered to look. But I'm not supposed to have an opinion." Thus, even the dean of admissions felt frustrated and impeded by the faceless, bureaucratic *other* that could hamper everyday activity.

The computers were large and clunky white machines yellowed with age, and the fluorescent lights were distracting. I found myself second-guessing myself constantly. If a question seemed easy to me, I nervously thought that I must have answered the previous question incorrectly. I found the reading comprehension section a little disorienting; in the past when I have taken a reading comprehension section on a standardized exam, there was a reading followed by five to ten questions. Not so here. On this exam, every reading passage was followed by only one question about that reading. Twenty questions meant twenty different reading passages, on topics as diverse as marine biology and George Washington; it thus required that I quickly shift my thinking twenty times. The following is a sample question from the website:[2]

> Leonardo da Vinci is not only one of the most famous artists in history, but he was also a botanist, a writer, and an inventor. Even though most of his inventions were not actually built in his lifetime, many of today's modern machines can be traced back to some of his original designs. The parachute, the military tank, the bicycle, and even the airplane were foretold in the imaginative drawings that can still be seen in the fragments of da Vinci's notebooks. Over 500 years ago, this man conceived ideas that were far ahead of his time.
>
>   The author of this passage is praising da Vinci primarily for his
>
> A. artistic talent
> B. intelligence
> C. foresight
> D. fame[3]

The sentence skills section was far trickier than I expected and required the test taker to complete sentences in different formats. Many of the questions I encountered seemed to be more about personal writing style than "correct or incorrect," and I found myself falling back on my ear for Standard English. A sample question from the Accuplacer website reads less ambiguously:

> *Although the sandpiper is easily frightened by noise and light, it will bravely resist any force that threatens its nest.*
>   Rewrite, beginning with
>   *The sandpiper is easily frightened by noise and light,*
>   The next words will be
>
> A. but it will bravely resist
> B. nevertheless bravely resisting
> C. and it will bravely resist
> D. even if bravely resisting

The arithmetic section was far easier than I expected. By question five, I realized that I could get a lot further by making estimates rather than actu-

Table 4-1. Accuplacer Test Scores

	Maximum Score	Passing Score (general admission)	Passing Score (ATB)	Mean Ravenwood Score (2008)	Mean National Average (2008)	Author's Score	Author's Percentile Rank (national, 2008)
Reading Comprehension	120	57	55	74.53	77.10	120	99.0
Sentence Skills	120	54	60	80.00	81.91	112	89.0
Arithmetic	120	36	34	52.06	60.25	113	96.0

ally doing the calculations, and this quickly sped up my test taking. For example, a sample question from the website reads:

Which of the following is closest to 27.8×9.6?

A. 280
B. 300
C. 2,800
D. 3,000

It thus became relatively easy to determine the correct answer without having to do all the calculations. Table 4-1 shows my scoring across these three areas, as well as passing scores in the college. I was relieved that the Oracle did not pronounce me immediately inadequate for my credentials. What did immediately strike me with surprise was that I did so well in arithmetic and relatively poorly in sentence skills.

The average Ravenwood student was in his or her thirties (as I was at that time) and had not encountered this kind of exam or this kind of material in quite some time. Although college-going high school students certainly feel anxiety when they sit down to take the SAT, they have become accustomed to the battery of exams that constitute assessment in schooling. For many of Ravenwood's prospects, however, such exams could be a decade (or more) in their past. In addition, despite having planned to study more for the exam, life had thrown a number of events at me, giving me only ten minutes or so to review the material before going in. I imagine that prospects who needed to make arrangements to leave work early or secure proper child care might be met with such distractions. Finally, the review materials I had did not match the exam content. Clearly, the consequences of these conditions on this precise moment are critical.

Like the SATs and ACTs, Accuplacer was a product, designed and sold for a particular purpose, articulated on the website as follows:

> At times, education professionals need additional information about students' academic skills to determine if developmental classes would be beneficial before the students take college-level work. *How do you accurately assess students' academic skills in order to effectively recruit, advise, and place them?* (emphasis in original)
>
> ACCUPLACER is a suite of computer-adaptive placement tests that quickly, accurately, and efficiently assess reading, writing, and math skills.
> ACCUPLACER:
>
> - Can reduce your assessment costs.
> - Allows you to assess using direct writing with scores available immediately.
> - Helps save your technical support dollars.
> - Allows you to deliver the right tests to the right student (individual customization).
> - Enables you to test in remote locations.
> - Allows you to facilitate institutional research through customized reports.
> - Can help you increase retention through correct course placement.[4]

Accuplacer is thus a product that is packaged and marketed as a suite of tools for the purpose of assessment of some sort of merit or intelligence. According to the College Board, 1,300 secondary and postsecondary schools use Accuplacer, although it was unclear exactly how the exam was being used across those institutions—whether as general assessment, admission requirement, course placement, or admission exam for pre-college secondary school programs. The company also provided a product brochure to specifically assist college administrators in determining appropriate scores for college admission.

Gregoire learned just how much of a product the exam was after allowing the Learning Center to bring in its students to take the exam to brush up on skills. He was harshly chastised by Dean Arriza because the college was charged $1.15 for every test taken. Regardless of the cost and how the exam was used, however, no one in the college knew whether this exam was a good predictor of success at the college. Neither Gregoire nor Gary, director of institutional research, had had the time to crunch the numbers.

Regardless, the College Board represented an important part of the educational infrastructure in which Ravenwood participated. All of the activity in that room around Accuplacer had implicated various players in the infrastructure: the test was designed by psychometricians for a private organization to be sold to the colleges, to be instantly graded and evaluated by computer, to place every test taker in a curve in relation to other test takers. The test was administered and overseen by one department (the Testing Center) and made meaningful by another (the Office of Admissions). There were also study materials, tutorials, the technology itself (both hardware and digital), and other elements of the network pulled into that room with me. Typically, the SAT and ACT were taken at particular sites and sent to the college or university, but at Ravenwood everything took place on campus, which allowed both closer control over the process and immediate reporting. There were other reasons for these choices as well.

Testing, Scores, Access, and Opportunity

One of the reasons that Accuplacer was selected for use at Ravenwood was because of another "class" of person that the college needed to measure, and attract as students, the Ability-to-Benefit (ATB) student. This was a particular program that allowed prospects without a general equivalency diploma (GED) to take an exam and, if they scored well enough, to enroll in courses at Ravenwood. After completing twenty-four credits at a certain GPA, these students could apply for their GED and receive it from the state. Although some colleges would openly advertise these sorts of programs, Ravenwood College never shared information about it on its website or in its advertisements, which suggested that it was somehow embarrassing. Prospects found out about this possibility through word of mouth.

Accuplacer was specifically required for use with ATB students who were carefully regulated in their testing process. ATB students were thus those who were fulfilling an equivalency of the high school diploma (GED) by taking college-level courses; this was not a remedial or independent program and as such students were anonymously mixed in with the general population. Prior to 2004, there were two separate exams in use at

Ravenwood, Accuplacer for ATB students and TABE (Test of Adult Basic Education) for everyone else. Both of these were very similar, and so it was decided that all prospects would simply take the same exam. As an outsider, I had difficulty uncovering who actually made this decision either because of bureaucratic momentum in which policies take on an agency of their own or because the individuals who enacted them were able to avoid ownership. Who made the decision about which exams to use and why? As with the setting of enrollment goals, no one was sure. Although there were many other possible areas for testing, Ravenwood used only the Accuplacer tests and scores for sentence skills, reading comprehension, and arithmetic. Presumably, efforts were not made to ensure that the pre-prepared study materials from the company corresponded to only those sections that the college used.

Although admissions processes were reviewed by accrediting bodies, there was no specific regulation of entrance requirements for any college or university in the United States, which was therefore at the discretion of the individual college administration. As long as a prospect was a high school graduate (or equivalent), colleges could utilize any exams, assessments, scores, essays, recommendations, or transcripts as the basis for admission. It is instructive that so many institutions rely on only the ACT or SAT. According to Gregoire, under an earlier director of admissions (whom I had never met), it was significantly easier to enter the college because only a cumulative score was required; there were no score requirements for individual sections. Thus, if a student did well enough in sentence skills and reading comprehension and failed arithmetic entirely, he or she could still pass the exam. This was later changed.

Whereas the regulation for most students was at the discretion of Ravenwood, ATB students were strictly regulated because they did not have a high school diploma or GED, and so passing scores were set by the College Board and then approved by the federal government. Credentials opened up opportunities not only symbolically but at times as enforced by regulations. There were no time limits, but usually it took students an hour to ninety minutes to complete the Accuplacer exam. Gregoire estimated that although about 90 percent of prospects with a high school diploma or GED passed the exam, only about a third of ATB prospects passed. After prospects finished the exam, Gregoire either sent the scores downstairs directly or e-mailed them to the Office of Admissions, without informing the student of his or her score. Indeed, many admissions counselors described this moment, of informing students that they had failed the exam, as one of the worst of their job. Aaron, for example, never used the term "fail" but preferred to say something like "it looks like the score is not high enough. It looks like this time it didn't go well." He was sure to "drill it in" that if it did not go well, it would be possible to take the exam again in two weeks. He also admitted that he occasionally lied and said, "It's very common that it happens and everyone passes on the second time." This lie often comforted students who failed the exam, but if after the second time, the student was still not able to pass, Aaron just did not know what to say. Aaron, who had a background in teaching and would later teach a course as an adjunct, felt that "everyone has potential" and found that he could just not take the look on applicants' faces when they found out that they had failed again. In such cases, he feared that he might start "preaching" about hope and doing better but worried that he would go overboard and sound like a "salesman."

An ATB prospect could retake the exam two weeks after the initial exam. If a prospect failed the second exam, he or she could retake it three months after the initial exam, but only if he or she provided proof of "intervention," which required documentation to confirm tutoring, the length of tutoring, and so on.[5] Dean of Students Arriza assessed the documentation to ensure that it was adequate to warrant a retest. Gregoire saw only one or two over the years who had sought out formal tutoring and returned to test again. This strict rule about retaking the exam applied only to these ATB students; admissions counselors encouraged students with a high school diploma to retake the exam as many times as necessary to pass.

Originally the Testing Center was operated through the Office of Admission, but at some point it was determined that it was ethically questionable to have the same people responsible for recruitment and assessment, and so the dean of students was given oversight of testing, as well as the employment of proctors whose performance was not in any way tied to the number of students gaining admission. Gregoire was meticulous in proctoring exams, checking paperwork carefully and especially photo identification. There were times when someone would leave the Office of Admissions on the first floor with paperwork in hand to take the exam and a different person would arrive on the seventeenth floor to take that exam. He recalled one such case when a prospect appeared in the Testing Center looking to take the exam but claimed to have left her photo identification downstairs in the Office of Admissions by accident. Gregoire had told her to retrieve it and return. Later, Madelyn (assistant director of admissions) returned with the prospect and the photo identification; only it was a different person. The prospect tried to persuade Gregoire that he was mistaken and that she was the person who had just been in the office looking to take the exam and had forgotten the identification, to which he responded, "Okay, who did you get to take your exam for you?" Anxiety can fuel such decisions.

By and large, undergraduate prospects were assessed purely on the basis of the Accuplacer exam and, if they had attended college before, GPA. Graduate prospects faced a more complex set of assessments, including a résumé, two recommendation letters, an essay, and undergraduate GPA. These additional requirements did significantly alter the process. Two different experiences with Dean Levitz were demonstrative.

On one afternoon in December 2008, the dean suddenly asked me to meet with him and an applicant in his office. She was applying for a graduate program, and at first I assumed that he wanted me to reinforce his narrative about the college, so I said a few good words about the college based on what I had seen. The dean stopped me, however, indicating that this was not his reason for asking me in. He said I was there to show others in the college how hard the Office of Admissions worked to make sure that "good" students got in. He then went on to explain that he liked what she had put together; she was organized and had a lot of promotions in her professional experience and had been recommended by a recent alumnus. He asked her to account for the poor grades documented on her undergraduate transcripts, with the understanding that in a graduate program a C is a failing grade and a B average is required to graduate. She explained that she had worked hard for her grades and done what she could to seek tutoring at that time.

Dean Levitz interrupted her and told his own story. In his day, he had gone to a small college in order to dodge the draft during the Vietnam War. He had not been invested in his education and had not really "worked for it," and he suggested that she had not really "worked for it" either. His biggest concern, however, was not the transcript but the essay. Up until this point, I had remained largely silent and pensive looking, but he seemed to want my support here. I chimed in about how important writing was not just in this program but for a graduate education and gave some general advice about how to improve one's writing. At this point, I was still unsure why he had called me in and how he expected me to contribute when his body language seemed to request my participation. When I finished my comments, Dean Levitz gave her the essay back and asked her to "take a red pen to it." She went outside, corrected, and rewrote her essay, while Dean Levitz and I chatted. He had told me that the essay had mechanical errors and missing words but that she had potential as a student. He felt she would make good contributions to Ravenwood. She started classes in January.

In September 2009, this same student stopped me in the hallway. She said she was not sure if I remembered her, but I had been in that office with her and Dean Levitz. She wanted to let me know that she appreciated that we had given her the chance and that she had been doing well in her studies. This was the sort of situation that demonstrated the ways in which I needed to carefully negotiate my presence and participation in the setting. My clothing and general appearance certainly resembled other administrators, and although staff members largely came to know me and my research projects, the incidental students that I encountered seemed less likely to differentiate me from members of the Ravenwood community. Months earlier in Dean Levitz's office, I had been identified as someone doing research on the college, but I am certain that such distinctions were not meaningful to the student at the time. There were two White men in an office discussing her application with her, and it had been clear that access might not be given. I congratulated her warmly but emphasized that I had nothing to do with the admission decision.

In this first case, the student had been given the opportunity to completely rewrite her narrative about herself and to "fix" the story itself. The dean instructed her on how to construct poor performance in a way that would not threaten her legitimacy. It eventually became clear to me that he had called me in as some sort of witness, to communicate to others (faculty? administrators?) how much care they took in assessing prospects' fit. The next case I share, however, was quite different, and the particular weaknesses found in the essay help to demonstrate how merit (or the lack of it) was being constructed.

About a month after the first case, I was meeting with Dean Levitz when a discussion of another prospect's application came up. He showed me the application essay, which was poorly written, including sentence fragments and misspellings (not unlike the previous case). The dean, however, was most disturbed by the conspicuous inaccuracies. For example, the essay suggested that Ravenwood was listed in *U.S. News & World Report* as the most diverse campus in America—yet Ravenwood rarely even appeared in the rankings and never at the top anything. Furthermore, the applicant invented a supposedly nationally recognized "research center" at Ravenwood with which she wanted to work but did not exist. Soon after this, Jaleel (her admissions counselor) stopped by to ask about the application and Dean Levitz was abrupt in his appraisal. He was upset that Jaleel had even brought the application to him, as this was a case where the prospect clearly "must" be rejected. The dean felt that this was clear because the prospect was not demonstrating the skills she needed to survive in the program, and letting her in would just be setting her up for failure. The problem, Dean Levitz insisted, was not that the essay was poorly written but that it demonstrated that there was "something wrong with her head. She's not all there." He indicated that this was the kind of student who would drive the faculty crazy and about whom other students would think, "who are these people who are getting into my class?" For this prospect, there was no talk about rewriting an essay, no desire to meet her, and no chance to negotiate access. Again, I did not normally have access to applications for reasons of privacy, and so it was always particularly instructive when I was specifically invited to review some aspect of an application. It also reinforced to me that Dean Levitz had a particular purpose in mind in both cases, although it is difficult to say exactly what.

On a number of occasions, I heard admissions counselors talk about some prospects loosely in terms of their mental health. During an interview with Bernard, Jaleel knocked on Bernard's office door to ask him to assist in dealing with a student who was a "head case." Bernard said he would later on, but after Jaleel left, Bernard had laughed; he had enough such students of his own. Questions of access to higher education were thus about specific scores and academic qualities, but assessment was also about whether the student should be affiliated with the current students. There were many aspects of personhood that could be marked for display in these contexts, and they overlapped and competed in many ways: mental health, scores, ways of talking, affiliated organizations, ways of dressing, professionalism, and other loaded terms populated the talk of applications and students. "Head cases" need not apply.

Embodied Acts of Affiliation: Race, Class, Carpeting

I had a question. It had been growing in my mind for some months, and when the opportune moment came, I asked it. Louisa, an admissions counselor, was someone with a personal interest in community activism, youth mobilization, and social change in communities of color; she herself was enrolled in a graduate program at a local, highly selective, national university. Before that, she had also been enrolled at one of the public universities in the region but was disappointed by what she had experienced there. She was very proud of her choice of a selective university and talked to me about it regularly. Ravenwood College drew on a narrative of social change, progressive policy, and empowerment for marginalized communities of color, which seemed to me exactly what Louisa was interested in studying. As a full-time admissions counselor, tuition at Ravenwood would be free, whereas the university she attended was extremely expensive. My question was: Why had she not enrolled at Ravenwood College, as some of her coworkers had?

When Louisa responded, I was surprised to hear that her sister was actually an alumna of Ravenwood; I had not known that Louisa had a sister, much less that she was connected with this institution. Louisa made it clear that although it was good for "someone like her sister" and it had a positive role to play in society, Louisa would *never* attend Ravenwood College. I asked what the college would have to offer in order to make Ravenwood a realistic option for her. Louisa said it was "impossible" but that this was not because of anything that Ravenwood had or had not done. She told me that she had had it set in her mind from when she grew up in "the Projects" that she would one day go to a selective university. For her, it was the ultimate obstacle to overcome. Louisa wanted to go to the best, and the selective university she attended was among them. She seemingly trusted in the accuracy of published college rankings and was therefore not willing to settle for anything less than the best. Reputation counted for a lot.

Echoing the Jeffersonian paradigm, she further suggested that institutions and students often naturally aligned, that there was a clear difference in the caliber of student if one were to compare community colleges with state colleges, city colleges, private colleges, or selective research universities. "If you let everyone into a school . . . if you have a little more selective [*sic*], you know you are dealing with people of a certain level." Despite some voices of dissent, there is a publicly acknowledged hierarchy to colleges and universities that are fueled by the various college rankings available in the popular media. And a major factor in calculating rankings is selectivity—that is, how many applicants were typically rejected. If it was "easy" to get into Ravenwood, some assumed that this indicated that the material covered in the classes would also be easy, or less challenging, or that the ease of access would translate into less commitment from the students. Louisa was among these.

Louisa claimed that she wanted to be challenged by her education and to know that she earned her degree through hard work. Although she felt the Master in Business Administration (MBA) program at Ravenwood was a little more selective, the undergraduate programs at Ravenwood just "took everybody." She thought that the open-access mission of the college was admirable, "but if you're going to do that, which I think is great to give the opportunity, let's give them the right resources and social support to be the best that they can be." Why not Ravenwood? The answer was related to how Louisa's personal history and life narrative connected to a complex social landscape in which institutions and individuals accumulate and mobilize symbolic capital; apparently, Ravenwood was not offering the sorts of capital that Louisa was looking for. She took Ravenwood's less-than-prestigious position for granted and seemed to suggest that Ravenwood both "marked" students in a particular way and that (collectively) students "marked" Ravenwood.

Why Not Ravenwood?

In the United States, race, class, and gender are interpenetrating ideological categories with which individuals must engage that hold particular historical positions in the meritocracy. Ravenwood College, serving largely working class women of color, struggled regularly with questions of merit as embedded in these categories. For example, Louisa also described how important it was that education could "show"; if one met a college graduate on the street, one should be able to "tell" that he or she had experienced a college education. She insinuated that this was not the case with Ravenwood students and did not like it when students used certain "slang" or "things that you should not." Louisa was not sure how to say what she wanted to say. Or, rather, it seemed she was trying to find a tactful way to articulate her thoughts. She suggested that being from the same background, she knew when to "turn it on" and when to "turn it off." Louisa was referencing visible (or audible) markers of class and race as connected to legitimacy, which was particularly relevant to her because of her own origins in "the Projects."

Louisa's comments reflect what other administrators and faculty referenced to me many times through the idiom of "professionalism," one of the more complex elements of symbolic capital available. There were students who did not behave as they should—talking out in class, using overly assertive language, not attending classes regularly—or who were just "unpolished." This idiom of professionalism seemed to implicate race and class in unspoken ways. Apparently, some students either could not or would not "turn it off," which was problematic when accumulating cultural capital.

Louisa was very much aware of the actions, gestures, words, and characteristics that identified her social origins and was able to either display or discard them, to take advantage of advantageous attributions and subvert disadvantageous ones. Again, many of her students (i.e., those she had recruited to Ravenwood) seemed either unable or unwilling to slip into the appropriate "theatrical costume" to affiliate them with the most appropriate categories. Louisa claimed that the public university system was not good enough, and even other selective universities would not be enough for her: Louisa wanted only the best, and she took it for granted that her highly selective institution was one of them. Her ways of speaking, moving, and acting needed to affiliate her with such an institution. And apparently her peers in such an institution either embodied the right categories or were able to "turn it off," as she was.

Of further importance is that in the United States, being marked as belonging to a particular race, even if one adopts the appropriate bodily dispositions, may not grant one access to "merit" as it is deployed by institutions in the meritocracy. Individuals are systematically marked through their very bodies—sometimes in observable traits (as in skin color), in choice of clothing, in ways of speaking and interacting, and even in ways of moving. Their positions in the meritocracy move in relation to these markings regardless of intellect, hard work, or other traits more publicly acknowledged as categories of merit. It is informative that this conversation about embodied markers of race and class took place at the same time as Louisa's refusal to ever attend Ravenwood herself—almost by means of explanation. Therefore, Louisa's struggle with how to classify individuals was itself part of a delegitimizing script that colored Ravenwood College as an institution; institution and the students within it mutually reinforced each other's position in the broader structure. Louisa did not want to be affiliated with the institution, because she did not want to be affiliated with the students at Ravenwood.

Louisa felt that students at Ravenwood did not "show" their education. Others explicitly described how race was a factor in whether prospective students would consider enrollment. Cole, tuition planner in the Office of Admissions, shared with me a simple observation whispered from a prospective White student who met with him about financial aid: "There are a lot of Black people around here." Perhaps the prospective student made the comment to Cole because he was White (many of the admissions counselors were people of color), and likewise Cole perhaps confided the story in me because I am as well. When the prospective student made the observation to him at the time, he did not know how to respond; he just became flustered and changed the subject. Although Ravenwood was clearly marked by a certain demographic profile of student inhabiting the space, race was not something that was easily or regularly talked about at Ravenwood (at least in front of a White, male anthropologist). Or rather, it was talked about in very specific and socially permissible ways or silenced completely. Many thoughtful works on color blindness and muteness are key here (see, for example, Bonilla-Silva and Dietrich 2011; Diaz de Rada and Jimenez Sedano 2011; Marx and Larson 2011; Pollock 2004, 2005, 2008; Staiger 2004; Ullucci and Battey 2011). Race was both ever-present and yet not spoken of. Other sorts of affiliation, however, were talked about in more explicit ways.

Why Not the Institute?

One day Bernard (another admissions counselor, who was also enrolled in a Ravenwood College graduate degree program) went to visit a nonaccredited institute that granted associate degrees. Again, *U.S. News & World Report* classifies institutions as first tier (most prestigious or best) through fourth tier (least prestigious or, through implication, worst).[6] For many, this was the key affiliation for an institution to have. In addition, it classified a number of institutions as "unranked": some institutional details were provided, but these institutions had incomplete data, alternative curricula, extremely small student populations, or other traits that made them difficult to compare with others in a consistent way. Ravenwood was in this category. The institute that Bernard visited was not even listed as unranked; it did not appear anywhere in the rankings. It was, for lack of a better term, untouchable.

Bernard had several goals for this visit to the institute, including to recruit potential students and pursue possible articulation agreements.[7] Bernard had made the connection with the institute when he recruited a graduate student named Haileen who happened to work at the institute. Haileen was highly critical of the institute and openly informed everyone that the purpose of her master's degree was so that she could "get the hell out of there." In fact, she had reportedly pleaded with Bernard to help her get a job at Ravenwood, but he had tactfully demurred. However, after the visit, Bernard let me know that he would not recommend that Ravenwood pursue any agreements or affiliations with the institute. Why not?

Bernard was shocked by what he saw when he entered the institute. It was floored with linoleum instead of carpet, the bathrooms were filthy, and the physical space was generally decrepit. The security guards napped at their stations, which were not equipped with telephones, computer terminals, surveillance monitors, or radios. In fact, much of Bernard's assessment of his visit to the institute was based on the physical appearance as a "shithole." He said that he understood Haileen's desire to come find a job at Ravenwood, because there was simply no comparison. The institute seemed to be a fly-by-night institution, and therefore he would not pursue relationships with them (although he would pursue their students). On reflecting on the legitimacy of the institute, we began to talk about Ravenwood; he thought that perhaps if someone from a more elite or selective university visited Ravenwood, they would have the same reaction that he did walking into that institute. He began to wonder whether Ravenwood's physical space (architecture, design, decoration, and so forth) marked its position in the hierarchy in a similar way to the institute.

Bernard's observations of specific, physical things (such as carpets) and embodied actions (such as sleeping security guards) reinforced his other assumptions about the classification of the institution as one that lacked accreditation and thus legitimacy. Merit and legitimacy were thus inherently comparative (as the rankings attest), inscribed and displayed in a number of things: from the physical and embodied to affiliation with other institutions. Symbolic capital is defined through the act of recognition. Of course, by no means does carpeting or closed-circuit security mean that the classroom experience was any better or worse, but these things did signify to Bernard an ensemble of other unseen traits (including financial security) of the institution. Bernard did, however, recognize those markings.

In Bernard's description of his visit to me, he said that institution was not a "real" college. I asked him whether Ravenwood was "real," and he said without hesitation that it was. He said that in the past it was kind of "sketchy" to him whether Ravenwood was real, but once he enrolled for his MBA at Ravenwood, he learned that the college was, in fact, so. The textbooks were the same as used in other colleges, the professors knew what they were talking about, and the work was real. Since entering the classroom himself, he had become far more confident that he was working for a "real" (or legitimate) college. Louisa, in contrast, had never attended a course at Ravenwood but did draw personal comparisons with her sister and with the students she recruited. Thus, reflections on merit were innately about recognizing various markers of symbolic capital, particularly for those who had not been in a classroom. Because Bernard had not attended classes at the institute, I asked how he could be certain that it was a "shithole" and not "real." Bernard admitted that he could not be sure, but being "real" was referenced by several observable, physical markers and by his own knowledge of the institute's rank and affiliations. In the end, however, he agreed that the test of the institute's merit would be what happened in the classrooms, but he was not willing to spend the time to find out. The campus aesthetic, the staff behavior, the public persona, and the general atmosphere all lent the impression that not much was happening in the classroom, but it was in the classroom itself that Bernard felt merit could be found. These signifiers were a shortcut.

According to my observations, Ravenwood College was not particularly sophisticated in its techno-bureaucracy and business practices; its marketing was not strong, its budgets and profitability were (relatively) small, and the administrators did not always manage information efficiently. Ravenwood did not carefully manicure representations of itself and was in many ways chaotic; for many, this demonstrated mediocrity. Compared with the institute, however, Ravenwood's legitimacy was self-evident. Just as Bourdieu holds that individuals demonstrate their class-bound taste through fine distinctions in everything from art to music, the institution itself would be transformed into a consumable object that marked the tastes of the student and the institution's capital. Linoleum, carpeting, or cherry wood parquetry?

Why not the institute? The answer was related to how Bernard understood the institute's position in the meritocracy. Bernard's assumptions about the institute's "untouchable" category were confirmed by specific markers, and affiliation was not an option. The decision to formally affiliate or not was centered in commensurability. As we will see in the next section, another key to this process was accreditation, which classified like institutions with like institutions. This membership was, of course, highly malleable in practice, but there were clear consequences for institutions that lacked membership. How an institution was classified had significant consequences for the institution and its students.

Narratives of Reputation and Accreditation

A large component of the *U.S. News & World Report* college rankings was reputation, or how well academics and higher education executives thought of a given institution. Part of being a "real" college included its reputation, which involved being affiliated with a group of peers: the colleges that institutions competed with for students. Even the term "Ivy League" originally designated a set of institutions that competed athletically with each other and were thus considered peers: Brown, Columbia, Cornell, Dartmouth, Harvard, Princeton, the University of Pennsylvania, and Yale. Such affiliations become part of both cultural and institutional narratives but also formal ones that included documents, figures, and reports that could also grant formal membership to regional associations. Institutionally, Ravenwood was regulated by a number of agencies but also included the voluntary, self-regulating accrediting body: the Middle States Association.[8] It seems everyone knows today that an institution should be accredited, but few seem to know exactly what that means. In fact, accrediting bodies are a complex of governmental, nongovernmental, and private, self-regulatory bureaucracies that assess standards of quality. Of course, these standards are themselves the product of historical moments, and what constitutes the demonstration of these standards is likewise historically constituted.

Regional accreditation did not actually bestow the institution with the right to grant degrees, as these rights and requirements are reserved by each state.[9] Although the federal government sets complex and elaborate regulations, particularly for the disbursement of financial aid and through the oversight of the Department of Education, accreditation associations are actually self-regulating bodies made up of member institutions. Originally, such associations were set to establish standards for those seeking education under the GI Bill in the 1950s, but by 2008–2009, they had taken on a far more complex peer-review-like role in maintaining standards. The Department of Education closely oversaw this process of self-regulating peer review but did not accredit institutions.

The consequences of accreditation included the ability of students to receive financial aid from the government and to apply for transfer credits among an institution's peers; a regionally accredited college would rarely accept transfer credits from an institution that was not accredited in the right way. Essentially, accreditation was about seeking and obtaining membership in a number of different associations of postsecondary institutions. There were a handful of postsecondary institutions that refused outright to participate in such memberships for philosophical or ethical reasons, but most college administrators saw this as highly suspect. Such institutions that refused accreditation ran the risk of being labeled "diploma mills," institutions that fraudulently sold degrees without any real schooling. For this reason, unaccredited degree granting was actually illegal in about a dozen states. Ravenwood held accreditation from the Middle States Association of Colleges and Schools and from the Department of Education in the state and was also member of other, similar associations.

Accreditation bodies assessed the institution in several important ways to determine whether it merited membership, which had to be reviewed on a regular basis. According to Middle States (2010):

> The Association is a non-governmental, voluntary organization of educational institutions, acting through their respective Commissions (as defined below), committed to excellence in all levels across the continuum of education, whose purposes are to encourage, advance, assist and sustain the quality and integrity of education. In order to achieve these purposes in the public interest, the Association shall establish appropriate criteria and levels of educational excellence and effectiveness, and work with other organizations, agencies, and institutions to achieve cooperation and coordination between and among schools, colleges and universities.[10]

Middle States' assessment was based on fourteen standards in which the college needed to demonstrate excellence and accomplishments through objective evidence; these were instructive and demonstrate the many layers of assessment involved.[11] Teams of auditors, made up of executives, faculty, and administrators from other member institutions, come in to gather the data and assess evidence. These standards constitute a formal, classificatory scheme that is "based on nothing other than the interest of individuals or groups in question have in recognizing a feature and in identifying the individual in question as a member of the set defined by the feature" (Bourdieu 1984, 475). Although formally articulated, the act of accreditation (and reaccreditation) is in practice loosely enacted by a team of member auditors who come to recognize the performance of those features (both in action and text). This is a formal encounter with great consequence.

In 2009, while I was conducting research, Ravenwood went through its accreditation review, which was immediately considered a top priority by the new president. A team of Middle States auditors would came to the college to review every record and every office to assess the institution against the fourteen standards. In order to make their stay more comfortable, Ravenwood offered to make identification cards for these auditors who sent their names, photos, and titles electronically. Identification cards were available when they arrived. More important, however, the information was used to create a flyer for staff with the names, photos, and titles of the entire auditing team. Everyone from front desk employees and security guards to faculty had this flyer ready so that they would know the team members on sight. In further preparation for the arrival of the team an institutional, nine-chapter, 142-page, self-study was written.[12] This study rewrote the recent history and broader narrative of the institution around the standards examined by the accreditation team.

In this report, the college built a complex narrative that acknowledged past difficulties but set the course for the future as optimistic. Gary, director of institutional research, gave some flair to these reports through titles like "Weathering the Storm" when referring to the sharp declines in enrollment and resultant layoffs. Completely absent from this report was any sense that the tensions, conflicts, or crises of the past carried over into the present or the future.

The narrative was supported by the campus climate during the brief team visit. In fact, the audit process was only a couple of days, and through pure accident of timing, I never encountered a single member of the accreditation review team. After a great deal of preparation for their visit, I arrived one day to hear that they had arrived, investigated, and left before I had even seen them.

The college had succeeded in impressing the team in the way that counted the most here: on paper. The sixteen-page report from Middle States to Ravenwood was overwhelmingly positive, with the message that although it had faced and would face many future challenges, the college "should take pride in the many actions you have already taken to address them." The report also described how the auditors were "impressed with the energy, enthusiasm, and excitement exhibited by the entire campus community during the visit which helped to bring the self-study document to life." The self-study and the visit erased the differences of opinion, the finger-pointing, the blame games, the interoffice conflicts and doubts: "Ravenwood knows its mission and the students it serves. It is confident in the knowledge that this type of education can truly change the lives of working adults." The college easily met all standards (although there were recommendations for each), and the admissions team in particular was able to present the following image:

> Ravenwood's Admission practices ensure that students have a reasonable opportunity to matriculate at the college. The admission policies and practices reflect the college mission. Processes within the enrollment services area facilitate cooperation with faculty, academic departments, and student services to allow for recruitment of a student who is a good fit for the institution. Leadership in the department has re-committed to "Experiential Curricula" and, therefore, seeks to ensure that, not only does all staff understand the unique mission of the college, but that they also understand their target market.
>
> The newly energized department has worked to re-establish relationships and articulation agreements with institutions that have historically been feeder schools. The Dean of Admission has sought to establish a marketing strategy and has reinstated a branding campaign which has increased the college's visibility. The college advertises via cable television, the Internet, radio, and print media. Furthermore, Admission materials have been redesigned for the college as well as individual schools.
>
> Comprehensive information is available regarding academic programs, placement testing, and transfer requirements.

In the first paragraph, institutional identity is secured and reinforced in texts and practices. In the second paragraph, we find that all of the energy focused on marketing and recruitment described earlier paid off for the dean, as Middle States' purpose in ensuring the "quality and integrity of education" drew very heavily on how the college was advertised. As with the self-study, the report from Middle States clearly demonstrates that all differences, disagreements, and conflicts were effectively erased. The many daily practices and challenges that I encountered throughout my time in Ravenwood were conspicuously absent. Again, the purpose of the visit was to witness the performance of specific institutional features in practice and text, to essentially confirm that the institution continued to display those markers that were deemed important by the collective of members. For accreditation purposes, Ravenwood was marked in the right ways. Regardless, the acts of classification and affiliation were powerful mechanisms through which merit was established. The narrative as laid down in the accreditation report was clearly only one interpretation of events in Ravenwood, in which sudden resignations, conflicts, personal agendas, and power struggles were absent or insignificant. The "act of recognition" transforms the thing itself, and collective representations shape the entire social order, as groups "progressively impose the representation of their existence and their unity, both on their members and on other groups" (Bourdieu 1984, 480). This process was in many ways a bureaucratic mechanism both for proclaiming inclusion in membership and for enforcing conformity among those members, or at least a surface display of symbolic conformity. Just as students were actively recognized for their membership in particular groups (as described to their detriment earlier in this chapter), so Ravenwood was recognized to its advantage.

Marking Ravenwood College

While the college assessed prospects and students, Ravenwood was, in turn, assessed by those prospects and students through a variety of tools. Just as Ravenwood's applicant and students struggled with legitimacy and relevance on the periphery, as a relative newcomer to higher education, Ravenwood also struggled with legitimacy; the connection between student and institutional assessment was mutually constitutive. Again, if we think about brands as "the ongoing articulation between brand tokens, a brand type and a brand ontology" (Nakassis 2012, 628), then the token of higher education is the alumnus him- or herself; the consumer is the token or, rather, will be at completion of study. Thus, a particular instantiation of the college brand is the alumnus, which further demonstrates the consequence of educational infrastructure's sorting function. The act of consumption locks in the consumer (student) and producer (college) in a dance of affiliation and mutual constitution of position in the meritocracy. Whereas in highly selective settings extremely fine distinctions needed to be made, Ravenwood occupied a position toward the mediocre bulge in the middle of the curve that implied that fewer such distinctions were necessary. Aaron, for example, became upset when prospects for the MBA programs wanted to know about rankings. To him, this tied directly to application assessment; at such times, he thought to himself, "I don't know where we rank, but we're not asking a lot out of you (in the admission process)."

Nevertheless, there were certainly those at Ravenwood who held to a more Jeffersonian paradigm that equated merit with selectivity—and as such felt that the college must find ways to demonstrate its merit. The sixty-five-page *College Assessment Plan, Footprint and Blueprint (2009),* prepared by Gary, was created to

> Provide evidence on how well students are achieving learning objectives at the course, program and institutional levels of the College, and how the College might improve teaching and learning;
>
> Supply data that evaluates the College's overall effectiveness in meeting mission-critical goals and strategic plans, including academic program offerings, support services and administrative structures, policies and processes; and
>
> Serve as a means of providing ongoing information in a systematic fashion that fosters a collegial culture of program and process improvement and evidence gathering necessary for informed decision-making and continuous improvement.

This report described and evaluated the various assessment devices that the college used; thirty-four in total. Gary's office was hidden on an upper floor near all of the other administrators and executives who populated the campus but whom few students met. From here, Gary, whose background was in psychology, sociology, and marketing, looked at numbers. He collected, analyzed, and reported on data, both to the college and its stakeholders.

Between stacks and boxes of papers and beneath paintings of all things nautical, I asked Gary what he thought of the college rankings and prestige and Ravenwood College. When I had brought up rankings, most admissions officers from outside of Ravenwood seemed skeptical of the accuracy of such systems but felt beholden to them because parents, kids, Boards of Trustees, and the general public paid attention to them. Many of the admissions counselors at Ravenwood suggested that such publications were well suited to the task of ranking and that there was something to them. Gary took a different perspective. Gary felt that the problem was really a data–institution mismatch, that is, that Ravenwood did not perform well using traditional metrics of merit. The solution, therefore, was to find assessment tools that would document and quantitatively prove the value of education at Ravenwood. Said another way, although the rankings did accurately measure some kind of merit, it was not the kind of merit that Ravenwood was good at; the college needed to find the right assessment tools to model what worked. According to Gary, the best such model for Ravenwood was a "value-added" model. Enter the *College Assessment Plan, Footprint and Blueprint*.

Both in my professional experience and in the context of other research experiences in higher education administration, the "value-added model" was commonly drawn upon in less prestigious institutions, although it was not always identified as such. The argument goes that although Harvard graduates are amazing, they were amazing when they were admitted. Elite institutions may only "add" a little bit to their students' achievements. In contrast, institutions such as Ravenwood may not have finished "products" (i.e., students) that can compete with Harvard, but Ravenwood "added" a great deal of "value."

Dean Mitchell of the School for Business and Technology spoke to me about this model through the euphemism of "heavy lifting." He suggested that at the elite universities, teaching was a cushy job because there was no heavy lifting involved; all one had to do was stay out of the students' way. At Ravenwood, in contrast, which was dedicated to a mission of access to those who have traditionally been marginalized by society, teaching required a lot of heavy lifting. It is a great deal of work to teach these students who have been described as "unpolished," "aggressive," and "vocal," all of which might evoke class, race, or even mental health connotations depending on context. Gary was the first to explicitly use the term "value added" with me, although others had drawn on the idea, and he saw it as part of the accountability and assessment direction that higher education was moving in.

One assessment tool used to measure "value added" was the Collegiate Learning Assessment (CLA) test,[13] and he was pleasantly surprised to find that Ravenwood did better than 40 percent of the institutions whose students took the exam. In fact, Gary said that when you control for other institutional demographics—minority, adult, women-focused institutions—Ravenwood's value added was even higher. The CLA used a cross-sectional sample, rather than longitudinal, and determined that although "cognitively" first-semester freshmen were at the same level as final-semester seniors, in other ways there were significant "authentic" improvements. Assessment therefore provided a powerful framework for demonstrating different kinds of merit, whether it be "cognitive" or "authentic" (terms used in the CLA). "Authentic" merit seemed to reference practical application of theory to practice, and Gary seemed to think that Ravenwood did well in this area.

"Authentic assessment" was in the CLA exam involved giving students a complex scenario in which they relied on a series of documents for resolving real-world problems. Gary's example was a "mayor's office" scenario in which an outbreak of swine flu was described in several different policy-like documents. After reviewing the documents, the student had to make policy recommendations in a narrative form. Students' performance was then assessed by the CLA team at the Council for Aid to Education (which designed and administered the test), who read them blindly with a six-point rubric across a series of performance areas. The second part of the CLA test assessed debate-like argument and found that more Ravenwood seniors did particularly well "punching holes" in the arguments of others, although they had a lackluster performance in defending an argument. The CLA, Gary felt, played well to the curriculum's strengths and was where Ravenwood could best demonstrate value added.

Gary collected such data in reams. His tiny office was filled with impressive reports on every shelf and others stuffed into boxes. Many of them had full-color graphs and charts, and many had been conducted by outside research companies. Gary felt that the big challenge for the college was in standardizing the assessment both of students and of their learning. When I asked whether his reports were being read or utilized by anyone on campus, he grumbled and said he was not so sure, but he was optimistic about the college's new self-study and strategic plan because they were data driven and seemed to be taken seriously by the administration. Indeed, Gary was the only person from whom I ever heard the CLA mentioned.

Essentially, assessment is a way to transform people and institutions into specific kinds of numbers that can be meaningfully translated across the infrastructure. This kind of work was so important to the institution that an entire department was dedicated purely to this purpose (although Gary was the only employee in that department). Various stakeholders were interested in Ravenwood College and could understand it only through certain assessment tools, from the Title V grant discussed in chapter 2 to the number of applications accepted according to *U.S. News & World Report*. These various assessment tools were actively used in the construction of merit or quality as a classification but also shaped practice.

Shumar (1997, 137–138) described how an institution had moved toward higher ranking by accepting only students with higher SAT scores and better academic records. The shift allowed the institution to lay claim to higher academic quality that could eventually increase demand for admission but put the institution at fiscal risk in the immediate (due to the reduced number of students). Because the ranking systems considered students only in the "daytime school" and not "night" school, each of those rejected applicants was offered admission to evening classes. As an evening student, "the potential student was assured s/he could take daytime classes, that costs were the same and the degree was the same. No future employer would ever know they came to the university through the less prestigious evening college" (Shuman 1997, 137). Thus, the college and administrators would engage in practices in response to classification systems (based on forms of bureaucratic assessment) that students would then have to deal with. Similarly, as seen earlier, Ravenwood seemed not to discourage the alteration of online application systems as it allowed for the canceling (or rejection of) a high number of applications and thus inflated the sense of selectivity.

Standardized testing was not only a powerful idiom through which merit was socially constructed but a hegemonic complex of activities and practices through which merit had to be demonstrated to powerful bureaucracies, both local and systemic. It was the terms through which both individuals and institutions were required to explain themselves and to legitimate their participation in those broader systems. Although individual institutions have decided to forgo such exams, this was only for institutions that were relatively secure in the sphere of higher education. Thus, institutional responses to such bureaucracy informs us about the institution's position more broadly. These numbers, like accreditation, marked Ravenwood as a legitimate college. However, not everyone bought into that.

Disrupting a Legitimate Ravenwood

In August 2009, an e-mail was sent by a Ravenwood alumnus to the president of Ravenwood College about a disturbing note on Wikipedia. Of course, any user could edit any page on Wikipedia, and a user had done so on the entry for Ravenwood College. The entry itself was little more than a paragraph about the college and its location, but a link had been inserted at the bottom simply titled "Students [*sic*] View." This was the object of the flurry of e-mails that circulated throughout the executive in-boxes at Ravenwood.

In the e-mail to the president, the student indicated that the "Students View" link connected users to a personal website, which I will call "Hate-Ravenwood.com." Administrators at Ravenwood were able to have the link from Wikipedia removed, although it was unclear how long it had been there and how many people had seen it. HateRavenwood.com, however, was an independent website, and there was nothing that the college could do about it. Although it was built as a WordPress blog, HateRavenwood.com had a registered domain name, which meant that the disgruntled student who set up this site was paying annual or monthly fees in order to send out negative stories and images about the college (the site seems to be inactive at the time of publication). As it was premised on a blog structure, the disgruntled student was able to not only post comments anonymously but to solicit other disgruntled students to do the same, although of course it was impossible to substantiate the origin of any of them. HateRavenwood.com contradicted nearly every legitimizing narrative employed by the college and emphasized the aspects of the college that seemed like a business.

A major theme of these anonymous, online entries was that listing a degree from Ravenwood College on one's résumé actually hurt one's chances of being hired, as "hiring managers" knew that Ravenwood was not a "real" college. Of course, in these virtual contexts it is impossible to determine much about who set themselves in opposition to Ravenwood's own narratives, aside from whatever markers one could glean from the text. Nonetheless, such individuals actively took institutional narratives and reinterpreted them in these spaces.

For example, the federal government initiated a number of changes to promote veteran access to higher education, and Ravenwood actively engaged with these policies as an opportunity to increase enrolment. In January 2009, the president of Ravenwood College laid out a policy that would take advantage of changes in financial aid to veterans that would allow them to attend Ravenwood essentially tuition-free. The dean of admissions asked his staff to begin brainstorming ways to recruit and serve veterans because every college in the region would attempt to recruit these same students, and the president's plan would give Ravenwood a strong position to start from.

Upon hearing of this campaign, one entry on HateRavenwood.com suggested that Ravenwood was not a "college" but actually a "sham" and a "business." It was suggested that the offer of free tuition would never actually be honored and that it was all a "gimmick" that would take advantage of brave servicemen and women. The anger and frustration on the site was palpable and directly challenged the narratives of Ravenwood as a legitimate college oriented toward social justice.

Another entry took note of Ravenwood College's recent marketing awards (which the college proudly displayed as part of a narrative that marked its legitimacy) as further evidence of their being a "sham." The author admitted that the college did effectively market itself but claimed that everything that he or she had been told was a "lie." The author called the administrators "snake-oil salesmen" and "city-slickers" and warned everyone to stay away. Such terms suggested a sleek and sophisticated scam at play; I doubt that many administrators at Ravenwood would find this term apropos. Although many administrators at Ravenwood were (in my opinion) dedicated to student empowerment, they were also underfunded and lacked sophisticated systems to manage the organization, responding to situations viscerally without careful forethought. The college was not well funded but constantly struggling with financial sustainability and threatened by layoffs. Finally, the administration of Ravenwood in general, and the staff in the Office of Admissions in particular, constantly seemed to be subject to forces beyond their control. Everything from the weather (rain affecting event attendance) to the economy (trends in unemployment), from the market (the ways others ranked or classified them) to the cost of tuition (which could not compete with the public university system), seemed to be beyond their control;

these were simply conditions with which they must deal. Apparently, colleges needed to pursue profit and financial security, but institutions marked as doing so had their legitimacy questioned. Case in point, although every institution has disgruntled students, accusations of illegitimacy based on having a profit motive or utilizing business models did not seem to mar selective universities that were obviously very profitable. Yet here, success in advertising, marketing, and business were described in these comments as being almost antithetical to the process of schooling.

Perhaps most wounding on HateRavenwood.com, however, was a post that was supposedly sent to the site owner from a "hiring manager." This hiring manager claimed to have encountered a number of Ravenwood graduates with minimal literacy and poor analytic skills and suggested that seeing the institution listed on a résumé would make him or her skeptical of any job candidate. Ravenwood would mark the students. More important, this hiring manager suggested that these Ravenwood graduates were "victims" from "disenfranchised" communities of color who had been sold "fraudulent credentials."

The hiring manager further suggested that many students had formerly been incarcerated or had gone through substance abuse rehabilitation and were the victims of exploitation by Ravenwood College. The college had been founded on the principles of social change and empowerment, and many persons I met had dedicated themselves to the pursuit of these ideals; this narrative was a key component of the legitimizing narrative used in the institution to describe itself. This post essentially suggested a complete corruption of the institution from savior (or at least facilitator of salvation) to predator and would suggest the fundamental flaws of higher education as capitalist enterprise: that whatever the intentions, the commoditization of schooling hurt more than it helped. Given the graduation ceremonies, positive alumni survey responses, and my own observations, I would argue that many employees of Ravenwood College clearly cared a great deal about servicing marginalized students. Some outside the college, however, saw what Ravenwood did as no more than exploitation of vulnerable markets.

There was little consensus about which institutions were legitimate, and one needed to interpret a variety of markings inscribed in students and institutions. Students were active, thinking agents, sometimes resisting the legitimacy-reinforcing narratives that Ravenwood laid down and going through bureaucratic processes in their own ways and on their own timelines. Merit and legitimacy were constantly under contention and dispute everywhere in the college but were mutually constituted by the faculty and students themselves. Thus, I heard a great deal of gossip about the quality of instruction and faculty: faculty who included exam questions with racist subtexts; faculty who taught only for twelve weeks so they could go on vacation; faculty who used Jewish holidays as an excuse for canceling classes; faculty who would take attendance and tell students to go home after ten minutes of class; faculty who did not teach. But likewise did faculty complain about students: graduate students who produced work at a community college level; papers that were "painful" to read; students who were unprepared; students who continued to deny plagiarism despite being caught red-handed. Faculty wondered how some students even got into Ravenwood. This led to a diametrically opposed position taken by admissions staff and faculty (in particular). Repeatedly, many faculty reported that it was their job to teach whoever was let in to the college. It was their responsibility to prepare as best they could any student who ended up in a classroom or who met the academic standards as set by the college. Poor-quality students were thus the result of poor admissions decisions. Admissions staff, conversely, insisted that the college had a mission of open access and empowerment for those who could not otherwise achieve it. Thus, it was their responsibility to give everyone a second chance, and it was up to the faculty to recognize those who had talent and to purge those who did not. Poor-quality students were the result of social promotion by faculty. This tension reflected some of the institutional conflicts and finger-pointing that I observed at other points. What were the explanations for the mediocrity of the college, and who was to blame? Of course, there were no simple answers here, and few people would point their finger any further than down the hallway. The college inhabited a space in higher education at the intersection of race (largely Black and Hispanic), gender (largely female), and class (largely working class and poor)—is it any wonder that it struggled with merit in the eyes of the general public? What does it take to be a "legitimate" college in America? And was Ravenwood "legitimate"?

Conclusions: On the Logics and Anxieties of Meritocracy

In the beginning of this chapter, I set out to examine the competing ways that members of the Ravenwood community and the institution itself struggled with and operated within the cultural order of merit in higher education—to see how Ravenwood marked students and how it was marked by students. This order was partly the result of a mutually constitutive process, an assemblage of activities and understandings that (re)produced everyone's position in the social structure. I have examined how symbolic capital was made visible and institutionalized through affiliation, standardized testing and assessment, institutional association and accreditation, embodied acts and material traits, and choice. In higher education, symbolic capital always marks one's merit, which becomes the basis for and legitimizes other classifications. Members of the Ravenwood community struggled with this process.

This chapter is not meant to argue that questions of merit and mediocrity are always resolved in the same ways nor that these are coterminous with notions of legitimacy. Both student and institution battled for legitimacy. For students, that legitimacy was bound up with everything from test scores and choices to embodied behaviors (accents, gestures) that signified race and class. For the institution, legitimacy was bound up with student traits, membership in associations, display of ranking, physical things (carpeting), and embodied behaviors (sleeping security guards). However, most important, it was also bound up with being affiliated with each other. The sorting infrastructure had consequence for individual students, staff, faculty, and the institution overall.

Ravenwood was regionally and nationally accredited and had been for many years. According to formal classificatory schemes, Ravenwood College was "real." Its being a real college, however, was not deeply internalized by students and faculty but was actively contested by students who were sensitive to the notion that what was true in a bureaucracy on paper was not the same as what was "real." Many of the accusations, both online and in classrooms, revolved around the notion that Ravenwood was not a legitimate college. The same was true for faculty. One afternoon while exiting the elevators I observed a couple of professors greet a third man. One professor introduced the other, with "come meet someone who works at a *real* college."

The performance, articulation, and marking of classificatory schemes are a critical aspect of class that should be examined as part of the complex of local practices and can be productively interrogated through the construct of brand in higher education. Merit is constructed both about students and about institutions in complex ways that reflect the competitive, American, higher-education marketplace and that are operationalized through the educational infrastructure. Whether these were deeply internalized dispositions or simply the practical strategies to obtain other forms of capital, individuals and institutions mutually reinforced the other's position through their affiliation. For these reasons, I argue that legitimacy, in this setting often parsed out through the idiom of being "real" and often taken for granted broadly but contested locally, should be understood and examined as a complex of symbolic capital that emerges from a variety of embodied and educational practices. Furthermore, it points to the very particular position that Ravenwood occupied in the educational infrastructure and how it related to other parts of that network. And one's symbolic position in that infrastructure was mutually reinforced through access to other sorts of capital: financial, in particular.

Chapter 5

FINANCING EDUCATION AND THE CRISIS OF SUSTAINABILITY

Hire more professors that actually want to teach and know their material.
Also, the tuition is too high for the courses they offer. It is way cheaper at
other institutions such as [public institution] and [public institution].

Lower the cost of tuition so students don't have to use the cost of the college
as a reason not to attend, or as a reason to have to leave.

The program is administratively, academically, and financially
subpar and overpriced.

Providing resources for single parents that want to return back to school such
as childcare in the area, and improve the conditions of the computer labs.

ANONYMOUS COMMENTS, RAVENWOOD GRADUATION SURVEY 2007–2008

In what ways does Ravenwood's financial situation drive the decisions
that it makes and how it operates? What does the anthropology of markets
help us see about this?

Just as with others forms of cultural capital, social capital, and financial
capital, Ravenwood's position in the meritocracy and its access to financial
resources were mutually constitutive. As we saw earlier, Ravenwood's approach to recruitment, branding, and converting applicants into students
was deeply informed by the resources it had available and the economic conditions of its students. And as has been demonstrated by the histories of
other institutions, it is possible to "purchase" one's way out of a particular
position in the meritocracy. (Beaver College's transformation to Arcadia University is demonstrative here; see Williams and Omar 2014.) A sudden and
large endowment can lead to facilities that are marked with eliteness, celeb-
rity faculty and scholars who are known in the right circles, and strategic

management of metrics that will lead to movement in rankings. Said plainly, for institutions and individuals alike, choice is constrained by cost. Ravenwood's lack of financial resources took away more options.

As institutions of higher education in the United States are simultaneously educational and entrepreneurial in nature, one of the most important aspects of educational infrastructure at the postsecondary level is the financial one. The ways that dollars flow into Ravenwood College are mediated through both the financial lives of applicants and students and also through the networks of private institutions that lend money to students and the local, state, and federal institutions that define and operationalize financial need. This chapter emphasizes the ways that these processes were enacted locally, the ways that they were framed within the local organizational culture, and the implications for understanding Ravenwood College.

Climbing out of the Red: Risk and Ravenwood College

At the end of December 2008, the weather took a decidedly blustery turn. The wind was whipping through the streets, and a mix of snow and hail came with it. The restaurant hosting Ravenwood's Christmas party was just a few blocks away from campus, but the admissions staff members and I huddled together and moved quickly to get out of the bitter weather. We were among the first to arrive, and we watched as the restaurant filled with warm partygoers holding stiff drinks. Many attended, and many attendees seemed ready to let loose. While Dean Levitz introduced me to faculty and board members, I began to hear word of a memo that was sent right before the party that had apparently brought a little extra joy to this celebration. A few days later, I had the opportunity to get my hands on a copy of the memo. Fall enrollments had proved stable, and for the first time in two years, the Board had approved an "end-of-year stipend" for all full-time employees, equivalent to about 5 percent of their annual salary. If the trend continued, the Board might approve cost-of-living salary increases and restore pension benefits. These were good omens—signs that Ravenwood College was moving in the right direction fiscally.

At the time of my study, higher education in early twenty-first-century America was filled with anxiety and risk, but as we have seen, Ravenwood occupied a position in the merit curve that was particularly precarious. Some of these risks were pertinent to all higher education institutions, as they were predicated on shifts in demography. It has long been understood that the Baby Boom represented a bulge in populations that coincided with American postwar prosperity, all of which led to increased enrollments at colleges and universities. Since the 1980s, colleges have attempted to mitigate what they knew would be a decline of students arriving at college straight out of high school. Many of these attempts involved expanding access to more minoritized students and nontraditional adults. Before the economic and housing crisis of 2008–2009, there had already been an awareness of the declining pool of customers who would potentially enroll in college, but as the crisis unfolded, a blanket of panic seemed to descend. In many ways, at the time of my writing, this blanket has not yet been lifted. As institutions of higher education have come to be dominated by corporate logics and profit motives, the fundamental demographic problem that preceded the economic crisis will not go anywhere—unless a radical shift in demographics goes with it. This reflects another fundamental contradiction in higher education as being both merit-based and capitalist. As described earlier, the logic of the Jeffersonian paradigm requires clean and clear standards of merit distributed in a normal curve and available to a very few. Capitalism, however, requires an endless pool of customers so that institutions can grow ad infinitum. If population grows steadily, then these two aspects can be managed, but in the face of population decline, they are put in opposition to one another. If merit is normally distributed, and the population shrinks, then the number of college-going students should likewise shrink. This is, however, understandably anathema to the business sensibilities that see college as a private enterprise and a private good. Colleges and universities should grow. As it seems that few institutions are willing to simply concede shrinkage, this also means that there will be a lowering of academic standards or increased competition for fewer students—or both. If the capitalist principles are adhered to, it is only an extension of logic that there will be many colleges and universities that shrink or close entirely. These were some of the pressures that Ravenwood admissions staff felt in 2006 and feared in 2009.

As we also saw earlier, Ravenwood sought to manage risks through enrollment strategies and markets, and those risks came to dominate many of the decisions that it made. But some risks were associated not with higher education in particular but rather with the class of institution to which

Ravenwood belonged, and were being discussed in higher education circles even during the course of the study. Kneedler (2008), for example, reported on the existing economic data on postsecondary schools in an attempt to predict which institutions might be most at risk of decline in the current climate. He found the current conditions to be most difficult for institutions with the following characteristics:

States with large numbers of private institutions.

The Northeast and high-growth regional or local urban cores and corridors now slowing.

Serving economically disadvantaged students.

Master's and doctoral (not research-intensive).

History of low fund-raising performance.

Serving high proportions of minority students (e.g., 20 percent or higher).

Founded by a religious group and now serving a wider clientele.

Urban/suburban.

To be frank, even during the course of this study, reading articles like Kneedler's filled me with anxiety for the Ravenwood community; aside from a lack of religious affiliation, Ravenwood College fit the bill. Stripling (2008) predicted that "problems may arise . . . for expensive colleges with relatively small endowments—substantially below $100 million—that rely heavily on tuition revenue." In 2015, Sweet Briar College in Virginia announced its closure, which was soon after blocked by dedicated alumni and members of the community, but it began a flurry of speculation about the security of small colleges. Moody's Financial Service announced predictions that college closures would triple by 2017 (Berman 2015; Woodhouse 2015), while others provided guidelines for how to identify mostly small, insolvent institutions that applicants should avoid (Selingo 2015). Burlington College in Vermont announced that its doors would close in May 2016, and there was a real sense that others could follow.[1] Again, Ravenwood also seemingly fit in the at-risk category. Every semester of this study, it was not clear to me whether the budget number would be met, and I released a great sigh of relief at the beginning of every semester when things seemed to fall into place. At the time of my writing, Ravenwood has managed to balance enrollment, revenue, and expenses, but the question of for how long still hovers.

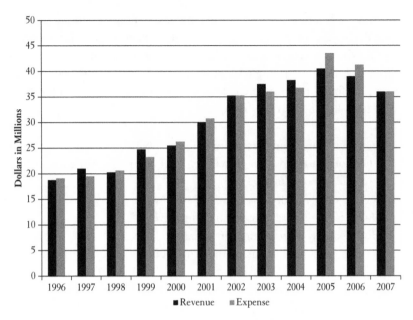

Figure 5.1. Revenue and Expenses at Ravenwood College, 1996–2007

These figures shaped the palpable tension at Ravenwood during the course of this study (see figure 5.1).

As described in chapter 3, Ravenwood College was not inexpensive, and Admissions had needed to justify the cost in its persuasive scripts about why to enroll by highlighting costs in terms of time to and probability of completion, with students maintaining the potential to earn an income throughout their education. Ravenwood's tuition rate was between $450 and $800 per credit, which translated into between $15,000 and $26,000 per year for most students (depending on the program). At public institutions with which Ravenwood regularly competed for students, the comparable in-state rates were between $3,150 and $4,600 per year.

As cost of attending college and student debt in the United States has steadily increased in recent years, many are beginning to ask whether higher education itself is helping to drive inequality. After all, recent trends seem to indicate a class-based cleavage that structures opportunity around access points across different sorts of institutions. William Julius Wilson (2012, B9) pointed out that, increasingly, children from affluent families attend institutions segregated from those from low-income families, while Bailey (2012, B10) noted that, mostly because of cost, low-income students are more likely to attend community colleges despite high academic skills. Wolin (2012, B8) noted the differential college completion rates across family income and an average unforgiveable student debt of $23,000. Such debates also spilled over into the Occupy Wall Street movement and the public discourse about college education that has remained, even if the social movement has faded. And yet, contradictions are rife. In 2011, the Pew Research Center released survey findings about the American public's perception of higher education that highlight these contradictions:

> A majority of Americans (57%) say the higher education system in the United States fails to provide students with good value for the money they and their families spend. An even larger majority—75%—says college is too expensive for most Americans to afford. At the same time, however, an overwhelming majority of college graduates—86%—say that college has been a good investment for them personally.[2]

Furthermore, according to this survey, 94 percent of Americans want their children to attend college. Thus, today the contradiction of cost and value is at the heart of college attendance in the United States, just as it was at the heart of admissions in Ravenwood.

Some of the risks that Ravenwood faced were particular to this institution and this historical moment. Although Ravenwood had cultivated a place in the educational market, it lacked brand recognition, it lacked prestige, and it did not quite seem to know how to get more of either. There were also those who thought of Ravenwood as an institution in transition. The energetic and authoritarian founders had driven the college in numerous ways, including in the constant pursuit of endowments and government grants. Flo Epstein painted a picture of Ravenwood in the late 1960s and early 1970s that was a stark contrast to the college that I encountered. Since then, Ravenwood's path had been less clear.

Epstein was small, soft-spoken, and unassuming. She had been brought into the college by the founder as a writer in the early years of its formation, when other kinds of possibilities hung in the air. At that time, the college focused its recruitment efforts on poor women who wanted to promote social change in their communities—and recruiters went out into neighborhoods to find such people. The admissions process included a group interview, where college staff and prospective applicants would sit in a circle and talk about themselves, the challenges they faced, and what could be done to improve local communities, which Epstein described as a "very sixties thing to do." At that time, federal grants largely covered the full cost of tuition for such students. It is not clear when, but at some point, Ravenwood adopted admissions processes more typical of most other colleges and universities—with all the trappings of application forms, test scores, and student loans. I was unable to reconstruct these transitions, but I imagine it was a gradual shift toward conformity rather than a single dramatic change. Epstein had been serving as a member of the Board of Trustees for one year when I met her, and she had a number of concerns. She told me:

> The college had so many financial problems recently that in some ways it has no choice. But on the other hand, if it were . . . clearer about its mission, I think it might help in solving these problems. And, it certainly is true—there were—there have been at times unrealistic expectations for growth. When the college wasn't clear about how to manage that growth—how to do what it does with a larger student body. So the board has a lot of issues to address, and I think it is just beginning to.

Some twenty years after the passing of the founders, the college had become almost completely reliant on tuition. Presidents and their administrations had come and gone, each with a different, often competing, vision for the kind of institution that Ravenwood should be. But the real transition was that the college came to rely less and less on outside funding, and the burden fell more and more on students as paying customers. At the time of this study, it certainly seemed to me that nearly every decision was one that sought to carefully balance the institutional mission with the financial context. The financial situation produced incentive for but was also exacerbated by shifts in leadership and goals. According to Ravenwood's old-timers, financial strain also contributed to a loss of focus on the school's mission.

The reality was that students were not able to handle the full burden of their educations, as the progressive mission that Ravenwood's founders had laid out was expensive. And Ravenwood's decisions, though driven in part by mission, were also driven by the practicalities of the marketplace. At times, such decisions even drove academic programming.

Market-Driven Programming

The August 2009 marketing report had several components. One component was descriptive and demonstrated the weakness of the Ravenwood brand; another component had recommended breaking into a new market: White women in their thirties (see chapter 2). Yet another impractical recommendation was addressed in this marketing report: the creation of a registered nursing program. Professor Bhatt, Business Programs chair, understood that a nursing program could potentially be a "cash cow" but was skeptical because it also required a massive investment up front in technology, labs, and clinical faculty. Although such a program could potentially yield a significant, tuition-paying student population, it would take many years of investment before it moved from producing costs to producing profits. Professor Bhatt was among those who felt that the marketing company just did not "get" Ravenwood College.

The research group also recommended that the college offer hybrid-blended online courses, more specific certificate programs, and more part-time options. These options had been explored by the college in the past in different formats by trial and error but with limited success. The faculty in particular believed that the LC Clusters were such a critical part of the college that they were unwilling to discuss part-time options that would dilute the Clusters. Largely made up of nontraditional, adult students, the Ravenwood student body seemed to be less savvy with technology than more traditional college students; reportedly there were students (and faculty) who were not comfortable using the Internet or e-mail, purchasing books online, or accessing Blackboard course software. Most applications and forms were still done by pen and paper. Although of course there were many students who were comfortable with technology, it seemed rather risky to invest in an online platform that could potentially disaffect the existing profile. Thus, part-time and online options did not seem practical.

The research group recommended moving toward two seven-week terms per semester, because working adults nationally had indicated a preference for that format. I never even heard this finding discussed, and few individuals seemed to take it seriously.

Other findings about adult-age college students were of greater interest, although I heard some administrators suggest that the college had paid

$40,000 to have a research group tell it things that it already knew. These included the following findings:

- According to respondents, the most important issues when deciding on a college in general were reputation of the institution, convenience of location, and affordability.
- In 2008–2009, the Internet was used to gather a tremendous amount of data about colleges in general and should therefore be the primary vehicle for marketing the college, supported by buses and billboards, personal contact through open houses, and personal referrals.
- On the whole, the cost of Ravenwood was deemed acceptable by respondents in the survey.
- More and more, college admissions applications at Ravenwood were being completed by applicants who had never had any contact with an actual staff person. The website needed to provide all relevant information and be user-friendly and attractive.
- Respondents rated the following traits of Ravenwood College very favorably: earning college credit with work-related activities; faculty as practitioners; the accelerate speed of completion for degree programs; and the frozen tuition policy.[3]
- The college should offer far more diversity of degree programs, including accounting, marketing, health professions, psychology, performing arts, graphic design, and criminal justice.

Although Ravenwood did not seriously consider the nursing program as an option, the limited number of degree programs was a constant frustration to admissions counselors, who at times felt that they had saturated the market. From this point of view, degree programs and their curricula were the product for sale, and Dean Levitz took a very close interest in all developments in academic areas at Ravenwood College. Whenever the college invested in developing a new academic program, it was investing a tremendous amount of money, time, and energy in hiring staff, designing curricula, getting state approval, and finally marketing and recruiting students. This investment did not always bear fruit.

In the wake of September 11, Ravenwood College had designed a new master's degree in emergency management to meet the growing (perceived) need for managing security and disaster. Ravenwood's existing programs were very much designed for working professionals, and it was felt that an emergency management program would be ideal to reach those working as nurses, paramedics, security teams, police officers, firefighters, and mental health professionals. Unfortunately, for nurses to be promoted, they needed clinical degrees in nursing; mental health professionals needed clinical credentials in psychology; and paramedics, police officers, and firefighters in the region received virtually no tangible benefit for obtaining a graduate degree. Most of the emergency management programs around the United States emphasized antiterrorist law enforcement and managing federal-level disasters and were designed for Homeland Security agents, rather than local firefighters or paramedics. Despite having a very dedicated faculty and some talented students, the emergency management program struggled to recruit more than a handful of students each semester. There were those who thought that the investment had not been paying off and that a marketing report like the one above could have foreseen some of the challenges that were being faced. Situations like this came to mind in August 2009 when I sat in on a marketing meeting that brought up the subject of new programs to be offered by Ravenwood.

I met with Dean Levitz, Admissions Counselor Jaleel, Danny from the advertising agency, and Professor Bhatt, the new chair of the Business Program, to discuss (among a variety of other topics) Professor Bhatt's report on the status of a bachelor's in health care management and proposed revisions to the current business degree programs. Although much of the recent marketing reports was positioned as either commonsensical or of little value, Professor Bhatt pointed out that they did vindicate many of the recommendations that he had been making about moving into health fields. Dean Levitz and Danny were visibly excited by the proposal for a new health care management program, which had been discussed for some years without progress. Professor Bhatt's report included projections both of national employment trends in this field and potential enrollments, course descriptions that included details about LC Clusters, and the names of an advisory board made up of leaders from the business and health professions. It also maximized the faculty skill sets and curriculum of the existing Business Program, allowing essentially a new major with only a limited number of new course offerings (and thus requiring only a limited number of new faculty to teach them).

The revisions to the existing business curriculum were equally impressive to Dean Levitz and Danny. By adding nine new courses into new LC

Clusters, Professor Bhatt was able to add three track concentrations in: entrepreneurship, accounting, and project management. These concentrations would give the appearance of a more diverse set of programs while actually utilizing virtually no new resources.

For the health care management program in particular, conversation moved quickly to recruitment and marketing to immigrant and international student populations. After some discussion, Dean Levitz indicated that he had $25,000 left in his budget, $18,000 of which he was willing to spend on international recruitment efforts in India and particularly the Caribbean. Dean Levitz brought up a nearby township that had suffered economically, but through recruiting almost exclusively from the Dominican Republic and Puerto Rico, a local college had been able to build a campus there. Danny, who had worked in postsecondary marketing for twenty years, suggested that running ads in a Caribbean newspaper was extremely inexpensive and that a strategic visit by a team of recruiters with strong materials would yield a large number of prospects. Professor Bhatt, who had worked for one of Ravenwood's competitors before his recent move to Ravenwood, said that at that institution he had been able to draw large numbers of students simply by setting up a recruitment program in a hotel, supplemented by advertisements in local newspapers. Danny was ecstatic, saying to Dean Levitz that he had been advising this approach to Ravenwood for nearly seven years. Danny asked where they would start.

Professor Bhatt, who was himself a Caribbean of South Asian descent, said that he wanted to go after Trinidad first because the competitor whom he had just left was heavily recruiting the Black population while ignoring the Indian one. He said this was a critical mistake because the Indian population would "sell every goat to make sure that one family member could go to school" and had a great deal of financial resources. Dean Levitz attributed that to the British educational system, which he saw as academically superior to those in former French and Dutch colonies. If recruitment went well in Trinidad, they concluded, they would then shift efforts to Jamaica, which also had a strong history of immigrants working in health management. The fact that it was also a former British colony went unspoken.

Academic programs were imagined here as products that needed to be pitched to particular students as consumers within niches. Ethnicities were used as a shortcut to understanding consumer behavior, in the same way that other markets were. According to Shumar (1997), the introduction of market segmentation, which radically transformed capitalist understanding of consumption, "saw the social field populated not with individuals but with demographic centers, social groups from a particular set of socio-economic backgrounds" (137). The implications of this approach were that it opened up entirely new segments of the population as consumers and suggested sets of behaviors and values for those consumers that could then be used to fabricate the most attractive image (or marketed fantasy). The production of these images, however, was not part of a carefully prearranged, systematic order but was negotiated by various persons.

Critically, as I have already argued, marketing for the college was largely understood as the selling of the institution as the vehicle for personal and professional mobility. But the decision to invest in new academic programs by necessity required the careful analysis in purely financial terms. For both the institution and the students, merit is seemingly pushed aside as a pressing concern in favor of financial exigencies. As the federal government divested support, students needed some other way to pay for the ever-rising expenses involved in the production of Ravenwood College and increasingly relied on a complex infrastructure of financial aid to fill in the gaps. In bureaucratic terms, this gap is quite easy to understand. There is the cost of education and the amount that the student can reasonably expect to pay toward that cost. The difference is the gap or, as most often described in official documentation, need.

Need, Merit, and Haste

Ravenwood College was a locus of activity, in which various policies, institutions, and systems came together in a dance of sometimes competing and sometimes complementary agendas. Although the idea of need was not difficult to grasp, the financial aid system used to determine need was possibly the most complex, heavily regulated, and consequential system that Ravenwood encountered regularly. In fact, the federal, state, and private system through which students could obtain funding for their education was so complex that most administrators did not even attempt to understand how it worked, leaving the process to the Office of Financial Aid. Aid could come in the form of student loans, scholarships, grants, or the Federal Work Study Program and was a powerful mechanism through which the state could exert itself on private institutions of higher education. For example, in March 2008, the U.S. Department of Defense identified steps to withhold federal aid to colleges that placed restrictions on Reserve Officers' Training Corps programs and military recruitment (Hermes 2008). Therefore, especially for tuition-reliant colleges, institutional policies and practices—even unrelated to financial matters—could be deeply influenced by the need to conform with financial aid requirements. In the conversion process described in chapter 3, one of the documents required to move from *incomplete applicant* to *completed applicant* was the Free Application for Federal Student Aid (FAFSA),[4] which was also the main tool for gathering financial data about students to calculate need. In other words, participating in the federal aid infrastructure was a required step in the process by which one moved through the admissions infrastructure at Ravenwood. In local parlance, the entire financial aid process was called the *packaging* of students for federal aid.

The FAFSA is a form, now primarily digital, designed to collect financial and demographic data from prospective students in order to determine financial need. Cole, the tuition planner at Ravenwood, noted that the FAFSA itself was a "gateway" into college as virtually every person interested in attending college in the United States is required to fill out the form. The exceptions included international students (who were ineligible for almost all forms of aid made available through the FAFSA) and "full-cash" students, including those who were "extremely" wealthy, whose families owned "cash" businesses,[5] undocumented immigrants, and certain "ethnic groups"[6] that Cole felt had a "distrust" of the system and thus avoided any sort of loans or financial aid processes.

After a student completes the FAFSA, an Expected Family Contribution (EFC) is calculated, which is an important operationalization of need. The EFC is what the federal government says the student's family is able to afford for educational expenses per year, in a range from $0.00 to $99,999.[7]

According to Cole, some "complex formulas" were used to determine EFC, which accounted for variables such as age, family size, income, and savings. These formulas changed from time to time as a result of what Cole thought were obscure regulations and legislation that "don't always get results that make sense." For example, one student with whom he worked was earning $41,000 per year, and his calculated EFC was $17,000. This meant that, theoretically, the government felt that the student's household could realistically contribute $17,000 per year toward education and continue to live on $24,000 per year. Given the cost of living in the region, Cole thought that this would be nearly impossible. This student was not even close to qualifying for aid. According to Cole, even having an EFC of $5,000 was enough to disqualify a student for a state grant. In this sense, it did not matter if a student's EFC was $5,000, $17,000, or $99,000—the odds of receiving any financial aid would be very low.

After the EFC was calculated, the Department of Education would send a Student Aid Report (SAR) and an Electronic Student Aid Report (ESAR) to the institutions that the student identified in the FAFSA. The report summarized all the basics: the demographic responses and, of course, the EFC. The student had an opportunity to revise the information, and the institution was informed how much the student would be eligible for in federal aid. Many colleges use the data in the ESAR to then recalculate need based on their own institutional formulas. Cole thought that there may have been a slight move toward more need-based aid and less merit-based aid, due to the economic climate at that time.[8]

FAFSAs were completely self-reported, but the Department of Education randomly flagged about 30 percent of them to audit every year. When a FAFSA was flagged, the college's Office of Financial Aid would need to audit the records of the flagged student, which would entail having the student (or the student's parents) bring in all of the documentation to verify the income and financial data described in the FAFSA. For many years the Department of Education had discussed linking information from the Internal Revenue Service with the FAFSA to automate the process, but this had not happened during this study.

After the Department of Education used these data acquired in the FAFSA, it would forward the information to the state in which the college operated. If, for example, it noted that a state resident was applying to a college within that state, it would send that data automatically to the state's Department of Education. State agencies would then repackage students along state guidelines—that is, recalculate need based on any local legislation. In some states, however, the formula was based on state taxes rather than federal taxes, so it would either recalculate from scratch, or the state would automatically fill in the data from its own tax records. Forms and documentation required for Ravenwood students were then sent to the student directly. Students were given an estimate of an award from the state and asked to verify their data, sign the form, and send it back to the state directly. When this process was complete, the students were considered packaged for state aid.

Other forms of aid were based less on need and more on merit. Students with merit (or at least particular, institutionalized, documented forms of merit) might be offered financial incentives because the college or university wanted to raise its profile, move up in the rankings, or otherwise attract a certain sort of student. "Merit" of this sort might be found in the name of the previous school, the GPA achieved at that school, a score on a standardized test, a powerful letter of recommendation, an impressive résumé, or a thoughtful essay. Ravenwood was atypical in how it operated, and so it may be helpful to consider how a typical institution operates before turning to Ravenwood's process.

A typical, traditional college applicant in his or her senior year of high school applies to four or five institutions, with the goal of enrolling in one of them the following fall. One or more of these colleges might offer early admission through March 15 (of the previous academic year) and strongly recommend that applicants complete the FAFSA before then in order to be eligible for aid. By April 15, directors of financial aid at those institutions might be pressured by their admissions offices to "package" all of the "early app" students so that they can send accepted students their "award letters." These are generally based on their parents' financial documentation, as many of these students are minors. Award letters are composed in the Office of Financial Aid and break down all of the forms of aid available to the student, from institutional awards to federal and state awards; they include awards based on need and merit, and may also point to loan eligibility. Institutional awards are often based on formulas that have been refined over many years to best meet recruiting goals. Aid like this is understood as essentially a recruitment tool, designed to attract or "yield" prospective students through financial incentives, and may actually be a blend of need and merit.

What usually works best, in this context, is a system of specific financial incentives (awards) that maximizes enrollments and minimizes cost but takes into account pressures that the dean of admissions might receive from individual admissions counselors, high school counselors, or coaches of athletic teams (although athletics is further regulated in other ways). Assuming that a student is accepted by more than one college, she would look for the best financial aid package for herself, perhaps even mentioning to admissions personnel what a competing institution had offered. In my interviews with administrators in the region, two described hiring a private research company that calculated the ideal amount of aid to offer every individual applicant. Such companies claimed that their formulas could identify exactly how much aid would be needed to attract a student without going over. For example, they might suggest that student X be offered exactly $2,000 in merit scholarship because offering less would push them somewhere else, but offering more would be a waste of funds. One of the colleges that was actively using such a company at the time of this study would not negotiate any financial aid decisions with applicants; whatever the company determined to be the optimum award was nonnegotiable. The other college had canceled the service because using it had proven ineffective in changing enrollment patterns or spending.

Students with high need were desirable because their funding was supplemented by federal and state agencies. As Cole saw it, given the state of the economy, students who were high achievers (and thus likely to be eligible for merit-based awards) had even more flexibility and leverage because such students could move into tier 2 colleges that were offering huge amounts of aid over tier 1 institutions. Of course, applicants with both high need and merit were in the most advantageous position of all. Institutions were interested in acquiring "meritorious" applicants because they would bring up the numbers used by ranking systems, which included metrics like average SAT scores and high school GPAs. Moving up in the ranking system would then potentially lead to an increase in applications. At that point, institutions would ideally be in a position to either follow a growth model, in which they would increase enrollments and thus become more profitable, or follow a prestige model, in which enrollments would remain unchanged while demand increased. A dean of admissions at a small liberal arts college in the region informed me that his institution follow a prestige approach because a growth approach would entail purchasing expensive real estate for new buildings, hiring faculty, and expanding administration. The college preferred to keep a steady enrollment at the current size and enjoy the security of knowing that there was high demand to get in. However, with tier 2 institutions throwing money at applicants to attract them, many tier 1 institutions were turning to their wait lists, which traditionally had remained untapped. Applicants were asking for more money, negotiating more, and making choices that weighed cost against prestige.

Although Ravenwood provided scholarships and grants to attract students or to induce certain behaviors, there were other stark contrasts here. In December, a flyer was distributed around the office that offered prospective students $1,000 if they completed applications and registered for courses by December 15 (for those starting classes in January).[9] Current students could receive a grant for $500 if someone they referred to the college enrolled.[10] Such awards were not actually based on need or merit but were rather incentives for speedy enrollment.

In addition, admissions counselors could grant to their applicants a merit-based scholarship ($4,500 renewed annually for graduate students, $3,000 renewed annually for undergraduates), although there was a great deal of disagreement among the counselors about the criteria and processes involved, and I was unable to locate written documentation of the criteria. A number of admissions counselors went months on the job without realizing that they could award such scholarships, assuming that doing so was part of the financial aid process. The office used an Microsoft Access file on a shared network drive in which staff filled in the scholarship information—the recipient, ID numbers, notes, name of admissions counselor, and the amount awarded—and then a letter was generated. Louisa, one of the admissions counselors, would immediately print a copy for herself, the student, and Financial Aid. She had no idea where this Access file came from, how it operated, if it was on a shared drive, or anything else; she only knew that if she completed the process, her applicant would be given the award. In fact, the only way she could locate the file was by clicking a link in an e-mail that someone had once sent her. Admissions counselors reported that "somebody" was managing and tracking that database, but they did not know whom. "It is in the system, so someone is watching," said Louisa. Maggie, another admissions counselor, was always careful to get her scholarships approved by Dean Levitz, but this was apparently unnecessary—and others suggested that the scholarship would go to whomever they decided without question.

Some admissions counselors reported that Dean Levitz required an undergraduate GPA of 3.0 for the graduate scholarship, yet it was the application as a whole that was being assessed. So, for example, Louisa herself would give the scholarship to every graduate student with a 3.0 or higher. If they were close to that GPA, she would cautiously offer the scholarship. If they had good essays, she would cautiously offer the scholarship. If the undergraduate GPA was "low," maybe even 2.1, then she would hesitate. She had a sense of whom her applicants were as individuals and used that knowledge to inform her decision. "If their essays are good, and they are passionate, and they really want to do it and I really believe in them, then I'll fight." She would take it to Dean Levitz and argue for the scholarship going to that student. In one case, an applicant had a bachelor's degree from a first-tier, national university, but her GPA was a 2.2. She also had a child, and a parent had died during her studies, but her essay was excellent and she had the experience. Louisa decided to award her the scholarship. She explained her reasoning: "I mean, I didn't have a good GPA in high school and I go to [Selective University] now." She felt that the score was not indicative of that student's potential and assessed merit partly on the basis of personal narratives. In contrast, when I spoke to Kenya (the newest member of the admissions team at that time), she had never given a scholarship to a prospective student, thinking that it required an undergraduate GPA of 3.9 or so. As we saw in chapter 3, former employee Roslyn suggested that when she was on staff, admissions counselors would simply award the scholarship to every applicant they processed. Even at the time of this study, the scholarships were being given out not strategically as an incentive for particular types of students that the college wanted to attract or based on a particular metric but rather at the complete discretion of the individual admissions counselor, without any systematically documented criteria.

In a private conversation, Cole railed against these scholarships because he felt they were not based on merit in any meaningful way. He had heard that originally the scholarship was dependent on maintaining a certain GPA after enrollment, but this had led to conflicts between faculty and students who might lose their scholarship if their grades were too low, so the college eliminated the GPA requirement. It was reported that the scholarship granted at admission was renewed annually automatically; students would not be reviewed in any way for that renewal.

There were other stark contrasts between institutions such as Ravenwood and what we might think of as the typical model. Applicants rarely applied to other colleges at the same time as to Ravenwood, and very little negotiation about financial aid took place. Because academic standards were lower, institutions such as Ravenwood were not necessarily willing to spend money on individual students, because doing so would most likely not significantly alter the college's position in the ranking systems. In fact, many people at

Ravenwood seemed unaware of the school's ranking, usually just assuming the worst. Finally, because of the speed with which prospects become students, the bureaucratic processes could operate very quickly, meaning that details that would inform aid decisions could be hard to come by. Rather, awards were used as an incentive to do things more quickly and to get applicants to commit to coming.

Ravenwood's somewhat atypical focus on speed had some unusual consequences. As mentioned, it was possible for Ravenwood prospects to apply; take and pass the entrance exam; complete the FAFSA; and register for classes in one day. Such applicants, however, could not be fully packaged until after they were already registered for courses. Therefore, some students did not receive an award letter and thus know whether they were eligible for aid—and, if so, how much—until weeks into their first semester. This was in direct tension with Ravenwood's tuition refund policy. At Ravenwood, like at most colleges, students who officially withdrew before attending classes could receive 100 percent of their tuition back (although fees were nonrefundable). Beyond this, however, the terms were as follows:

Withdrawal during the
First week	75% reimbursed
Second week	50% reimbursed
Third week	25% reimbursed
After the third week	0% reimbursed

Although such reimbursement policies were typical in the region, the speed of enrollment was not. Students might discover only in their third week that they would be receiving no financial aid of any kind, but at that point, the college would reimburse only 25 percent of what they paid, which amounted to many thousands of dollars. Rather than engaging in the type of negotiation between offers that might take place in more traditional settings, Ravenwood students often found themselves committed to the institution before it was even clear to them how much it would cost.

Cole felt that the reason that this happened at Ravenwood was the rush to get "asses in classes." Ravenwood had suffered losses and was perpetually operating in crisis mode. In order to sustain itself, the college was unwilling to lose a single student. Theoretically, it was possible to calculate the financial aid much more accurately, so that even without an official letter, students would have had a good sense of the type of financial aid they would qualify for before enrolling. Providing this information would have entailed catching the errors made by students that created these problems, not deviating from deadlines (i.e., you must complete the FAFSA by a certain date), and spending fifteen to thirty minutes with every applicant going over all of the documentation. Unfortunately, the Office of Financial Aid and the Bursar's Office were dangerously understaffed, and so staff barely had the time to process paperwork at all, much less individually counsel every prospect for thirty minutes. Throughout the course of this study, the Office of Financial Aid never had more than three employees (which included a director and two counselors). Because Ravenwood accepted students on a rolling basis, with starts in the fall, spring, and summer, the Office of Financial Aid was perpetually behind.

In fact, the pace of all aspects of administration at Ravenwood was hectic. Nothing had to happen "next year"—everything had to happen "now." The market was imagined as precarious and risky; survival was paramount. Rather than taking time to plan or strategically negotiate with students to maximize affordability, there was the constant crisis of sustainability. There always seemed to be a backlog of paperwork in the Office of Financial Aid, as well as heightened tensions and anxiety. It seemed a far cry from its former self, at least as described by Flo Epstein.

Student Loans and the Securities Sausage

The world of student loans and financial aid represent an entire and complex network laid atop and intersecting that of college admissions. Need was calculated, federal and state awards were granted, institutional awards (based on need or merit) were granted, and the student could still not afford the cost of attendance. At that point, private lenders were happy to step in to provide loans to fill that gap. Provided for by about sixty different lenders (e.g., Sallie Mae, Citibank, PNC, HSBC, TD, Commerce), in 2008–2009, student loans required a minimum credit score of around 580 and, unlike other loans, would not be discharged after bankruptcy or sometimes even death.

The business of student loans was complex, and practices were in flux. Generally, it was expected that, for all of the loans given out, about 3 to

4 percent would default. At the time of this study, many lenders would sell this student loan debt as asset-backed securities (ABS) as soon as they acquired it. This requires some explanation.

Let's say a group of lenders give loans to a variety of students attending a variety of different colleges. Some lenders specialize in specific institutions; others work nationally with nearly everyone. The lenders might predict a return of investment of around 3 percent, so that if they gave out $100 million in loans, they would expect to make $3 million. However, managing all of those loans could be tedious, and their repayment could take years, and so many lenders would bundle their loans and sell them in the ABS market.[11] Cole described this as the "student loan sausage." On the ABS market, the debt was undifferentiated and sold to various investors looking to make a profit, who had no idea where the loans were coming from—hence, the sausage metaphor. Similarly, investors picking up this student loan debt would be unable to differentiate what they were purchasing. Students were not involved in this process and often did not realize who owned their debt, as the conditions of the loan had not changed.

Banks and other lenders spent a good deal of time developing relationships with colleges and universities across the country. Most students were not particular about the lending institution they borrowed from and would just select whichever lender was at the top of the page when they met with their financial aid counselor.[12] Furthermore, many administrators who worked in financial aid offices had spent time working for lenders and vice versa. Cole himself had worked for a prominent lender with strong ties to Ravenwood before becoming a tuition planner. Out of curiosity, Cole and I began to review the data about loans at Ravenwood.

In doing so, we noticed that over a one-year period, the number of private bank loans jumped from about $350,000 to about $1.4 million. Cole said, somewhat proudly, that this was in part due to his previous work with the prominent lender for which he used to work a few years ago. Because this particular lender was getting so much business from Ravenwood, it wanted to offer a "perk" in the form of a specific class of loan, which allowed many people to go to college who never could have otherwise. Cole insisted that the lender actually lost money on this risky set of loans but considered it a "thank you" and a sort of incentive for the college to continuing doing business with it.[13] Essentially, about $1 million was offered for loans to students who were otherwise considered ineligible for them. In the face of ongoing media coverage of questionable mortgage lending, I asked nonchalantly if Cole would consider this "predatory" lending. He said "absolutely not," because the conditions of the loan were no different than for any other student (i.e., they did not change the policy or charge a higher interest rate). It was a program for the benefit of marginalized students who might not otherwise be able to attend college.

Cole did note, however, changes in student lending. During the economic crisis of 2008–2009, investors became infuriated when default rates on student loans rose from 3 or 4 percent to between 5 and 7 percent. The value of the securities dropped. Lenders grew nervous, because even if they gave out more student loans, they faced increased risk of never being able to collect them, and they had a harder time selling them on the ABS market because investors were worried about the possibility of defaults. Therefore, many lenders were getting out of the student loan business entirely or had raised their criteria so high for private loans that they were actively discouraging clients from applying. Cole had lost his job with the prominent lender after it reduced its student loan involvement (and after having provided $1 million in loans to unqualified borrowers). He was attempting to piece together a job at Ravenwood College as a tuition planner.

Thus, at the time of this study, many colleges were increasing tuition— at private institutions because expenses continued to rise and at public institutions due to cuts in state funding. Federal aid was generally dropping for students, there were far fewer lending institutions, and those that remained in the market imposed increasingly strict lending requirements. It was becoming even more difficult for students to figure out how to pay for higher education, despite the fact even many entry-level positions required a college degree. Cole had observed how transformations in personal finance over the years affected this process. Even fifteen years ago, a parent would have approached the financial aid process having lived in a home for fifteen years, built up equity, maintained low credit card debt, established a retirement fund on the side, and maybe held a car loan that required regular payments; essentially, they were fiscally secure. In his experience, parents today were coming into financial aid with major credit card debt and no equity, because they had already spent it in building an addition to the home that they bought at an already inflated price two years previously. According to Cole, these parents had no financial "wiggle room—not an inch." They were over-burdened as it was, and he thought that 50 percent of home equity loans were being used for education.[14]

Cole suggested that the College Cost Reduction and Access Act of 2007 significantly changed the student loan process, including the reduction of special allowance payments for lenders, the reduction of lender insurance rates, and the doubling of lender origination fees (see U.S. Congress 2007). Cole described the act as being led by "Democrats"[15] who did not like private banks making a profit from student loans and so added more restrictive and fixed costs. Because costs were fixed (rather than based on a proportion of the total), a bank would have the same cost whether lending $2,500 or $10,000. This encouraged banks to lend greater amounts of money to students, while discouraging them from lending to those who needed only small loans. It also pushed out a lot of lenders who did not want to deal with any of the new regulations. Loan limits had been increased for independent students (i.e., adults not living at home with their parents, as was common at Ravenwood), which had eased the hurt for Ravenwood College. In the end, however, Cole felt that policies like these would essentially just throw up further barriers for accessing education. From his point of view, loans were indications of students' commitment to their own future.

Meritocratic Commitment as Coffee Grounds

The financial aid process was mysterious to many at Ravenwood, and most admissions counselors were not fully aware of how it worked. For them, the Office of Financial Aid was that magical place where students were packaged. For example, the loan authorization form was given as part of the application process, although Admission Counselor Aaron was initially not entirely sure what it was used for. At first, he described it to students as almost like a FAFSA, a document that authorized the college to examine the prospect's finances in order to determine need for a student loan. From conversations with other admissions counselors, though, he learned that this was incorrect, and he began to describe it differently. This form authorized the college to receive the student loan money directly, rather than having the lending institution give the money to the student, who would then write a check to Ravenwood. Aaron found the lack of clarity about the form's purpose—what it was authorizing—troubling. What also bothered Aaron was that at most other colleges where there was "overage" (i.e., more loan money than tuition cost): the college would write a check for the difference and give it to the student. At Ravenwood, if there were any excess funds coming in, the college would apply that money to the next semester. This form authorized the college to do so.

Aaron felt that this was inappropriate because he felt that Ravenwood's students, particularly the many low-income students, could use that money for buying books or other general expenses. Aaron was not sure how to handle this form because he could not imagine why any student should authorize the college to act as such. Nadira was an alumna of Ravenwood College and had been through the process many times herself. She said that she tried not to get involved in making one option sound better than another; she presented the options of the loan authorization form and stepped back so that students could make their own decisions. Nadira felt that the loan authorization served two purposes: first, it was a convenience because, like an auto-payment, one never need worry about sending a check in on time; and second, it ensured that the money was being spent in the right place—and some people did not trust themselves with money. Aaron's problem with the form and its policy, however, was that it implied that students were somehow incapable of making those sorts of decisions for themselves. Aaron set himself against a particular point of view that interprets and imagines students vis-à-vis market sensibilities.

Market sensibilities require that one understand human activity as the result of free-market agency alone and presume that every individual is responsible for his or her own state through his or her own actions. In present times, there is a constant need to produce one's self as a marketable product or project.[16] For example, such discourses in the media about the 2008 economic crisis in real estate implied that although the banking industry acted inappropriately, certain people—who should not have had credit or loans in the first place—mishandled their personal finances. The subtext thus implied that the most important criticism of the banking industry concerned not its lending practices but rather that banks had mistakenly taken certain borrowers to be capable of making sound financial decisions, when they were not. From this point of view, the bank itself was a sort of victim. In this discourse, "certain borrowers" seems to reference poor people of color but also points to a lack of merit broadly. The implication is that these were persons from the bottom of the curve who did not "merit" the trust to begin with.

This line of thinking was reflected in the ways that some Financial Aid staff at Ravenwood College talked about their students, particularly through the contrasting idioms of "commitment" and "hand-holding." "Commitment" here referenced both a fluency in the educational and financial infrastructure and a willingness to overcome obstacles to attain personal goals—perhaps equivalent to "grit." "Hand-holding," in contrast, referenced what students needed when they lacked commitment; they needed someone to hold their hand through every little activity. Through these idioms, market-fundamentalist understandings were coded in discussions about students and their education as being solely the result of individual, personal, meritocratic traits.

Most administrators I encountered did not embrace these market-fundamentalist positions and described "hand-holding" simply as being part of the job. As first-generation students or those who came from disadvantaged backgrounds, these students required more guidance through administrative processes, which the counselors provided. The dean of students, for example, saw her role as partly one related to student advocacy, which included guidance through bureaucracy. Financial Aid staff with whom I interacted, however, found it particularly frustrating. At the new student orientation, Randolph, the director of financial aid, complained to me about students needing too much attention and voiced admiration for elite university students, where his peers informed him that students would come to the office to meet with a person only if something went "wrong." At all other times, according to Randolph, those students at selective institutions handled registration, financial aid, and many administrative procedures remotely through the college's online systems. In contrast, Ravenwood was bogged down with face-to-face meetings and paperwork: registration was still completed on paper, and students needed to literally acquire signatures and physically move from office to office. Although this struck me as being related to available resources in Ravenwood, Randolph felt that this was related to students having their hands held too often and becoming dependent on the college. He felt that the "real" world did not work that way and that the college was "crippling them" through so many walk-throughs and orientations.

On numerous occasions, in conversations with Randolph (usually brief, as he was perpetually busy in Financial Aid) and Cole (at greater length and depth, as time allowed), I found that hand-holding was used as a vehicle for describing weakness and dependency. One afternoon Cole and I were discussing recent concerns with retention of current students. He argued that by and large this problem of retention was due to a lack of commitment among students. To defend this position, he produced an article from the *Chronicle of Higher Education*, in which a proprietary college classified its entire student population with the colors of a traffic light: green indicating high levels of commitment and ability, yellow indicating lower such levels, or red indicating little commitment or ability. He then said that he believed that "they" (pointing a finger out into the Office of Admission) needed to be better at filtering out those who lacked commitment. He felt that those students who had dropped out in their first semester had simply "changed their minds" about education; his only explanation was that they lacked commitment.

I disagreed. By this point in the research, Cole and I had developed a friendly relationship, and I felt that my disagreement would allow me to probe his opinions more deeply but not threaten our relationship. I therefore challenged his interpretation, which I felt placed all of the blame for dropping out on the students themselves. These students were working adults, and I suggested that perhaps they did not know what it was like to take fifteen credits a semester, have two kids, work full-time, and pay $8,000, and that it would be understandable that some might have "bitten off more than they could chew." Although he admitted that such factors might have played some minor role, Cole felt it had less to do with their actual condition and more to do with their individual perception. He suggested that these students had neither real estate nor investments in Wall Street, and so most of them were not actually being affected by the crashing economy. Although maybe a few had lost their jobs, he insisted, most of them were just scared by what they heard in the media. Of course, evidence suggests that recessions are actually more impactful for the kinds of communities Ravenwood served (Hoynes, Miller, and Schaller 2012).

I further challenged Cole by asking about the rising cost of consumables: food, fuel, utilities, and so on. I used coffee as an example: at one time, a cup of coffee could be had for under a $1 but had risen to nearly $2 in some places. "If you think a cup of coffee is more important than your education, then you definitely lack commitment," he said. He was certain that these students were dropping out not because of economic hardship but because of a personal lack of commitment to their education. Attending college, he felt, meant making sacrifices, and those students who dropped out were just unwilling to make those sacrifices. Those who had actually lost their jobs, he said, should have been even more committed to their education because the consequences would be that much more important.

I suggested that students might have commitment to education but not to paying $8,000 a semester for it; Ravenwood was private and not inexpensive. Perhaps, I suggested, these students were pursuing education in other places. Cole could not understand why someone would "change their mind" about college because of cost, as it was a pure market transaction: "if you buy a car for $X and they tell you that you will have to pay $700 a month, where is the confusion? You don't have to experience it—you're told what the cost will be." He agreed that these students might lack some "financial sophistication" due to inexperience in such matters, but now that he was there as a tuition planner, it should no longer be a problem. Cole argued that the main challenge was that the admissions process was not even trying to measure "commitment" to education; counselors just collected documents and checked off the boxes. Drawing on my example of the rising cost of coffee, he described the process of recruitment as being like brewing coffee: he said that "the coffee filter was not fine enough and so you get a lot of grounds in your coffee—and those need to be spit out—and it is a good thing that they are spit out."

This view of the educational process as a straightforward market transaction and the lack of students' financial sophistication also intersected with notions of merit; when the grounds (students without commitment) were let in, the entire cup of coffee (the college) was spoiled. Cole felt that qualified students in the classroom would see the students next to them and wonder about their admission, knowing that that these other students were not "qualified" to be there. Although this view as not widespread across the participants in this study, it is notable that it seemed to arise most frequently among those who worked with finances.

Cole felt that if the college was "healthy in enrollment," it would make "tougher decisions" about rejecting students who did not display commitment. Instead, the college kept doing everything possible to pull in the "red" students—the ones who lacked commitment and therefore might drop out in the first semester. His notion of "qualified" here was couched not in terms of academic performance but rather in his understanding of personal commitment, or what some call "grit."

Cole's interpretation of students reflected a market-fundamentalist sensibility, which seemingly positions all outcomes as the result of agency, personal empowerment, and rational choices over broader structures or contexts. Ravenwood's students were predominantly women of color, and over 90 percent were receiving financial aid. Cole saw the changes in enrollment numbers as completely about the perceptions and choices of autonomous, individual students. He would not consider that there might be valid, logical reasons why someone might drop out from Ravenwood. Furthermore, he did not see the conditions under which the college operated as contributing to these problems, aside from letting in students who should not be there.

Policies at Ravenwood were variously interpreted and actively contested by different stakeholders. A policy might be seen as predatory by some and as fiscally wise by others, crippling by some and empowering by others. Every student and his or her motivation, personality, and status were to be interpreted and classified and were part of how enrollment numbers were accounted for. More important, however, given the college's progressive history and curricula, even individuals who considered themselves politically liberal would find themselves embracing key market-fundamentalist tenets.

Although many liberal or progressive administrators in Ravenwood did not explicitly buy into market fundamentalism, they did embrace education as a personal investment in the future and individual, agentic choices as a vehicle for mobility. This was seen in both the advertisements and recruitment scripts described earlier, where the possibilities for mobility were tied to notions of individual choices. Neoliberal understandings of self-authorship, work ethic, and confidence (à la Demerath, Lynch, and Davidson 2008) were tied up at Ravenwood with a progressive curriculum that embraced a philosophy of personal empowerment and the promotion of social justice. It seemed difficult to effectively engage Cole's ideologically consistent (although fallacious) assumptions about merit when one lacked the tools to articulate a consistent opposition. Indeed, some of these administrators may have internalized the lack of prestige and the decline in enrollment, as demonstrated by comments that the ranking systems that positioned Ravenwood on the bottom were perfectly accurate.

Conclusions: Anxiety in Educational Markets

The financial pathways within educational infrastructures were considered to be extraordinarily complex and constantly shifting based on government policy, but both students and administrators at Ravenwood College needed to be fluent in them. Or, rather, there was great consequence tied up in having fluency about the ways that capital flowed through the infrastructure. However, as suggested throughout, this infrastructure was laden with meaning, and college administrators at Ravenwood struggled to remain relevant in a competitive, knowledge-production market—particularly given the ways that merit has historically been conflated with markers of race and class. The administrators struggled with how to make sense of the decline in enrollment and the students that they encountered daily and to minimize the impact on future operations. I have attempted to further show how certain neoliberal tenets were configured around these issues and the contradictions and conflicts this produced among administrators.

The mission of Ravenwood, even as currently articulated, was progressive and laudable, but operating under that mission of servicing disadvantaged and nontraditional students was also expensive. Ravenwood's survival in the contemporary educational market required that administrators keep the bottom line in mind and treat students as paying customers in specific market niches. In many ways, Ravenwood College's challenges resembled the challenges of its students. Access to financial resources opens up more choices while also creating a cushion in the event that a risky choice taken will not be devastating if failed. Like students who were saddled with debt and were struggling to compete in a tight job market, Ravenwood found itself in a very competitive, credential-production marketplace but without access to many resources. A heavily resourced student has likely been better prepared for the path, has leveraged that preparation into multiple offers, and may not have to focus on cost as the primary driver. A student without access to resources may have few options to attend college, both because he or she has not had a lifetime of preparation for it and because cost is prohibitive. An institution with many resources may decide to enter a new market with new programs and rely on other program enrollments to keep the institution financially stable. An institution without such resources both has less to invest in such a program and is taking a greater risk, as there may be no cushion in the event that it does not do well. Access to resources, in many ways, protects one from the marketplace. For students and institution in more precarious economic situations, such choices are more heavily risky.

Therefore, many of the challenges that Ravenwood faced were tied to its financial difficulties and to a growing paradox between its progressive curriculum and mission and business decisions that had to be made in order to survive in the marketplace. Decisions, whether at the policy or individual level, often needed to be made with the financial context in mind.

The acquisition of capital has a complex relationship with notions of merit. Although in the educational context, merit and capitalism seem to produce certain contradictions and tensions, in the broader economic world, the two align in ways that cohere around a simple and clear narrative of success. People who earn more money do so because they produce more value than those who earn lower salaries, or so the thinking goes. Wealth itself therefore can be seen as a mark of success in the meritocracy, while the "lazy" and "unskilled" are justly punished for their inadequacies with low incomes. Or, more colloquially, "you get you what you pay for." But what can be done with those institutions without brand recognition or access to resources? What options are there?

Conclusion

Whither Ravenwood College?

The suggestions that I have in effort to improve the educational experience at Ravenwood is to concentrate more on the writing skills number one, and number two offer more incentive for the students to give them the feel of being in college. I have a 19 year-old who will be attending Ravenwood College this Sept.! And I wish Ravenwood had more to offer so she would get the total experience of being a college student.

My initial experience at the beginning of Fall 2006 was great at Ravenwood College. I was surrounded by working professionals such as myself and well versed and experienced professors. However, during my time there everything went downhill. Some of the best professors I had left the school and many of the new professors were not even [subject-major] professionals and acted as though they could care less about teaching at Ravenwood and were just collecting a check. The morale of the college is at an all-time low, students have to endure a rude and incompetent staff, poor resources with the school for almost $40k per year. . . . I would not recommend this school to anyone because I do not feel like it is worth the money I spent. I am quite sure I can get a better experience at a host of other schools for the same amount of money while offering quality professionals and service and resources. It is very unfortunate that the [academic program] has such promise and is so unique but Ravenwood fails to tap into the resources throughout [the region].

On the job training will be a good idea because for me [it] was not possible to find a job till now on my field of study. In other words, I have a master degree, but not the job of my degree.

I would highly recommend anyone to the school, because it has worked for me, and I was accepted at my worst so I appreciate what was done for my self-esteem. Much thanks to those professors that help change my life for the better. Thank you.

Anonymous comments, Ravenwood Graduation Survey
2007–2008

Everyone seems to agree that higher education is in a crisis, at nearly every layer. If one were to go by the alarmist rhetoric found in blogs, editorials, news programming, and popular books, American higher education is failing at nearly every level. It is too expensive (Dannenberg and Voight 2013; Gerald and Haycock 2006; U.S. Government Accountability Office 2007; Vedder 2012), it does not prepare people either for particular jobs or for careers (Arum and Roksa 2010, 2014), nor does it teach anyone anything of value even at the elite levels (Deresieqicz 2014; H. Lewis 2007). Of course, some of these concerns are rooted in very real histories of structural inequality, and therefore focus on how traditionally minoritized or marginalized populations go unserved (Harper 2015) and where racialized tension is going un-redressed (Jayakumar 2015). While some point to the complacent and comfortable lifestyles of faculty as the source of the high cost, others have pointed at higher education's infatuation with athletics (Fisher 2009; Miller 2003; Vedder 2004), added layers of administrators and luxury-level facilities and capital investments (Vedder 2004), and declining funding from the public sector (Center on Budget and Policy Priorities 2013; Tandberg 2010) as the culprits in increasing tuition rates. Certainly, the fiscal outlook is equally bleak for academics and academic labor (Manicone 2008; Youn 2005), which seemingly mitigates the faculty labor factor as a major cause for increased costs.[1] With new technological and digital innovations comes a growing anxiety among faculty that "robot graders" and massive open online courses will replace human instructors and face-to-face contact entirely. As with K–12 education, higher education has become a contested battleground about labor, accountability, cost-effectiveness, and (in alignment with thinking of education as infrastructure) a collective fantasy about our future as a country. If all of higher education is in crisis, what does this say for our collective future?

Institutions must navigate these crises and tensions and manage risk, all while holding to their educational missions (as suggested by Zemsky, Wegner, and Massy 2005). Although some of these crises may be manufactured or exaggerated (in the vein of Harvey 2005), it is also true that some institutions may not survive these crises—as we have seen with recent events in Sweet Briar College and Burlington College. For now, Ravenwood College still stands. Although *U.S. News & World Report* no longer deploys "tiers" to describe institutions in the same way, it is still in the business of assigning ordinal ranks to every institution of higher education in the United States.

Ravenwood remains unranked, acknowledged as existing but unsuitable for "proper" ranking because of a lack of data. Since my original study, Ravenwood has reopened one of the extension campuses that had closed, although its enrollments have not changed significantly. Ravenwood seems to be pushing along at its particular point in the stratified curve.

In the United States, a complex educational infrastructure has been constructed that facilitates the flow of people, knowledge, and meanings into a heavily stratified, meritocratic curve, which then also acts to legitimate their position in that curve. Although some think that these institutions are too different to even be compared, I argue that this infrastructure supports a hierarchy of excellence and is built to manage and regulate the circulation of people within it. It is an infrastructure that is decentralized across various institutions with competing needs and agendas and is subject to the political, economic, and social tensions of the day; it reflects a single continuum of merit in higher education. Consistent with the audit culture described by authors like Strathern (2000), Apple (2005), Hall (2005), C. Shore (2008), and Shore and Wright (2015), "benchmarks," "performance indicators," and other standardized, numerical metrics have infiltrated many aspects of work and school, and so a large part of that infrastructure is dedicated to measurement and classification for various bureaucracies. Ravenwood is assessed, evaluated, and positioned every single day in multiple ways. Ravenwood's applicants, students, and alumni experience the same, as they attempt to navigate that infrastructure in empowering ways. The institution and all of the individuals who participate in it mutually constitute each other's positions. Once more, I am not attempting to determine whether these metrics accurately measure what they are purported to, nor am I suggesting that all credentials lack substance; rather, I have attempted to explore how the confluence of these metrics position Ravenwood College and the value of its credential in a particular place in the hierarchy and what the consequences are for how it operates. Although it may be true that, to many, the current practices at Ravenwood lead to its classification as "mediocre," it is also true that its classification as "mediocre" leads to its current practices. Thus, the ways that various administrators interacted with numbers, deployed persuasive scripts, moved individuals through the admission funnel, and handled Ravenwood's financial precarity were partly a logical way to handle their position in the meritocracy. But such ways of doing also kept them in that position.

In many ways, Ravenwood was atypical of private, nonprofit institutions of higher education in the United States, which have traditionally drawn on affluent, White student populations. Rather, Ravenwood's history aligned more closely with the sorts of missions and projects of public institutions, while its curricular structure was somewhat unique. It served nontraditional, underserved, minoritized students in a nontraditional way and bucked many of the conventions of the field. In fact, there was evidence to suggest that it was once even more radical, given how Flo Epstein described a group admissions interview structure that was eventually put aside in favor of more traditional application processes (see chapter 5). But the Jeffersonian paradigm of education premised on sorting has also been premised on the scientific management logics of standardization, and these measures in turn leave very little room for difference. Thus, even though Ravenwood met every formal criterion of institutionally required legitimacy, it still did not fit in neatly; standardized measures serve as incentives that standardize institutions. Partly, Ravenwood's extraordinariness acted to position it as mediocre.

The consequences of how Ravenwood interfaced with the infrastructure were not only about routines and activity but also about meaning. The educational infrastructure is not a value-neutral machine for moving things but is layered with symbolic and emotional meanings, and it is teeming with inequality. The infrastructure, built to accommodate the needs of the traditional, White, middle-class eighteen- to twenty-two-year-old who had been living with a parent, was premised on the approaches of selective institutions. Former president Hartwick and his team were often derided for moving Ravenwood away from teaching and toward research activities—in essence, shifting the ways that the institution interfaced with the infrastructure as a whole. This movement seemingly contradicted the "special spirit" of Ravenwood and a mission of service to and empowerment of particular, marginalized communities. Or if we consider the Jeffersonian paradigm of education described in the opening of this book, the semiotic understanding of meritocracy could seemingly not accommodate both a move toward more prestige and an embrace of access to nontraditional students. The infrastructure is designed in a way that those two are put in opposition to one another, and faculty in particular reportedly saw this moment as a betrayal. Paradoxically, the Hartwick administration's tenure also aligned with a lowering of admissions standards (at least as reflected in admission rates), fluctuations in enrollments, ethically questionable practices, and increased financial precarity.

Although higher education has largely been corporatized along a profit-focused logic, the relationship between institution and consumer can be sharper and more intense here than in other "industries." This is partly because which college or university one attends is not only about economic choices, but also speaks to the ways that persons have navigated other sometimes seemingly unrelated aspects of the infrastructure many years before seeking higher education. Further, as the U.S. admissions system draws on both academics and other abstract elements of character and leadership, it is seemingly the applicant's whole being that is being assessed as worthy of access or not. No wonder the process is anxiety laden. I also argue that the discourse about reputation or brand here is so much more formidable because rather than the consumer purchasing a token of the brand (as in this particular instantiation of shoe is a token of Nike), the consumer becomes a token of the brand (as in this particular graduate is an instantiation of Ravenwood). Thus, the consumer's future, aspiration, and sense of self become seemingly tangled up with the institution for a lifetime, a notion cultivated by every Office of Alumni Affairs that seeks to obtain donations from graduates. The logic of those donations are not only to show gratitude to the alma mater but also to continuously support the institution's position in the meritocratic curve: if the brand declines in value, so does every alumnus affiliated with it. Of course, I do not wish to suggest that one's undergraduate studies are the only variable in determining life path, reputation, and success. Far from it.

It is certainly true that data have suggested that obtaining an undergraduate education in any institution is statistically very impactful on income achievement,[2] although how much impact which particular institution one attends is a question that is a bit more complex.[3] However, despite evidence to the contrary, this understanding of the relationship between college brand and career achievement is a critical aspect of recruitment and admissions to any institution. Informing students that any bachelor's degree is as good as any other is not a good way to persuade this particular student to attend this particular college. Thus, regardless of whether that college brand is consequential, it is absolutely essential that every institution persuade its applicants, students, and alumni that it is consequential. These institutions are in the business of conferring symbolic capital, and so it is critical that others recognize their value. Clearly, this was an area that Ravenwood struggled with, both in terms of being recognized by others and in terms of its legitimacy being contested.

Related to these issues, and largely unspoken throughout this study, are the additional dimensions of merit as aligning with race, class, and gender. As with any ethnography, the human relationships developed with participants is so much at the center of the research project that there are limits on what one can access. My being a White, heterosexual, male anthropologist from an elite institution with a background in administration here engaging with administrators very deeply shaped how I was perceived, what I was able to gain access to, and how messages were packaged for my ears. Some participants were defensive, some apologetic, some instructive, and some silent. These factors, among many others, may demonstrate why so much of my data highlights formal organizational structures and informal practices at Ravenwood. I encountered very little explicit talk about race, class, and gender, although it seemingly infiltrated every conversation and practice in unspoken ways. This is also likely a result of the ways that the broader infrastructure has been reconfigured around the shifting discourse of political correctness, in which even the noticing of difference can be equated with discrimination. Thus, Pollock (2004) has expertly elaborated thoughtful ways of examining color muteness or color blindness in educational discourses.[4] Although these were socially and culturally real ways that staff and faculty thought about students, there were only limited institutionally approved ways available to talk about those differences and their impact on Ravenwood. It has been well documented how professions and career paths that are historically associated with Whiteness, maleness, and affluence hold more symbolic capital and prestige while offering higher remuneration.[5] Not only was Ravenwood overwhelmingly made up of adult, working-class women of color, but many of the undergraduate degree options were also those considered "paraprofessional" or "vocational."

Ravenwood College thus found itself in a peculiar position. Although Ravenwood inhabited a "mediocre" position, moving the institution along any of a series of paths away from that mediocrity also seemingly pushed it up against its mission. Moving toward the traditional means of reproducing symbolic capital and prestige would be both risky (because it had cultivated a particular niche and elaborated certain ways of doing things that worked for the institution) and a betrayal of the student body and the mission laid out by the founders. When administrators spoke of increasing diversity at Ravenwood, it was often done in a way that suggested attracting more students who were better prepared by traditional K–12 schooling, scored better on standardized tests, and could bring Ravenwood more stability and prestige. Given the nature of the United States' historical and contemporary structural inequities, this implies a desire to attract more people who were White, male, and/or middle class.

As mentioned, it was not only its student body, however, that was nontraditional at Ravenwood. Courses could only be taken in Learning Community Clusters, there were no electives, the capstone was central to the experience, courses were often misaligned with the traditional three credit-hour course, and there were only select applied or vocational majors. SATs and ACTs were not a central part of the admissions process. Many of the metrics drawn upon by college ranking guides were relatively unimportant. Thus, there had been other conversations about abandoning some or all elements of the curriculum to better align Ravenwood with the conventions of other institutions of higher education. Transitioning into Ravenwood, either as a student or as an employee, required shifting expectations about how a university curriculum was structured and took some time to explain to newcomers. Although many felt that this educational experience was at the center of Ravenwood's "special spirit," it complicated transfer experiences and did not conform with the ways most universities operated. Some expressed the sentiment that moving away from this structure was another sort of betrayal. Others expressed frustration at its rigidity. As with many aspects of life at Ravenwood, there was little consensus about what should be done, although there seemed to be a good deal of dissatisfaction with the way things were being done.

From my perspective as an outsider, there seemed to be very little time for careful forethought at Ravenwood. Its precarious financial situation and rolling admissions throughout the year required constant work just to acquire enough students so that the college could continue to exist, suggesting an almost "culture of poverty" model for institutional orientation to the future. Long-range planning was a luxury the college did not have. There was always anxiety beneath the surface that this semester would see a decline and that the institution as a whole would suffer; layoffs or worse could be in the future. Ravenwood seems to be doing well at the moment. But given its cost, its population served, and a growing sense that online and/or proprietary higher education will continue to penetrate the market, some might think it unlikely that Ravenwood will survive the next few decades. There would also be some who might say "good riddance." From the market-fundamentalist perspective, this book may just be documenting an institution's final days as the invisible hand of the market swings down upon it. Ravenwood may be a dinosaur—an artifact from a different era of higher education better suited to a museum than to a marketplace.

What are the faculty and staff of Ravenwood to do with that interpretation? What are the students and alumni to do with it? What is to happen to the "special spirit" that does not seem to fit in with the contemporary higher education marketplace? Ravenwood did not have the resources to challenge broad cultural understandings of merit or conventions of higher education. It seems as if the only institutions with the resources necessary to challenge such presuppositions are the ones that do very well in the current climate. At Ravenwood, there was a sense that any attempt to move itself up the meritocratic curve was one that would move it away from its mission, its exceptional history, and the special spirit that resonated with so many of its nontraditional students. Yet staying where it was had proven to be challenging from a fiscal perspective. In other words, it was trapped in a paradox where to be less mediocre would include trying to be more like everyone else. And that is extraordinary.

In 2008, the election of Barak Obama filled the Ravenwood community with hope, hope that there was a place for this institution and these students in the meritocracy. How will Ravenwood's story be rewritten under a Trump administration? Time alone will tell. At their heart, the stories of such institutions are not about networks, bricks, brands, policies, or curricula. Ravenwood's story is a human one, about one institution's struggles with categories it did not produce and with which it did not neatly fit. Ravenwood College had to "sell" hope to attract students, but also needed to locate hope in a marketplace that seemed incompatible with its mission. Some thought that Ravenwood was mediocre, but the notion of mediocrity seemingly erases this nuance into a monotonous and meaningless uniformity that requires neither deep analysis nor deep thought. There are extraordinary, worthwhile, and hopeful stories in such "mediocre" places just waiting to be written down.

Notes

Preface

1. Various popular calls have been made to forgo higher education completely, and a small decline in college enrollments in the United States can be clearly noted, although the most recent declines are found in the for-profit and community college sectors ("National Change in College Enrollment by Sector, Spring 2013 to Spring 2014" 2014).

2. This is attested to by internal reports and the data presented in this book.

3. There are almost too many to count, from classics such as Foley 1990 and Macleod 2008 to more recent works such as Adely 2012 and Brown 2015.

Introduction

1. All personal names, including "Ravenwood College," are pseudonyms and have been changed to protect the identities of the research participants.

2. Ravenwood College's "Undergraduate Adult Student Graduate Student Market Analysis," completed August 10, 2009.

3. Again, this internally produced marketing report ("Undergraduate Adult Student Graduate Student Market Analysis," August 10, 2009) was based on a consulting firm's

research and concluded that, among identified peer institutions, Ravenwood had the lowest visibility and the lowest mean rating. According to this same report, 55 percent of respondents in the region were "not at all familiar" with Ravenwood, and 40 percent were just "somewhat familiar" with it.

4. Much of the demographic data in this section come from Ravenwood's internal document "Self Study for Middle States Commission on Higher Education Comprehensive Accreditation Review" (2009).

5. As multiple categories may apply and data are self-reported, these numbers may not add up to 100 percent.

6. Although these rates are certainly high, Reisberg (1999) reported on a study of dropout rates across types of institutions roughly associated with tiers and selectivity and revealed that among the least selective institutions the average dropout rate was 46.2 percent. Astin and Oseguera's 2005 work suggests that only 58 percent of entering freshman graduate from the same institution within six years. This provides a better context for these figures.

1. Extraordinary Mediocrity

1. I am referring here to the cognitive, scientific, or intellectual "genius" as represented by someone such as Albert Einstein or Stephen Hawking and less so the figure of the artistic or musical genius, which holds a different position in the present cultural discourse about achievement.

2. Although De Botton (2004) sees these matters in terms of status anxiety, others have explored ways that other sorts of anxiety can be layered into these experiences. Walkerdine's (2006) work on class-based border crossing is illuminating in that it highlights how post–World War II educated women who were able to obtain some degree of social mobility also experienced a constant, anxious-laden need to manage a self-image that made them feel like an imposter in privileged settings and a traitor in nonprivileged spaces; they inhabit a liminal world that can lead to pathology and tension. Added racial and ethnic tensions are also explored through works such as Fordham and Ogbu 1986. De Botton is silent on the added layers that class, race, and gender bring to these anxieties.

3. But even the genius such as Gates, intellectual or entrepeneurial, is the product of more than just individual traits. Mialet (2012) has provided a powerful and thought-provoking account of "genius" in the form of Stephen Hawking—not the man but the icon and enterprise. In doing so, she charts the ways that Hawking serves as a node for activity around which several collectivities produce the icon role he inhabits. This is not to deny Hawking's extraordinary competencies but rather to interrogate the work (done by colleagues, graduate students, physicists, journalists, filmmakers, archivists, designers, assistants, nurses, and Hawking himself) that goes into producing the public figure and legend. Whether or not one possesses merit, we must consider and account for the tremendous amounts of activity in identifying and proclaiming the relative merit of persons in a meritocracy. After all, does someone possess merit if it is not acknowledged by others? Mialet challenges us to consider merit not as a fixed quality but rather as repre-

senting different sorts of positions in the social structure as emerging from a lot of activity and as evaluated by social institutions in relation to others. But it is not only geniuses who are at the center of such activity—there are bureaucratic machines that engage in such activity that we have all encountered.

4. Broadly, the notion of identifying children for continuous cultivation and schooling for the aim of taking on the mantle of government can be traced back even to Plato's *Republic*, which is also where the term *aristocracy* is coined.

5. The "Jeffersonian paradigm" does not belong only to Jefferson, and certainly it is not clear that he would support twenty-first-century manifestations of it. Nor is this the only tradition of "meritocracy" in American history, as unpacked well by Kett 2013. I instead use the term to point to a bundle of philosophical position and polemics within educational circles that have endured across the breadth of American history.

6. Conant was appointed president of Harvard University in 1933, founded the Educational Testing Service (ETS), and segued into a life serving U.S. presidents and adorning the cover of popular magazines.

7. Conant was nearly obsessed with operationalizing a meritocracy but was not concerned with the plight of women or people of color. He considered himself an enemy of aristocracy premised on the inheritance of wealth and yet was a supporter of oligarchy premised on intellect. He was a stern democrat and proponent of peace who was also involved in the development of chemical weapons during World War I and the atom bomb during World War II (Karabel 2005, 141).

8. Jefferson himself was far more complex, and this letter represented only one dimension of his positions, but the ideal described in this letter to John Adams took an iconic place in the argument that Conant was laying out to the public.

9. Conant's vision for meritocracy was apparently limited to specific White, Protestant males. Karabel's (2005) insightful, historical look into the admission policies of elite universities highlights how the present-day, American college admissions process was designed primarily as a means to prevent access to non-White males. In particular, Eastern European Jews of the early twentieth century were so adept at test taking that universities were being flooded by them, causing a panic in elite circles. This panic was, in some ways, related to the Jeffersonian notion that these spaces were not just for learning but were primarily a site for identifying future leaders. As such, access to these spaces by Jews directly contradicted turn-of-the-century cultural sensibilities of merit. It was also self-serving in that those with affluence and influence grated at being sorted into the same pile as these "undesirables" and could thus potentially abandon these spaces entirely, not unlike the "White flight" that historically occurs in residential neighborhoods when people of color begin to move in in large numbers. Partly, then, the goal of such admissions policies was to retain elite students. Conant was key in reinventing what that merit would look like and how it would operate; Jefferson's ideal was at the heart of this process. Fundamentally, this is the beginning of Offices of Admissions that primarily aim to keep people out rather than recruit people in.

10. The Pioneer Fund is a foundation dedicated to exploring the relationship between heredity, race, and eugenics and has been identified by some as an extremist hate group. Although *The Bell Curve* itself has been widely discredited in academic circles, foundations such as this one continue to pursue the same line of inquiry, as do more

popular works by nonacademics, such as the works of Wade (2014). This is to suggest that there is an enduring line of thinking where these notions continue to be promulgated.

11. I am here focusing on a few particular critiques, but many others have been put forward. For example, Fischer et al. (1996) make numerous other critiques of *The Bell Curve*, including the logic that equates test taking with intelligence. For example, although *The Bell Curve* does account for change as the result of childhood development, it fundamentally sees intelligence as a fixed, inherited, and biological trait. But, by this logic, an eighteen-year-old kid who is well versed in the culture and practices of testing is actually "smarter" than her highly educated parents, who would score lower because they are less able to recall from memory necessary formulas that they have not needed in thirty years. This would suggest that the parents actually lost IQ points over time. Or, as private test preparation classes do tend to yield higher scores on tests, this would suggest that IQ points can be gained over just a few months of study. Either way, this notion of IQ is not fixed but demonstrably variable. More recent critiques have come from Fendler and Muzaffar 2008, Guskey 2011, and Nisbett 2013.

12. This built on earlier works by figures such as Mehan (1973), who "showed that child and adult were helping each other get through a difficult situation in which they were plagued by arbitrary inappropriate questions made up by people far away for purposes of securing and legitimizing a bell-curved social structure with smart successful and dumb failing children. His achievement was to find intelligence where others found failure and to press the question of why a society would invest so heavily on failing its children" (as pithily summarized by McDermott and Raley 2011, 43).

13. This is more fully explored by Fendler and Muzaffar 2008.

14. Even Herrnstein and Murray (as shown by Claude S. Fischer et al. 1996, 31) had to do a tremendous number of mathematical operations to take the scores that they used for their analysis in *The Bell Curve* and turn it from a skewed curve into a normal one (i.e., the actual data they were working from in the book titled *The Bell Curve* was not distributed into a bell curve until they reworked the data).

15. A number of works have continued to consider how particular forms of instrumentation point to a discourse of measurement and an audit culture that have infiltrated contemporary bureaucracies and markets, including Strathern 2000, Hall 2005, and Shore and Wright 2015.

16. If Ivy League universities represent the height of that "above normal" category, then it is not unsurprising that the individuals in position of power and institutionally recognized merit would not welcome newcomers to their symbolic-capital-producing machine. Rather, they would find ways to justify the existing power hierarchies as legitimate by using whatever measures available. Indeed, much of *The Bell Curve* reads like a therapeutic essay to the elite: the message between the lines is that you (the reader) deserve your privilege because you are inherently better than your peers. It even explicitly panders to the readers at times: "Most of the readers of this book—this may be said because we know a great deal about the statistical tendencies of people who read a book like this—are in preposterously unlikely groups, and this reflects the degree of partitioning that has already occurred" (Herrnstein and Murray 1996, 47). They therefore

suggest that anyone who picks up their book is obviously on the above-normal part of the curve.

17. Fordham (2008) is clear that the cause of this tension was not other Black children but rather larger social structures and cultural modes of seeing that put racial identity and performance in White institutions in opposition to one another. Many women are put into a similar situation when they are asked to make educational and professional decisions in terms of their plans for motherhood and family—the two are considered in opposition to one another and must be reconciled. The point is not that women are oppressing one another (even if women have strong opinions on this issue) but rather that women have an added layer of tension to resolve when making professional decisions that men (even those who are parents) do not. Finally, one should consider the implications for poor, working class, and largely rural White males, whose own life paths are also not aligned with cultural models of achievement.

18. Cuadraz (2006), for example, examined ten years of life histories and educational trajectories of Chicana/o doctoral students as they have learned to cross borders marked by both race and class. Despite the heterogeneity of the experiences represented in these narratives, because these Chicanas/os had acquired some institutionally recognized success, Cuadraz described how their personal stories took on a mythic character that highlighted their individual choices and personal traits over the broader social and structural forces that shaped the ways opportunity unfolded in their lives. Exceptions to structural barriers do not challenge the power of the meritocratic myth but rather seemingly act to prove that social mobility is achievable if one simply follows the right formulae and never gives up—that is, the American dream.

19. Again, it is important to remember other traditions of merit and egalitarianism, even as we explore this particular, influential strand. There is certainly a good deal of evidence that Conant, drawing on Jefferson, was uninterested in expanding educational opportunities for everyone "except for members of a tiny cohort of intellectually gifted men" (Lemann 1999, 44) and even argued that Nazism and totalitarian regimes in the era were partly a result of overeducating its population (Karabel 2005, 153).

20. This is not to suggest that these credentials do not have value. In fact, the anxiety about credentials is very much driven by the differential values that credentials have.

21. Labaree's (2010) work does an excellent and more thorough job of exploring the contradictions of the American education system in general and as it has emerged from American history.

22. For a fascinating look at skills discourses, see, for example, Urcioli 2008.

23. A great deal of this body of literature has focused on technological and material pathways, such as with post-Soviet electrical systems in Russia (Collier 2011), the water supply in South Africa (von Schnitzler 2008) and Mumbai (Anand 2011, 2012), or roads in Albania (Dalakoglou 2010) or Russia/Mongolia (Pedersen 2011). These works have each highlighted the ways that these material pathways converge into networks or systems that then require assemblages of technical, administrative, and financial techniques to manage. Hughes (1993), for example, highlights how the invention of the light bulb was followed by the production of an infrastructure to handle the financial and managerial aspects of an expanding marketplace for electric light. Özden-Schilling (2016),

meanwhile, has considered the ways that private interests are cultivated through electronic data infrastructures in support of a deregulated electricity market and industry.

24. These considerations also align with the approaches that Latour has taken in examining the structure of social institutions in the production of everything from scientific fact (Latour and Woolgar 1979) to French law (Latour 2009).

25. Some have criticized the move toward materiality and circulation in infrastructure, arguing that it depoliticizes and dehumanizes what are complex social scenes and draws on "non-hierarchical, analytic language" that obscures inequality (Koenig 2016). It can also be seen as downplaying human agency. I align myself more with scholars (such as Appadurai 2015; Kipnis 2015) who see value in this mode of analysis but also take seriously the notion that there is plenty of space for human meaning making, ethics, and agency to be productively incorporated into this framework.

26. Reality television and competition programming draw on a similar fantasy about transcending the limits of our lives. As Crapanzano (2003) observed, "I am put into contact with a becoming that is unfolding at a distance. Hope allows me to take refuge in myself in order to see life unfold around me" (9).

27. I see this turn to infrastructure not as a move to positivistic or functionalist approaches to understanding education and culture but rather as aligning with Bourdieu's larger project to reconcile different theoretical traditions that are often interpreted as, but are not necessarily, oppositional (Bourdieu 1984, 1988; Bourdieu and Passeron 2000).

28. This move was part of the project to reconcile the theoretical traditions of Marx, Weber, and Durkheim. Marx's work emphasized the historical and economic drivers of social phenomena and Weber's the interpretivist, socially constructed nature of them.

29. Although sensitive to the relation between agent and structure, early work on social reproduction did seem to emphasize the deterministic, hegemonic aspects of structure.

30. For Bourdieu, cultural capital (e.g., knowing how to play a violin) opens up access to social capital (e.g., privileged networks, such as access to an elite university) and is made visible and meaningful through recognition by others as symbolic capital. Playing violin and performing hip hop both figure into how people are classified, but structurally, violin playing is potentially rewarded with scholarships while hip hop performance is not. In this vein, merit can thus be understood as having at one's disposal cultural knowledge, which opens up access to social networks and invests visible, symbolic capital that acts to legitimate or make self-evident the distribution of other forms of capital possessed by individuals or institutions (such as financial capital). Although institutions are particularly powerful spaces for concentrating other forms of capital (economic, political, and so on), symbolic capital itself cannot be "institutionalized, objectified or incorporated into the habitus" (Siisiäinen 2000) because it reflectively emerges from sets of embedded practices.

31. Furthermore, Bourdieu (1984) argues that classification is as much a matter of "being-perceived" as it is "being," and thus systems of classification are always related to embodied "theatrical" performances (483). For Bourdieu, this intersection of practice and reproduction reconciled a false dichotomy in social theory that holds discrete, objectively bound groups (à la Durkheim) in opposition to the collection of subjective, aggregate accounts of classifications (à la Garfinkel.) These practically performed classificatory

schemes are thus a forgotten aspect of a class struggle "aimed at transforming the categories of perception and appreciation of the social world itself" (483).

32. As when a woman of color (with readily apparent skills and competencies) felt marginalized in the workplace because she had chosen to attend Spelman (a historically Black college) even though she could likely have attended a more traditional, elite university.

33. The symbolic importance of higher education resonates with Arum and Roksa's (2010) findings, who have drawn on statistical measures to argue that very little is actually learned in higher education. Rather than focusing on learning, they argue, students are busy socializing or working to pay for very high tuitions and costs.

34. The newest educational buzz word for this decontextualized, meritocratic individualism is "grit," which, as elaborated by Duckworth et al. (2007) and taken up by a number of popular books (Ginsburg 2011; Tough 2013), is a combination of persistence and self-discipline that is considered more important than inate ability. Other popular books have risen in response, pointing out the tautological nature of the argument (people who persist tend to be persistent) or the nearly compulsive fear of failure that it engenders (such as Kohn 2014).

2. How to Sell Hope and Mobility

1. For example, an institution relying entirely on local students is at risk if the regional economy suffers, while an institution that draws from across the United States would be less subject to those fluctuations. There is thus a form of financial security that comes from "diversifying students" but also security that comes from "sticking with what you're good at." These two can be at odds.

2. This was near the lowest among a set of similar institutions in the region, some of which ran as high as 72 percent.

3. Of course, Ravenwood, a small, relatively obscure college, was in no position to challenge cultural and social mores more broadly. It had been disciplined by the marketplace and bore the brunt of its economic downturn with layoffs and campus closings. All it could do was insinuate its own brand into the individual's self-as-future-project.

4. I am not referencing "script" as a written or memorized talk, nor as some internalized, deterministic act. Rather, I am suggesting that there are a variety of speech acts (in this case, largely persuasive) that are loosely outlined by individuals prior to deployment from which they later draw upon and mobilize in creative ways. It was necessary to elaborate and deploy such persuasive scripts because Ravenwood as an institution held a precarious position in the marketplace (see also Posecznick 2015).

5. See the now seminal Pollock 2005.

6. As the similarity in Professor Bhatt's arguments demonstrate, individuals tended to acquire and elaborate specific ways of laying out persuasive arguments, which I refer to here as "scripts." Although the details would vary from telling to telling, they held some consistency over time. In a similar way, Professor Stubbs did draw on some of the same scripts that Dean Martinez did (mentioning powerful people of color), but these scripts were differently nuanced.

7. Maggie was arguing that such opportunities may be more significant than found in business—an argument she would leave out when dealing with potential business students.

8. Further incentives include the facts that international students were more likely to complete their course of study, as dropping out would be a violation of F1 status that could lead to (in the worst-case scenario) deportation. International students were also ineligible for any financial aid and were thus "full cash" students.

9. About thirty states require college students to show evidence of certain immunizations as a condition for enrollment. A few years ago, Ravenwood had been remiss in ensuring that its students were all immunized and was fined many thousands of dollars by the state for not doing so. Since then, Ravenwood has invited a nurse to come on campus to provide these immunizations free of charge during heavy recruitment periods.

10. Louisa took pride in her mixed heritage, which reportedly included European, Native American, and Hispanic ancestry. She was dedicated to community work and had taken the position, in part, because it would give her the opportunity to work with the Hispanic community more closely.

11. In China and East Asia, Kipnis (2011) informs us, educational competition, differentiation, and desire emerges out of encounters with the West (through processes of nation building and industrialization) but also out of deeply entrenched traditions in which hierarchies are legitimated through state-sponsored examinations.

3. It's All about the Numbers

1. Madelyn herself was also responsible for recruiting toward her own enrollment goal.

2. The exam and processes for taking the exam will be taken up more fully in chapter 4.

3. Note, this is not the same as the enrollment goal, which is usually substantially higher (and optimistic) than the budget number. The budget number is also less publicly available.

4. Note, of course, that this way of thinking also perpetuates existing population patterns in an institution. It is the rationale for individual admissions counselors to continue cultivating well-worn persuasive scripts rather than elaborating new ones. It also means, however, that occasional marketing campaigns might be devised to break into new markets or to expand the field of prospects.

5. Different members of the Ravenwood community referred to this period of time by different terms, but all seemed to hold an ominous tone. It brought up memories of layoffs, budget problems, loss of benefits, and general uncertainty.

4. Being a "Real" College in America

1. The number of "test-optional" colleges and universities seems to be increasing; out of over 4,000 institutions, approximately 850 do not officially require standardized tests

for Admission. This is therefore about 20 percent of institutions (see Capuzzi Simon 2015).

2. Although certainly arbitrary, it seems to me that the sample questions on the website were easier than the actual questions.

3. As the exam is computer adaptive, the questions change every time the exam is taken. As such, specific items from the exam I took were not available. All samples here were retrieved from "Accuplacer Sample Questions for Students" (2016). Note that the format and structure of the exam may have changed somewhat since I encountered it in 2008–2009, and there may have been other sections of the exam available that Ravenwood was not drawing on.

4. Although available in 2009, this particular language no longer appears on the Accuplacer website or in the Accuplacer materials.

5. See Koyama 2010 for some of the problematic elements of requiring private, outside tutoring.

6. *U.S. News & World Report* has since reconfigured its tier-based hierarchy, but this was the one in use at the time of the study.

7. Such agreements were made between colleges to lay out coursework equivalency to facilitate easier transfer. For example, a student from a college with such an articulation agreement with an associate's degree in business would be able to enter Ravenwood College with a set amount of credits ready to go, rather than needing the transcript individually reviewed. Such agreements would often be made between institutions accredited through the same regional agencies.

8. The Middle States Association includes institutions in Delaware, the District of Columbia, Maryland, New Jersey, New York, Pennsylvania, Puerto Rico, and the U.S. Virgin Islands.

9. Institutions receive regional, national, specialized accreditation. The six regional accreditation agencies in the United States accredit about 98 percent of degree-granting institutions of higher education. National accreditation is largely nondegree in orientation (65.1 percent) and for-profit (79.5 percent) ("The Fundamentals of Accreditation: What Do You Need to Know?" 2002). Although the Department of Education does not differentiate these, regionally accredited postsecondary institutions rarely accept transfer credits from a nationally accredited one.

Specialized accreditation associations largely emphasize a specific industry, discipline, vocation, or religious outlook. For example, the American Bar Association is one such body for law schools; others include the American Dental Association, the Association to Advance Collegiate Schools of Business, the American Veterinary Medical Association, and the Accreditation Board for Engineering and Technology.

10. Retrieved July 5, 2012, from http://www.middlestates.org/Purpose.html.

11. The first standard emphasized the college having clear and meaningful goals, objectives, and a mission statement. The second examined effective planning, resource allocation, and sustainability, while the third standard more specifically assessed the fiscal solvency and resources available to the institution. The fourth examined effective leadership and mechanisms of governance, while the fifth assessed whether staff and administration were qualified (broadly defined) for their professional positions. Standard

six was one of the most arbitrary as it assessed the institution's "integrity," which seemed to include a certain moral character. Standard seven assessed how well the institution assessed itself, its processes, and its students. The eighth standard was particularly important for this research, as it assessed college admissions processes. The ninth standard emphasized student support services. The tenth assessed faculty in terms of their credentials, academic environment, and teaching; and the eleventh evaluated particular curricula, coursework, and degree programs. The twelfth and thirteenth standards examined various aspects of the educational programs, general education and specialized educational offerings, respectively. The final standard assessed how well and with what criteria the college assessed student learning.

12. This report was the result of a few years of work, bringing together contributions from executives, faculty, and administrators from across the college. It was polished and reconfigured by Gary for the purpose of accreditation review.

13. Note that Gary articulates the goal of CLA as focusing on "value added," while the test designers usually focus on its nuanced approaches to understanding critical and analytic thinking through problem-solving, real-world scenarios. This is the same instrument that Arum and Roksa (2010, 2014) draw on in their work.

5. Financing Education and the Crisis of Sustainability

1. A number of blogs and websites, mostly run by academics, track various aspects of university closures. R. Brown (2016), for example, maintains an impressive blog documenting the closing, merging, and renaming of an extremely extensive list of institutions throughout American history and across every state. Batesal (2016) maintains more detailed profiles on the closings of about two hundred colleges and universities.

2. Pew Research Center, "Is College Worth It?" May 15, 2001 (retrived on September 30, 2016, from http://www.pewsocialtrends.org/2011/05/15/is-college-worth-it/).

3. If a student remained continuously enrolled every semester, Ravenwood College would not raise tuition. The tuition would often go up, but it would only be for new students or for someone who dropped out and later returned, as he or she would come in at the new rate. All of this also meant that every student in the college was paying a different tuition rate.

4. The FAFSA is utilized by the U.S. Department of Education to determine financial need for the purposes of college attendance.

5. Cash businesses are those that generate a great deal of cash, including small stores and contractors.

6. By "ethnic groups," Cole to me seemed to be referencing Black Americans. On numerous occasions, administrators discussed this sort of distrust for institutions or loans as specifically common among prospective Black American students.

7. "The Expected Family Contribution (EFC) is a measure of your family's financial strength and is calculated according to a formula established by law. Your family's taxed and untaxed income, assets, and benefits (such as unemployment or Social Security) are all considered in the formula. Also considered are your family size and the number of

family members who will attend college during the year" (retrieved on June 8, 2016, from https://fafsa.ed.gov/help/fftoc01g.htm).

8. Although very difficult to assess broadly, a number of more elite institutions (including Harvard, Yale, and Cornell) did make the news when they announced new programs that "vary in scope and generosity, but most either replace loans with grants for all students or significantly decrease the debt burden for families below a certain income threshold—on average, about $75,000 per year" (Farrell 2008, A23).

9. This $1,000 would be credited toward the student's current balance.

10. Likewise, this $500 would be credited toward the student's current balance.

11. ABS collateralized by student loans were one of the four major asset classes in this market (along with home equity, auto loans, and credit cards).

12. Eisenberg and Franke (2008, B16) reported on serious ethical scandals that were breaking at that time in which "lenders have reportedly provided student-aid administrators with significant benefits—payments for service on advisory committees, stock and stock options, and trips to conferences at posh resorts—in exchange for favorable treatment, including placement on a college's list as a 'preferred lender.'"

13. Unlike "inappropriate" contributions made to individual employees as covered by Eisenberg and Franke (2008), this was considered a business incentive.

14. This was Cole's figure, and I have no source to back him up at this time.

15. Note that it was George W. Bush who signed the law.

16. This position dates back to the misappropriation of the "culture of poverty" (O. Lewis 1966), which suggested that those who lived in poverty were victims of their own self-perpetuating, almost dysfunctional way of life. From this position, it is the autonomous individual's perceptions and choices that lead to his or her condition. Despite being heavily criticized by nearly every quarter of academia, the idea still resonates with neoconservative policymakers, who argue that any public welfare only creates dependency and that what everyone in poverty needs is simply "good values."

Conclusion

1. Endless editorials, blogs, and articles in academic circles speak to the deep anxiety about the decline of tenure and the rise of contingent faculty labor, including Berlinerblau 2014; Dunn 2013; June 2014; and Schmidt 2014. The depth of academic stratification has been of growing emphasis. See, for example, stories of faculty on food stamps (*Chronicle of Higher Education* 2012) or about the death of Margaret Mary Vojtko, a twenty-five-year veteran contingent faculty member at Duquesne University, who was so impoverished at the time of her death that she could not afford electricity (Lindsay 2013).

2. This is demonstrated in any cursory review of median annual earnings by education level available from the U.S. Census Bureau.

3. As Dale and Krueger (2002) point out, in some studies, where one applies has greater consequence on income than where one attends. That is, applicants who applied to very selective institutions performed as well as those who attended selective

institutions—even if the former did not gain admission. Similar conclusions were reached by Brewer, Eide, and Ehrenberg (1999).

4. Others have also examined the historical origins of color-blind policy as a means to reinforce existing structures and inequities in the Unites States, including Anderson (2007); Bonilla-Silva and Dietrich (2011); Marx and Larson (2011); and Ullucci and Battey (2011).

5. For example, these career paths include teaching, nursing, and social work in comparison to professorships, medical doctors, and psychologists.

REFERENCES

"Accuplacer Sample Questions for Students." 2016. https://secure-media.collegeboard
.org/digitalServices/pdf/accuplacer/accuplacer-sample-questions-for-students.pdf.

Adely, Fida J. 2012. *Gendered Paradoxes: Educating Jordanian Women in Nation, Faith, and Progress.* Chicago: University of Chicago Press.

"Administrative Compensation Survey for the 2009-10 Academic Year." 2010. Knoxville, TN: The College and University Professional Association for Human Resources. https://www.cupahr.org/surveys/files/salary0910/AdComp10ExecutiveSummary .pdf.

Anand, Nikhil. 2011. "PRESSURE: The PoliTechnics of Water Supply in Mumbai." *Cultural Anthropology* 26: 542–564. doi:10.1111/j.1548-1360.2011.01111.x.

———. 2012. "Municipal Disconnect: On Abject Water and Its Urban Infrastructures." *Ethnography* 13: 487–509. doi:10.1177/1466138111435743.

Anderson, James D. 2007. "Race-Conscious Educational Policies versus a 'Color-Blind Constitution': A Historical Perspective." *Educational Researcher* 36: 249–257. doi:10.3102/0013189X07306534.

Appadurai, Arjun. 2015. "Mediants, Materiality, Normativity." *Public Culture* 27: 221–237. doi:10.1215/08992363-2841832.

Apple, Michael W. 2005. "Education, Markets, and an Audit Culture." *Critical Quarterly* 47: 11–29. doi:10.1111/j.0011-1562.2005.00611.x.

Arum, Richard, and Josipa Roksa. 2010. *Academically Adrift: Limited Learning on College Campuses.* Chicago: University of Chicago Press.

———. 2014. *Aspiring Adults Adrift: Tentative Transitions of College Graduates.* Chicago: University of Chicago Press.

Astin, A., and Calvin B. T. Lee. 1972. *The Invisible Colleges: A Profile of Small, Private Colleges with Limited Resources.* New York: McGraw-Hill.

Astin, A., and L. Oseguera. 2005. *Degree Attainment Rates at American Colleges and Universities, Revised Edition.* University of California, Los Angeles: Higher Education Research Institute.

Bailey, Thomas. 2012. "Equity and Community Colleges." *The Chronicle of Higher Education*, July 2. http://www.chronicle.com/article/EquityCommunity-Colleges /132643/.

Bastedo, M. N., and O. Jaquette. 2011. "Running in Place: Low-Income Students and the Dynamics of Higher Education Stratification." *Educational Evaluation and Policy Analysis* 33: 318–339. doi:10.3102/0162373711406718.

Batesal, Paul. 2016. "America's Lost Colleges." http://www.lostcolleges.com/.

Berlinerblau, J. 2014. "Teach or Perish." *Chronicle of Higher Education*, January 19.

Berman, Jillian. 2015. "Why More U.S. Colleges Will Go under in the next Few Years." *MarketWatch.* http://www.marketwatch.com/story/why-more-private-colleges-are -closing-2015-03-25/print.

Bok, Derek. 2003. *Universities in the Marketplace: The Commercialization of Higher Education.* Princeton, NJ: Princeton University Press.

Bonilla-Silva, E., and D. Dietrich. 2011. "The Sweet Enchantment of Color-Blind Racism in Obamerica." *ANNALS of the American Academy of Political and Social Science* 634: 190–206. doi:10.1177/0002716210389702.

Bourdieu, Pierre. 1984. *Distinction: A Social Critique of the Judgment of Taste.* Cambridge, MA: Harvard University Press.

———. 1988. *Homo Academicus.* Stanford, CA: Stanford University Press.

Bourdieu, Pierre, and Jean-Claude Passeron. 2000. *Reproduction in Education, Society and Culture.* 2nd ed. London: Sage.

Bourgois, Philippe. 1996. "Confronting Anthropology, Education, and Inner City Apartheid." *American Anthropologist* 98: 249–265. http://onlinelibrary.wiley.com/doi /10.1525/aa.1996.98.2.02a00020/full.

Bourgois, Philippe, and J. Schonberg. 2009. *Righteous Dopefiend.* Berkley: University of California Press.

Brewer, D., E. Eide, and R. Ehrenberg. 1999. "Does It Pay to Attend an Elite Private College? Cross-Cohort Evidence on the Effects of College Type on Earnings." *Journal of Human Resources* 34: 103–123.

Brown, Amy. 2015. *A Good Investment? Philanthropy and Marketing of Race in an Urban Public School.* Minneapolis: University of Minnesota Press.

Brown, Ray. 2016. "College History Garden." http://collegehistorygarden.blogspot.com/.

Capuzzi Simon, Cecilia. 2015. "The Test-Optional Surge." *New York Times*, October 28.

Cavounidis, Costas, and Kevin Lang. 2015. *Discrimination and Worker Evaluation* (NBER Working Paper Series 21612). Cambridge, MA: National Bureau of Economic Research. doi:10.1017/CBO9781107415324.004.

Center on Budget and Policy Priorities. 2013. "States Made Deep Cuts to Higher Education, New Report Finds." http://www.cbpp.org/press/press-releases/states-made-deep-cuts-to-higher-education-new-report-finds.

Chitty, Haley, and Justin Draeger. 2007. "Summary of the College Cost Reduction and Access Act (H.R. 2669)." In *National Association for Student and Financial Aid Administrators.*

Chronicle of Higher Education. 2012. "4 Academics on Food Stamps," May 6. http://www.chronicle.com/article/4-Academics-on-Food-Stamps/131782.

Collier, S. J. 2011. *Post-Soviet Social: Neoliberalism, Social Modernity, Biopolitics.* Princeton, NJ: Princeton University Press.

Council for Higher Education Accreditation. (2002). *The Fundamentals of Accreditation: What Do You Need to Know?* Washington, DC: Council for Higher Education Accreditation. http://www.chea.org/pdf/fund_accred_20ques_02.pdf.

Crapanzano, Vincent. 2003. "Reflections on Hope as a Category of Social and Psychological Analysis." *Cultural Anthropology* 18: 3–32. doi:10.1525/can.2003.18.1.3.

Cuadraz, Gloria Holguin. 2006. "Myths and the 'Politics Myths Chicana / O Exceptionality': Interpreting of Achievement Narratives." *Oral History Review* 33: 83–105.

Dalakoglou, Dimitris. 2010. "The Road: An Ethnography of the Albanian–Greek Cross-Border Motorway." *American Ethnologist* 37: 132–149. doi:10.1111/j.1548-1425.2009.01246.x.

Dale, Stacy Berg, and Alan B. Krueger. 2002. "Estimating the Payoff to Attending a More Selective College: An Application of Selection on Observables and Unobservables." *Quarterly Journal of Economics* 117: 1491–1527.

Dannenberg, Michael, and Mamie Voight. 2013. *Doing away with Debt: Using Existing Resources to Ensure College Affordability for Low and Middle-Income Families.* Washington, DC: Education Trust.

De Botton, Alain. 2004. *Status Anxiety.* New York: Pantheon Books.

Demerath, Peter. 2009. *Producing Success: The Culture of Personal Advancement in an American High School.* Chicago: University of Chicago Press.

Demerath, P., J. Lynch, and M. Davidson. 2008. "Dimensions of Psychological Capital in a U.S. Suburb and High School: Identities for Neoliberal Times." *Anthropology and Education Quarterly* 39: 270–292.

Deresieqicz, William. 2014. *Excellent Sheep: The Miseducation of the American Elite.* New York: Free Press.

Desante, Christopher D. 2013. "Working Twice as Hard to Get Half as Far: Race, Work Ethic, and America's Deserving Poor." *American Journal of Political Science* 57: 342–356. doi:10.1111/ajps.12006.

Diaz de Rada, Angel, and Livia Jimenez Sedano. 2011. "Variations on Diversity and the Risks of Bureaucratic Complicity." In *A Companion to the Anthropology of Education*, edited by Bradley A. U. Levinson and Mica Pollock, 408–424. Oxford, UK: Wiley-Blackwell.

Dixon-Román, Exekiel J., Howard T. Everson, and John J. McArdle. 2013. "Race, Poverty and SAT Scores: Modeling the Influences of Family Income on Black and White High School Students' SAT Performance." *Teachers College Record* 113 (April): 1–33. doi:http://dx.doi.org.ezp3.lib.umn.edu/10.1016/j.acalib.2014.10.008.

Duckworth, Angela L, Christopher Peterson, Michael D. Matthews, and Dennis R. Kelly. 2007. "Grit: Perseverance and Passion for Long-Term Goals." *Journal of Personality and Social Psychology* 92: 1087–1101. doi:10.1037/0022-3514.92.6.1087.

Dunn, Sydni. 2013. "Visiting Professorships Take on New Uses in Changing Market." *Chronicle of Higher Education*, February 4. http://www.chronicle.com/article/Visiting-Professorships-How/136953.

Eisenberg, Meyer, and Ann Franke. 2008. "Financial Scandals and Student Loans." *Chronicle of Higher Education,* June 29. http://www.chronicle.com/article/Financial-ScandalsStudent/1677.

Farrell, Elizabeth. 2008. "The Changing Face of Student Aid." *Chronicle of Higher Education*, April 4. http://www.chronicle.com/article/The-Changing-Face-of-Student/34821.

Fendler, Lynn, and Irfan Muzaffar. 2008. "The History of the Bell Curve: Sorting and the Idea of Normal." *Educational Theory* 58 (1): 63–82.

Fischer, Claude S., Michael Hout, Martín Sánchez Jankowski, Samuel R. Lucas, Ann Swidler, and Kim Voss. 1996. *Inequality by Design: Cracking the Bell Curve Myth*. Princeton, NJ: Princeton University Press.

Fisher, Brian. 2009. "Athletics Success and Institutional Rankings." *New Directions for Higher Education* 2009 (148): 45–53. doi:10.1002/he.

Foley, Douglas E. 1990. *Learning Capitalist Culture: Deep in the Heart of Tejas*. Philadelphia: University of Pennsylvania Press.

Fordham, Signithia. 2008. "Beyond Capital High: On Dual Citizenship and the Strange Career of 'Acting White.'" *Anthropology & Education Quarterly* 39: 227–246. doi:10.1111/j.1548-1492.2008.00019.x.227.

Fordham, Signithia, and John U. Ogbu. 1986. "Black Students' School Success: Coping with the 'Burden of "Acting White."'" *Urban Review* 18: 176–206.

Gerald, Danette, and Kati Haycock. 2006. *Engines of Inequality: Diminishing Equity in the Nation's Premier Public Universities*. Washington, DC: Education Trust.

Ginsburg, Kenneth R. 2011. *Product Details Building Resilience in Children and Teens: Giving Kids Roots and Wings*. Elk Grove Village, IL: American Academy of Pediatrics.

Graham, S., and S. Marvin. 1996. *Telecommunications and the City: Electronic Spaces, Urban Places*. London: Routledge.

Guskey, Thomas R. 2011. "Five Obstacles to Grading Reform." *Educational Leadership* 69 (3): 16–21.

Hall, Kathleen. 2005. "Science, Globalization, and Eductional Governance: The Political Rationalistes of the New Managerialism." *Indiana Journal of Global Legal Studies* 12: 153–182.

Harper, Shaun. 2015. "Black Male College Achievers and Resistant Responses to Racist Stereotypes at Predominantly White Colleges and Universities." *Harvard Educational Review* 85 (4): 646–75.

Harvey, D. 2005. *A Brief History of Neoliberalism*. Oxford: Oxford University Press.

Hearn, James C., and C. Hearn. 2015. "Academic and Nonacademic Influences on the College Destinations of 1980 High School Graduates." *Sociology of Education* 64: 158–171.

Hermes, J. J. 2008. "Defense Department Finalizes Rule Barring Restricted Campus Recruiting." *The Chronicle of Higher Education*, March 28. http://www.chronicle.com /article/Defense-Department-Finalizes/40712.

Herrnstein, R. J., and Charles Murray. 1996. *The Bell Curve: Intelligence and Class Structure in American Life.* New York: Free Press Paperbacks.

Ho, K. 2009. *Liquidated: An Ethnography of Wall Street.* Durham, NC: Duke University Press.

Hoxby, Caroline, and Christopher Avery. 2013. "The Missing 'One-Offs': The Hidden Supply of High-Achieving, Low Income Students." *Brookings Papers on Economic Activity*, December: 1–66. doi:10.3386/w18586.

Hoynes, Hilary, Douglas L. Miller, and Jessamyn Schaller. 2012. "Who Suffers during Recessions?" *Journal of Economic Perspectives* 26 (3): 27–48. doi:10.1257/ jep.26.3.27.

Hughes, T. P. 1993. *Networks of Power: Electirication in Western Society, 1880–1930.* Baltimore: Johns Hopkins University Press.

Jackson, John L., Jr. 2010. "On Ethnographic Sincerity." *Current Anthropology* 51 (S2): S279–S287. doi:10.1086/653129.

Jayakumar, Uma M. 2015. "The Shaping of Postcollege Colorblind Orientation Among Whites: Residential Segregation and Campus Diversity Experiences." *Harvard Educational Review* 85 (4): 609–646.

Jefferson, Thomas. 1959. "Chapter 15: Equality. Thomas Jefferson to John Adams, 28, October 1813." In *The Adams-Jefferson Letters: The Complete Correspondence between Thomas Jefferson and Abigail and John Adams*, edited by Lester Cappon, 387–392. Chapel Hill, NC: University of North Carolina Press. http://press-pubs.uchicago.edu /founders/documents/v1ch15s61.html.

Johnson, Cathryn, Timothy J. Dowd, and Cecilia L. Ridgeway. 2006. "Legitimacy as a Social Process." *Annual Review of Sociology* 32: 53–78. doi:10.1146/annurev.soc.32 .061604.123101.

Jones, Jessika. 2011. "College Costs and Family Income: The Affordability Issue at UC and CSU." California Postsecondary Education Commission. http://files.eric.ed.gov /fulltext/ED517535.pdf.

June, Audrey Williams. 2014. "Without Summer Jobs, Some Adjuncts Must Fight for Unemployment Benefits." *Chronicle of Higher Education*, June 20. http://www.chronicle .com/article/Without-Summer-Jobs-Some/65975.

Karabel, Jerome. 2005. *The Chosen: The Hidden History of Admission and Exclusion at Harvard, Yale, and Princeton.* Boston: Houghton Mifflin.

Kett, Joseph. 2013. *Merit: The History of a Founding Ideal from the American Revolution to the Twenty-First Century.* Ithaca, NY: Cornell University Press.

Khan, Shamus. 2012. *Privilege: The Making of an Adolescent Elite at St. Paul's School.* Princeton, NJ: Princeton University Press.

Kipnis, Andrew B. 2015. "Agency between Humanism and Posthumanism: Latour and His Opponents." *HAU: Journal of Ethnographic Theory* 5 (2): 43–58. doi:10.14318/ hau5.2.004.

Kneedler, Richard. 2008. "The Economic Crisis—I." *Inside HigherEd*, October 23. https://www.insidehighered.com/views/2008/10/23/economic-crisis-i.

Koenig, Dolores. 2016. "The Year 2015 in Sociocultural Anthropology: Material Life and Emergent Cultures." *American Anthropologist* 118: 346–358. doi:10.1111/aman.12530.

Kohn, Alfie. 2014. *The Myth of the Spoiled Child: Challenging the Conventional Wisdom about Children and Parenting.* Boston: De Capo Lifelong Books.

Koyama, Jill. 2010. *Making Failure Pay: For-Profit Tutoring, High-Stakes Testing, and Public Schools.* Chicago: University of Chicago Press.

Kusserow, Adrie. 2004. *American Individualisms: Child Rearing and Social Class in Three Neighborhoods.* New York: Palgrave McMillan.

Labaree, David. 2004. *The Trouble with Ed Schools.* New Haven, CT: Yale University Press.

———. 2010. *Someone Has to Fail: The Zero-Sum Game of Public Schooling.* Cambridge, MA: Harvard University Press.

Lareau, Annette. 2003. *Unequal Childhoods: Class, Race, and Family Life.* Berkley: University of California Press.

Larkin, Brian. 2013. "The Politics and Poetics of Infrastructure." *Annual Review of Anthropology* 42: 327–343. doi:10.1146/annurev-anthro-092412-155522.

Latour, Bruno. 2005. *Reassembling the Social: An Introduction to Actor Network Theory.* Oxford: Oxford University Press.

———. 2009. *The Making of Law: An Ethnography of the Conseil d'Etat.* Cambridge, UK: Polity Press.

Latour, Bruno, and Steve Woolgar. 1979. *Laboratory Life: The Construction of Scientific Facts.* London: Sage.

Lemann, Nicholas. 1999. *The Big Test: The Secret History of the American Meritocracy.* New York: Farar, Strauss and Giroux.

Lewis, Harry. 2007. *Excellence without a Soul: Does Liberal Education Have a Future?* New York: Public Affairs.

Lewis, Oscar. 1966. *La Vida: A Puerto Rican Family in the Culture of Poverty—San Juan and New York.* New York: Random House.

Liebow, Elliot. 1993. *Tell Them Who I Am: The Lives of Homeless Women.* New York: Free Press.

Lindsay, Ellis. 2013. "An Adjunct's Death Becomes a Rallying Cry for Many in Academe." *Chronicle of Higher Education*, September 19. http://www.chronicle.com/article/An-Adjuncts-Death-Becomes-a/141709.

Macleod, Jay. 2008. *Ain't No Makin' It: Aspirations and Attainment in a Low-Income Neighborhood.* 3rd ed. Philadelphia: Westview Press.

Madan, Amman. 2007. "Sociologising Merit." *Economic and Political Weekly* 42: 3044–3050. http://www.jstor.org/stable/4419817.

Manicone, Nicholas. 2008. "Legal Remedies for Contingent Faculty." *Academe* 94 (6): 32–34.

Marx, S., and L. L. Larson. 2011. "Taking off the Color-Blind Glasses: Recognizing and Supporting Latina/o Students in a Predominantly White School." *Educational Administration Quarterly* 48: 259–303. doi:10.1177/0013161X11421923.

Mattelart, A. 1996. *The Invention of Communication.* Minneapolis: University of Minnesota Press.

———. 2000. *Networking the World: 1794–2000.* Minneapolis: University of Minnesota Press.

McDermott, Ray. 2004. "Materials for a Confrontation with Genius as a Personal Identity." *Ethos* 32: 278–288. http://onlinelibrary.wiley.com/doi/10.1525/eth.2004.32.2.278/abstract.

McDermott, Ray, and Kathleen D. Hall. 2007. "Scientifically Debased Research on Learning, 1854–2006." *Anthropology and Education Quarterly* 38 (1): 9–15. doi:10.1525/aeq.2007.38.1.9.9.

McDermott, Ray, and Jason Duque Raley. 2011. "The Ethnography of Schooling Writ Large, 1955–2010." In *A Companion to the Anthropology of Education*, edited by Bradley A. U. Levinson and Mica Pollock. Oxford, UK: Wiley-Blackwell. doi:10.1002/9781444396713.ch3.

Mehan, Hugh. 1973. "Assessing Children's Language Using Abilities." In *Comparative Sociological Research*, edited by J. Michael Armer and Alan S. Grimshaw, 309–343. New York: Wiley-Interscience.

———. 2012. *In the Front Door: Creating a College-Going Culture of Learning*. Boulder, CO: Paradigm.

Meneley, Anne. 2004. "Extra Virgin Olive Oil and Slow Food." *Anthropologica* 46 (2): 165–176.

———. 2007. "Like an Extra Virgin." *American Anthropologist* 109 (4): 678–87. doi:10.1525/AA.2007.109.4.678.Meneley.

Mialet, Helene. 2012. *Hawking Incorporated: Stephen Hawking and the Anthropology of the Knowing Subject*. Chicago: University of Chicago Press.

Miller, Ryan. 2003. "The Role of Athletics in Higher Education." *Major Themes in Economics,* Spring: 31–47.

Moore, Robert E. 2003. "From Genericide to Viral Marketing: On 'Brand.'" *Language & Communication* 23: 331–357. doi:10.1016/S0271-5309(03)00017-X.

Nader, Laura. 1972. "Up the Anthropologist: Perspectives Gained from Studying Up." In *Reinventing Anthropology*, edited by Dell Hymes, 284–311. New York: Pantheon Books.

Nakassis, Constantine V. 2012. "Brand, Citationality, Performativity." *American Anthropologist* 114: 624–638. doi:10.1111/j.1548-1433.2012.01511.x.

"National Change in College Enrollment by Sector, Spring 2013 to Spring 2014." 2014. *Chronicle of Higher Education*, August 18. http://chronicle.com/article/National-Change-in-College/147313/.

Nespor, Jan. 1994. *Knowledge in Motion: Space, Time, and Curriculum in Undergraduate Physics and Management*. Knowledge. London: Falmer Press.

———. 1997. *Tangled up in School: Politics, Space, Bodies, and Signs in the Educational Process*. Mahwah, NJ: Erlbaum.

Nisbett, Richard E. 2013. "Schooling Makes You Smarter: What Teachers Need to Know about IQ." *American Educator* 37: 10–19, 38–39.

Obama, Barack. 2013. "Morehouse College Commencement." http://www.realclearpolitics.com/video/2013/05/19/obama_if_you_think_you_can_just_get_over_in_this_economy_just_because_you_have_a_morehouse_degree_youre_in_for_a_rude_awakening.html.

Ortner, Sherry B. 2005. "Subjectivity and Cultural Critique." *Anthropological Theory* 5: 31–52.

Özden-Schilling, Canay. 2016. "The Infrastructure of Markets: From Electric Power to Electronic Data." *Economic Anthropology* 3: 68–80. doi:10.1002/sea2.12045.

Pedersen, M. A. 2011. *Not Quite Shamans: Spirit Worlds and Political Lives in Northern Mongolia.* Ithaca, NY: Cornell University Press.

Pollock, Mica. 2004. "Race Bending: 'Mixed' Youth Practicing Strategic Racialization in California." *Anthropology & Education Quarterly* 35: 30–52.

———. 2005. *Colormute: Race Talk Dilemmas in an American School.* Princeton, NJ: Princeton University Press.

———. 2008. *Because of Race: How Americans Debate Harm and Opportunity in Our Schools.* Princeton, NJ: Princeton University Press.

Posecznick, Alex. 2015. "Provoking Aspiration: Risk-Management through the Cultivation of Future Selves in College Recruitment." *Policy Futures in Education* 13: 639–661. doi:10.1177/1478210315579549.

Reardon, S. F., L. Fox, and J. Townsend. 2015. "Neighborhood Income Composition by Household Race and Income, 1990–2009." *ANNALS of the American Academy of Political and Social Science* 660: 78–97. doi:10.1177/0002716215576104.

Reisberg, Leo. 1999. "Colleges Struggle to Keep Would-Be Dropouts Enrolled: Dropout Rates by Selectivity of Institution." *Chronicle of Higher Education*, October 8. http://www.chronicle.com/article/Colleges-Struggle-to-Keep/20295.

Ryan, Camille L., and Kurt Bauman. 2012. *Educational Attainment in the United States: 2013.* Washington, DC: U.S. Census Bureau. https://www.census.gov/content/dam /Census/library/publications/2016/demo/p20-578.pdf.

Scheper-Hughes, Nancy. 1993. *Death without Weeping: The Violence of Everyday Life in Brazil.* Berkeley: University of California Press.

Schmidt, Peter. 2014. "Debate over Faculty Power Flares before Federal Labor Board." *Chronicle of Higher Education*, March 31. http://www.chronicle.com/article/Debate -Over-Faculty-Power/145635.

Selingo, Jeffrey. 2015. "How to Spot a College about to Go out of Business." *Washington Post*, March 11. https://www.washingtonpost.com/news/grade-point/wp/2015/03/11 /how-to-spot-a-college-about-to-go-out-of-business/.

Shore, C. 2008. "Audit Culture and Illiberal Governance: Universities and the Politics of Accountability." *Anthropological Theory* 8: 278–298. doi:10.1177/1463499608093815.

Shore, C., and Susan Wright. 2015. "Audit Culture Revisited." *Current Anthropology* 56: 421–444. doi:10.1086/681534.

Shumar, W. 1997. *College for Sale: A Critique of the Commodification of Higher Education.* London: Falmer Press.

———. 2014. "Wither the Welfare State: The New Global Adventures of Higher Education." *Learning and Teaching* 7: 92–104. doi:10.3167/latiss.2014.070107.

Shumar, W., and J. Canaan. 2008. *Structure and Agency in the Neoliberal University.* Hoboken, NJ: Taylor and Francis.

Siisiäinen, Martti. 2000. "Two Concepts of Social Capital: Bourdieu vs. Putnam." Paper presented at *IST Fourth International Conference.* Dublin, Ireland.

Soares, Joseph A. 2012. *SAT Wars: The Case for Test-Optional College Admissions.* New York: Teachers College Press.

Snyder, Thomas, and Sally Dillow. 2012. *Digest of Education Statistics 2011.* Washington, DC: National Center for Education Statistics.

Staiger, Annegret. 2004. "Whiteness as Giftedness: Racial Formation at an Urban High School." *Social Problems* 51: 161–181. doi:10.1525/sp.2004.51.2.161.

Stevens, Mitchell L. 2007. *Crafting a Class.* Cambridge, MA: Harvard University Press.

Stevens, Mitchell L., Elizabeth A. Armstrong, and Richard Arum. 2008. "Sieve, Incubator, Temple, Hub: Empirical and Theoretical Advances in the Sociology of Higher Education." *Annual Review of Sociology* 34: 127–151. doi:10.1146/annurev.soc.34.040507.134737.

Strathern, Marilyn, ed. 2000. *Audit Cultures: Anthropological Studies in Accountability, Ethics, and the Academy.* London: Routledge.

Stripling, Jack. 2008. "Big Trouble, Potentially, for Little Colleges." *Inside Higher Ed,* October 17. http://insidehighered.com/news/2008/10/17/moody.

Suchman, Mark C. 1995. "Managing Legitimacy: Strategic and Institutional Approaches." *Academy of Management Review* 20: 571–610.

Sunderman, G. L. 2010. "Evidence of the Impact of School Reform on Systems Governance and Educational Bureaucracies in the United States." *Review of Research in Education* 34: 226–253. doi:10.3102/0091732X09349796.

Tandberg, David A. 2010. "Politics, Interest Groups and State Funding of Public Higher Education." *Research in Higher Education* 51: 416–450. doi:10.1007/s11162-010-9164-5.

Tough, Paul. 2013. *How Children Succeed: Grit, Curiosity, and the Hidden Power of Character.* New York: Mariner Books.

Trencher, G., M. Yarime, K. B. McCormick, C. N. H. Doll, and S. B. Kraines. 2013. "Beyond the Third Mission: Exploring the Emerging University Function of Co-Creation for Sustainability." *Science and Public Policy* 41: 151–179. doi:10.1093/scipol/sct044.

Tuchman, G. 2011. *Wannabe U.: Inside the Corporate University.* Chicago: University of Chicago Press.

Ullucci, K., and D. Battey. 2011. "Exposing Color Blindness/Grounding Color Consciousness: Challenges for Teacher Education." *Urban Education* 46: 1195–1225. doi:10.1177/0042085911413150.

Urciuoli, Bonnie. 2008. "Skills and Selves in the New Workplace." *American Ethnologist* 35: 211–228. doi:10.1111/j.2008.1548-1425.00031.x.

U.S. Congress. 2007. *College Cost Reduction and Access Act.* HR 2669. 110th Cong. https://www.govtrack.us/congress/bills/110/hr2669.

U.S. Government Accountability Office. 2007. *Tuition Continues to Rise, but Patterns Vary by Institution Type, Enrollment, and Educational Expenditures.* Washington, DC: U.S. Government Accountability Office.

Varenne, Hervé. 2001. "The Culture of American Education: The Beijing Lectures 2001." http://varenne.tc.columbia.edu/hv/edu/beijing01/bei01.html.

———. 2007. "On NCATE Standards and Culture at Work: Conversations, Hegemony, and (Dis-)Abling Consequences." *Anthropology and Education* 38: 16–23.

Varenne, Hervé, and Ray McDermott. 1998. *Successful Failure: The School America Builds.* Boulder, CO: Westview Press.

Vedder, Richard. 2004. *Going Broke by Degree: Why College Costs Too Much*. Washington, DC: American Enterprise Institute for Public Policy Research.

——. 2012. *Twelve Inconvenient Truths about American Higher Education*. Washington, DC: Center for College Affordability and Productivity.

von Schnitzler, Antina. 2008. "Citizenship Prepaid: Water, Calculability, and Techno-Politics in South Africa." *Journal of Southern African Studies* 34: 899–917. doi:10.1080/03057070802456821.

Wade, N. 2014. *A Troublesome Inheritance: Genes, Race, and Human History*. New York: Penguin.

Walkerdine, Valerie. 2006. "Workers in the New Economy: Transformation as Border Crossing." *Ethos* 34: 10–41.

Wiley, Andrea S. 2007. "Transforming Milk in a Global Economy." *American Anthropologist* 109 (4): 666–677. doi:10.1525/AA.2007.109.4.666.Wiley.

Wilk, Richard. 2006. "Bottled Water: The Pure Commodity in the Age of Branding." *Journal of Consumer Culture* 6 (3): 303–325. doi:10.1177/1469540506068681.

Williams, R. L., Jr., and M. Omar. 2014. "Applying Brand Management to Higher Education through the Use of the Brand Flux Model: The Case of Arcadia University." *Journal of Marketing for Higher Education* 24: 222–242. doi:10.1080/08841241.2014.973471.

Willis, Paul E. 1977. *Learning to Labour: How Working Class Kids Get Working Class Jobs*. Farnborough, UK: Saxon House.

Wilson, William Julius. 2012. "The Role of Elite Institutions." *The Chronicle of Higher Education*, July 2.

Wolin, Richard. 2012. "Fading Glory Days." *The Chronicle of Higher Education*, July 2.

Woodhouse, Kellie. 2015. "Moody's Predicts College Closures to Triple by 2017." *Inside Higher Ed*, September 28. https://www.insidehighered.com/news/2015/09/28/moodys-predicts-college-closures-triple-2017.

Youn, Ted. 2005. "The Academic Job Market Is Bad for All of Us." *Academe* 91 (6): 27–30.

Young, Michael. 1958. *The Rise of the Meritocracy, 1870–2033*. London: Thames & Hudson.

Zemsky, Robert, Gregory Wegner, and William Massy. 2005. *Remaking the American University: Market-Smart and Mission-Centered*. New Brunswick, NJ: Rutgers University Press.

Index

CPSIA information can be obtained
at www.ICGtesting.com
Printed in the USA
LVHW040603200620
658462LV00002B/238